'This is an excellent, and long overdue, book on youth gangs in Australia drawing on 15 years' experience in the field. Rob White has produced a very readable and illuminating book that will be required reading for anyone with an interest in criminology or youth: it rightly deserves to become a classic text.'

—Andy Furlong, University of Glasgow, UK

'Critically engaging with international literature of "youth gangs" research and based solidly on wide-ranging and long-term empirical study of the area throughout Australia, *Youth Gangs, Violence and Social Respect* is a valuable contribution to study in this field. Rob White's writing is as accessible as it is perceptive.'

—Scott Poynting, University of Auckland, New Zealand

'Authoritative and provocative, theoretically engaged and empirically grounded, White's book makes a major contribution to the controversial and contested research literature on youth "gangs". The wide-ranging coverage and sharply focused analysis speaks eloquently to "gang" questions in Australia and elsewhere. A must read for researchers, teachers, students, practitioners and policymakers with interests in modern urban youth.'

—Barry Goldson, University of Liverpool, UK

'Rob White has produced a timely and important new contribution to the growing body of work that might be called critical global gang studies. Casting his eye over empirical data from diverse ethnic groups over 20 years of his gang research in Australia he concludes that gangs are but a symptom of massive structural inequalities in society and are themselves not the main cause of so many of our related social problems. Critiquing the bulk of criminal justice and criminological gang studies that through pseudo-scientific positivististic approaches reify and dehumanize the gang, White convincingly argues that only a humanistic, contextual and critical criminological lens can fully appreciate the complexity of the gang phenomenon. This work helps to broaden our global appreciation of the gang and rescue the study of this deeply complex social phenomenon from the parodic treatments to which it has been increasingly subjected. An important addition to any serious social scientific library.'

—David C. Brotherton, John Jay College of Criminal Justice, USA

'Youth gangs fuel moral panics and media headlines. Rob White's readable yet rigorously argued book debunks taken for granted assumptions providing new ways of understanding the lives of young people, their relationships with each other and the role of violence. Based on conversations with young people and years of research the book is essential reading for all those interested in the reality behind the headlines.'

—Jude McCulloch, Monash University, Australia

Youth Gangs, Violence and Social Respect

Exploring the Nature of Provocations and Punch-Ups

Rob White

University of Tasmania, Australia

First published 2013 by
PALGRAVE MACMILLAN

Palgrave Macmillan in the UK is an imprint of Macmillan Publishers Limited, registered in England, company number 785998, of Houndmills, Basingstoke, Hampshire RG21 6XS.

Palgrave Macmillan in the US is a division of St Martin's Press LLC, 175 Fifth Avenue, New York, NY 10010.

Palgrave Macmillan is the global academic imprint of the above companies and has companies and representatives throughout the world.

Palgrave® and Macmillan® are registered trademarks in the United States, the United Kingdom, Europe and other countries.

ISBN 978–1–137–33384–1

This book is printed on paper suitable for recycling and made from fully managed and sustained forest sources. Logging, pulping and manufacturing processes are expected to conform to the environmental regulations of the country of origin.

A catalogue record for this book is available from the British Library.

A catalog record for this book is available from the Library of Congress.

Contents

Figure and Tables

Figure

Tables

Acknowledgements

Youth and community workers contributed greatly to this project in many different ways, over many years. A partial list of those who have assisted the research process and/or provoked serious concerns about the research includes: Hatice Vural, Mary Malek, Elissar Mukhtar, Christina Radburn, Dave Palmer, Debbie Wong, Vanessa Phillips, Jodie Schluter, Cheryl Cassidy-Vernon, Kim Sattler, Siyavash Doostkhah, Katherine Yuen, Thuy Shaw, Ron Mason, Debbie Draybi, Katrina Marino, Meredith Hunter, K. Janke, Kavitha Chandra-Shekeran, K. Biddle, A. Wells, A. Hackett, L. Gosling, Mick Hearn, Helena Stewart and Carmel Guerra. My sincere thanks – and apologies – to those who participated or helped out in the various studies but whose names do not appear here.

Members of the OzGang Research Network were instrumental at crucial times and included Hass Dellal, Gerald Daniels, Carmel Guerra, Scott Poynting, Santina Perrone and Paul Tabar. In addition to much volunteer labour and participation, the national youth gangs research project benefited from a grant from the Australian Research Council.

At the University of Tasmania, people such as Hannah Graham and Eve Hicks were vital to the preparation and collation of the gang transcripts. As per usual, so too were Della Clark, Denise Jones, Lyn Devereaux and Sally Thurley, who were and are, as always, the backbone of university administration and culture. Bridget Stewart kindly read the draft manuscript and provided valuable comments, as did Scott Poynting, and Di Heckenberg has perused various writings about youth over the years.

Permissions have been generously granted from various publishers to draw upon previously published material.

From the Australian Research Alliance for Children and Youth:

'Youth Gangs, Violence and Anti-Social Behaviour', *Australian Research Alliance for Children & Youth*, April 2007.

'Anti-Gang Strategies and Interventions', *Australian Research Alliance for Children & Youth*, April 2007.

From Routledge:

White, R. (2011) 'Gangs and Transnationalisation', in B. Goldson (ed) *Youth in Crisis? 'Gangs', Territoriality and Violence*. London: Willan/Routledge.

From the Australian Clearinghouse for Youth Studies:

White, R. (2009) 'Indigenous Youth and Gangs as Family', *Youth Studies Australia*, 28(3): 47–56.

White, R. (2007) 'Taking It to the Streets: From the Larrikins to the Lebanese,' ed. S. Ponyting & G. Morgan, *Outrageous!: Moral Panics in Australia*, Hobart: ACYS Publishing.

Finally, my thanks go to Palgrave Macmillan, and especially Julia Willan and the rest of the editorial staff and production people, all of whom have ensured that this has indeed become a book.

1
Doing Gangs Research

Introduction

The concept of 'gang' is highly contentious and controversial. This is a mantra that will be repeated throughout this book. The ambiguities surrounding what a gang is and what gangs do are precisely why the term is both powerful and predictable in public discourses of disorder and danger. Gangs connote predatory and violent action, usually by groups of young men. The concept encapsulates notions of aggression, viciousness, chains of brotherhood forged in combat, and codes of obedience and behaviour that discipline individuals to the group's norms and values. Yet, simultaneously, the idea of gangs has a certain appeal, based on images and portrayals that emphasise shared purpose, strong group bonds, explosions of excitement and adrenaline, and financial and social gratification in the here-and-now. Even the fictionalised accounts of gangs embody these aspects of uncertainty and complexity when it comes to their good and their bad features.

Much of the present-day concern with the gangs question stems from negative media treatment of young people, which more often than not is framed in terms of the threat posed by gangs. This is reinforced politically by populist accusations that youth gangs are a major social evil today. Branding certain young people 'gangs' has allowed for widespread vilification of particular groups of street-present young people and created political space for the imposition of draconian forms of social control over their behaviour and, indeed, their very presence in the public domain. Moreover, exceptional and dramatic events, such as the English riots of 2011 and the Cronulla riots of 2008, provide platforms for the exposition of a form of 'gangs talk' that reduces complex social problems to simple answers and solutions. Gangs are easy to blame [1].

1

Within the academy, division exists between two schools of thought. On the one hand, there are those who argue that 'gangs' are basically a social construction, mainly born out of moral panic, and that to label someone or a group in this way misconstrues their lived realities and provides only a negative picture of who they really are and what they really do. On the other hand, there are those who claim that gangs are 'real', that they do engage in harmful criminal activity, and that policy and policing responses need to be developed to counter street-level thuggery and criminality of this kind. As with the common-sense notions of 'gang', however, the answer is far more complicated than either a hardcore 'realist' or 'social constructionist' position may imply [2].

Social problems, such as those purported to be associated with the presence of youth gangs, are constructed through a combination of material and cultural factors. There are things going on in the lives of these young people that demand our attention. The study of 'gangs' is the study of real, existing problems. However, while the problems may be 'real', the definition, magnitude, impact, risk and origins of youth gangs are open to interpretation and dispute.

One task of this book is to unpack the multiple realities of youth gangs in Australia, in order to both affirm substantive problems and dilemmas experienced by many young people today, and deny the reduction of these to individual choice and specific types of youth social formation. The foundations of the book have been built on direct conversations with young people over many years, and in many different places and settings. They have also drawn upon the study and experiences of researchers on young people in places other than Australia. First-hand accounts and a broad range of analytical literature thus constitute the core materials upon which the present narrative has been constructed.

Studying youth gangs

Doing gangs research involves a number of complex ethical, conceptual, procedural and methodological issues [3]. At the very beginning of such research, for instance, there are significant problems stemming from the use of particular types of gangs research methodologies. This is illustrated in current debates in the US over the development and use of gang databases [4]. A crucial point made in the debates is that certain types of legislated data collection end up being too inclusive and stigmatising of young people. The question of research definition of gangs is thus highly politicised, especially when linked to the question of government intervention and policy. What academics do, matters, especially from the point of view of social control. US-style gangs research, which heavily influences the methods currently being adopted as part of the Eurogang Research Network agenda, has tended to be strongly positivist in orientation, with great emphasis on quantitative criminological investigation – precisely the type of methodology that lends itself to the creation of databases (and the associated politics linked to the use of these). Fortunately or unfortunately, depending upon your point of view, there has been very little quantitative investigation of the gangs phenomenon in Australia (a rare example being a survey we carried out in Perth high schools several years ago).

Meanwhile, few social scientists (and one can surmise that this includes many of those debating the database) seem to actually engage in close-up first-hand observation of young people, to discern what they actually do with their time and to understand and value the meanings they bring to this. The 'social problem' of gangs is structurally generated, but analysis tends to see it in terms of population attributes (e.g., being poor) rather than stemming from dynamic social processes that also implicate the powers that be (e.g., police brutality or neoliberal economics). Those who do get close to the action are considered rogue sociologists; similarly, those who critique conventional understandings and conventional criminal justice interventions are viewed with suspicion if not outright hostility by those with a stake in maintaining the (academic as well as political) *status quo* [5].

The doing of gangs research is thus fraught with a number of ethical as well as methodological and conceptual issues. For present purposes I want to briefly illustrate a couple of issues that one has to be sensitive to in undertaking such research. To do this I will initially draw upon our experiences in interviewing young people in Melbourne in the mid-1990s, my first foray into the complex world of youth gangs research [6].

For this particular research we decided to interview young people from diverse ethnic backgrounds, including Vietnamese, Turkish, Pacific Islander, Somalian, Latin American and Anglo-Australian. The research consisted of interviews with 20 people each from five different areas of Melbourne (a total of 100 people) which reportedly had a high incidence of 'ethnic youth gang' activity, and interviews with 20 young people with an Anglo-Australian background in order to make comparisons with the ethnic-minority interviewees.

Specific local areas were the initial focus of the research, based on the assumption that certain ethnic-minority groups tended to reside or hang around in these locales (e.g., Vietnamese Australian youth in Footscray). However, we discovered early on in the research that a more sophisticated and complex pattern of movement often took place. Indeed, it was often the case that there were certain corridors within the metropolitan area within which young people moved. While these corridors were not suburb specific, they did range in specific territorial directions (e.g., fanning out from the city centre toward the western suburbs for one group; mainly concentrated along the coastal beaches for another). In addition, many of the young people did not in fact live in the place where they spent most of their time.

There was considerable variation in how the samples of young people were selected, and in the nature of the interviewer–young person relationship. As much as anything this had to do with the contingencies of social research of this kind: the diverse communities and the sensitivity of the subject matter were bound to complicate the sample selection and the interview process in varying ways.

The social connections and research opportunities of each community-based interviewer influenced the specific sample group for each defined ethnic youth population as follows:

- The **Anglo-Australian** young people were selected at random. They were drawn from local schools and from the local shopping centre.
- The **Vietnamese** sample was based upon prior contacts established by the interviewer, who had had extensive experience in working with and within the community.
- The **Somalian** sample comprised individuals chosen at random on the street, and recruitment of primarily female respondents was done through friendship and family networks. This form of sample selection was influenced by the nature of gender relations within the community, especially as this relates to street-frequenting activity.
- The **Pacific Islander** sample was shaped by the fact that two separate interviewers were involved, each of whom tapped into different groups of young people. In one case the young people who were interviewed tended to be involved in church-related networks and activities, which skewed the sample towards a particular demographic. In the other, the sample was mainly drawn from young people who were severely disadvantaged economically and who had experienced major family difficulties.

- Two interviewers were also involved with the **Latin American** young people. Each had difficulties in obtaining random samples due to the reluctance of individuals and agencies to participate in the project. Accordingly, the sample was constructed mainly via family members and friends who assisted in the process of making contact with potential subjects.

- The **Turkish** sample likewise involved two interviewers, reflecting the cultural mores of having a man interview the young men and a woman interview the young women. Again, family and friends were used extensively in the recruitment of interview subjects.

The composition of the sample and the dynamics of the interview process were thus bound to be quite different depending upon the group in question. So too were the social experiences and social position of the particular group.

For example, in cases where the interviewer was not known to a particular migrant family, the young people (and their parents) tended to be suspicious about what was going on, suspecting that perhaps the interviewer was a government employee sent by child-protection services to determine the fitness of the family to raise children (which, in turn, stifled frank discussion). In another instance, there was longstanding antagonism between the particular ethnic-minority young people and Anglo-Australians. Given that one of the interviewers was Anglo-Australian, and given the high degree of intervention into their lives by social welfare agencies of various kinds, some of the young people may have been very suspicious of the questions being asked. There were also instances where young people may have been reluctant to speak about certain matters. This was most apparent in the case of some refugees who were deeply suspicious regarding questions about authority figures, such as the police. In a similar vein, 'gangs' meant something quite specific for many respondents from war-torn countries. In their experience, 'gang' referred to men brandishing weapons who roam the streets robbing people, pilfering, raping and engaging in all manner of serious offences, including murder. Such 'gangs' clearly do not exist in Australia.

While there was considerable variation in the sampling and interview contexts, the research findings indicated strong lines of commonality across the diverse groups. In other words, regardless of specific methodological variations, the information conveyed through the interviews proved to be remarkably similar and consistent across the sample groups. This continued to be a feature of subsequent work as part of a national study that involved interviews with up to 50 young people in each capital city of Australia, including Canberra.

Over time, for both the national research and a Perth-based school survey, we found that gang identification was a useful indictor of youth behaviour. Accordingly, for the purposes of the research, young people were asked two interrelated questions in order to identify their gang status:

- Do you consider your special group of friends to be a gang?
- Are you a member of a gang?

These questions are related to what Klein refers to as the 'funnelling technique', as a means to operationalise the distinction between gangs and other kinds of non-gang youth-group formations [7]. The main aim of this kind of analysis was to provide insights into the nature and prevalence of gangs and gang membership, as well as to develop a picture of gang behaviour and those factors contributing towards its prevalence. That is, the purpose of the study was to investigate the background, behaviours and attitudes that contribute to gang membership and/or identification.

As the research proceeded, we learned to be more precise in targeting specific people and specific issues. For instance, in later work the interviewees included:

- core members of the group
- peripheral members of the group
- ex-members of the group

Discussions with individuals also helped to clarify the processes whereby one was deemed to be a core, peripheral or former member, and the social factors (e.g., age, being at school, gender) that influenced entry to and exit from the group.

Central themes

As indicated, this book is the culmination of years of scholarship and research on youth gangs in Australia. Over the course of the last three decades I have been engaged in various studies of young people. These have included their engagement in the criminal economy through to diverse street-present youth-group formations. In the specific case of 'youth gangs', the interest has translated into discrete studies in Melbourne, Perth and across the nation. From Darwin to Canberra, Hobart to Adelaide and Brisbane to Sydney, young people have been interviewed and surveyed about their street activities, their friendship networks, and the meaning they attach to everyday events and interactions.

This flurry of academic activity has led me to several key conclusions – and propositions – about the nature of youth gangs in Australia.

First and foremost, I am convinced that the main problem here is not gangs *per se* but youth violence. Groups of young people, predominantly young men, are regularly engaged in harmful and, at times, lethal street violence. Frequently this is stirred by alcohol and illicit drug use, within the cauldron of intense rivalries and group oppositions at the local community level. Violence has become a method of relating to others in its own right, and a preferred means of resolving conflicts in the first instance. Violence is one of the key hallmarks of youth today (and, indeed, of yesteryear), most especially for young men. Hence the subtitle of this book: 'Exploring the nature of provocations and punch-ups'. Whether this is a particularly new phenomenon is difficult to ascertain, but certainly the historical evidence suggests that it is not. A social problem with a history nonetheless remains a social problem.

Second, youth gangs and youth groups are so highly variable and changeable in nature that they become elusive to both define and pin down concretely for any length of time. It is for this reason that for the most part I have avoided the use of specific gang names here. The social landscape within which gangs are inscribed is so constantly shifting that groups come and go rapidly, along with their monikers and tag signatures. It is not the continuity of any specific group that stands out but rather its emergence and disappearance within a short time span. As such, reference to specific groups and specific gang members as if they have persisted, or will persist, for any meaningful length of time is fruitless.

Yet 'gangs' in some form or another do exist. While the human content of the gang may vary as new kids join up and old ones leave (a typical pattern), or this particular gang forms in this neighbourhood while the one down the road dissolves (again a typical pattern), the gang nonetheless exists regardless of how transient its membership or its formation. But gangs always exist in relation to something else – a community, a locality, a cohort of students, an ethnic identification, class and gender dynamics, drugs availability, criminal organisations, bikie gangs and so on. Gangs always stem from, and are part of, larger collectivities and communities of people.

Typically, gangs comprise mainly, if not exclusively, male members. Likewise, they tend to form in working-class neighbourhoods where economically life is tough and opportunities are limited. Moreover, in many cases, gang membership is overlain by ethnic identification and group experiences of racism and social put-downs. Certain neighbourhoods have foisted upon them negative reputations, while particular youths become targets for police attention and media vilification. Studying gangs is thus basically about studying communities, about determining who is connected to whom, how and why. It is about the ways in which masculinity is constructed on the streets, and how social respect is gained and lost through physicality and violence.

Issues of class are fundamental to understandings of gangs and gang-related behaviour. As demonstrated throughout this book, social marginalisation, economic hardship and institutional humiliation provide the grounding upon which the edifice of gang formation is constructed. Yet the nature of core gang activities, in particular fighting, also illustrates that for street-frequenting youth, masculinity is primarily a matter of using the male body in certain ways. Coming to grips with who we are and who we want to be is hard enough for the most ordinary of us. For the dispossessed and disenfranchised, it overlies their daily interactions and sense of being in ways that reflect the nature of the street itself.

Who young people are is who they present they are. Respect is forged in the context of wider forces beyond one's control, such as structural unemployment, and must be won using the personal tools at hand – in this case, fists, knees, arms, head and, by extension of one's body, knives, guns and poles. One's place on the street and in the social hierarchy involves a struggle for *self-respect* as much as a struggle for *social respect*. The process depends upon young people taking responsibility for their actions, but this in turn is shaped by the social resources available to them as provided by the outside world. Being treated 'right' and gaining and keeping respect is partly a matter of plugging into existing street culture and its 'code of the street' [8]. Youth gangs provide an outlet for young men to exercise their manhood in particular ways, to exhibit to the world around them their prowess and standing – as defined and celebrated within the street-oriented environment. Respect won on the street presents as an alternative to that of mainstream institutions and their markers of success. It is this alternative moral economy that makes the gang attractive, not just the exhilarations of collective action.

How best to categorise people and experiences in ways that provide accurate and sensitive portrayals of social life is part of an ongoing conundrum for youth gangs research. This has been a perennial problem for me over many years and likewise has a bearing on how I think about gangs and gang-related issues. For instance, as part of the national youth gangs research, interviews with young people in each capital city were arranged. The main subjects of the study were young people who claimed to be, or who were identified by local youth and community workers as being, members of youth gangs. In other words, the sample was entirely contingent upon local groups that were identified as gangs, not ethnicity as such. However, in virtually every location around the country, ethnicity turned out to be central to which groups were deemed to be 'gangs' and who the gang members were. Ethnicity was also central to relationships at the local level between the gang members and other youth. Social being, which encapsulates consciousness of self and the ways in which one negotiates everyday life, is thus very much intertwined with ethnic background, as well as class and gender.

Within the Australian and many other national contexts, it is clear that we need to appreciate more than ever the ways in which ethnicity is socially constructed ideologically and materially in the lives of young people. For those engaged in the study of youth gangs, this is amongst the most important features of such research. Accordingly, this is reflected in the substantive discussions of gang life throughout this book. Moreover, in the light of the fact that indigenous young people constitute a separate and unique category of young people – as members of the first peoples of Australia – and as such warrant their own story and own analysis, this too is reflected in particular passages and chapters.

The media and youth gangs

The media are directly implicated in both the formation and the continued encouragement of youth gangs. They do this in various ways. First, they create a cultural climate within which negative perceptions of young people are in the foreground. Hardly a day goes by, for example, when there is not some reference to young 'offenders' in newspapers, on radio talkback shows and in television news coverage. The persistence and pervasiveness of such reporting and commentary mean that it is hard not to be fearful of crime and to be suspicious of young people.

Second, much of the coverage of youth crime is couched in the language of 'youth gangs', and especially 'ethnic youth gangs'. The latter is especially the case in Australia, but is certainly not unique to this country [9]. This reinforces the perception that groups of young people are 'out of control' and 'terrorising' ordinary citizens. Thus any portrayal of 'youth' tends to be linked to criminality, and the media discourses on 'law and order' frequently portray youth groups as criminal gangs.

Third, in order to sell a story, the media often attempts to get young people directly involved through interviews and pictures. If there is no gang as such, then at times young people have been asked to 'pretend' to be gang members 'for the camera'. Not only is this unethical and a gross misrepresentation of actual youth-group formations but it can, ironically, lead to the identification of some young people with gang membership. That is, the thrill and excitement of media attention may amplify the desire to be seen as a gang member. Reputation and status thus may be artificially created but have material and longer-lasting consequences for the young people and communities involved.

Youth gangs are increasingly perceived to be a problem. However, empirical study is needed in order to ascertain whether or not gang-related activity is on the rise; whether there is an increase in youth gangs as such or simply in the conflicts between diverse groups of young people generally; and to whom youth gangs are a problem (i.e., to other gangs, to members of the general public, to non-gang young people, etc.). In other words, we cannot assume that gangs are a problem simply because the media says so.

Intensified moral indignation around particular marginalised groups of people whose actions have been regarded as deviant is evident with regard to racialised portrayals of particular ethnic-minority communities in Australia. It is frequently the case, as well, that particular events are seized upon by the media to reinforce the 'ethnic' character of deviancy and criminality in ways which stigmatise whole communities. The extra visibility of young ethnic-minority people feeds the media's moral panics over gangs, as well as bolstering a racial stereotyping based upon physical appearance. But ethnic targeting is only one manifestation of how the gangs problem is portrayed.

The transnational flow of information and images of youth gangs provides fertile ground for the projection of underlying social anxieties, in many different societies, onto 'youth gangs'. Gangs have proved to be politically popular 'folk devils' for a long time, and there are indications that this will continue in the 21st century [10]. From the ill discipline of youth to the lack of respect for their elders, youth gangs provide handy reasons for what is wrong in the world today. Explaining riots and mob violence through the discourse of youth gangs has ensured its continuity as a stock explanation for social disorder, much of which originates in structural inequalities and involves young people who have been set adrift from the social supports of the society within which they live.

And so it goes. Talk about gangs, especially in the media and by politicians, tends to be made by those who do not know much about gang lives or the worlds inhabited by gang members [11]. This allows for the employment of simplistic and stereotypical definitions and pronouncements. It also feeds quickly into heavy handed attacks on the cultures and activities of street-present youth.

By contrast, and as demonstrated by and throughout this book, most dedicated researchers of gangs fail to agree on just about everything and anything to do with gangs – their membership, their size, their make-up, the impact of gender, the rituals (or not) guiding violence, their continuity over time, the degree of threat or harm they pose, their prevalence, their demise. The list goes on. This observation alone reinforces the notion that 'gangs talk', which reduces social problems to gangs, is both illogical and intensely ideological.

Youth gangs are not a simple phenomenon but are highly variable and fluid. Likewise, purported solutions to the 'gang problem' that do not reflect this complexity and ambiguity can basically do more harm than good, since they tend to reinforce the marginalisation and repression that generate youth resistance in the first place.

Conclusion

Issues of identity and inequality are central to how and why particular groups become linked with gang processes and discourses. Matters relating to territory, youthful male bravado and histories of intergroup conflict (and, in some cases, interfamily conflict) are at the heart of the gang violence that occurs. In most cases, violence is also precipitated by the influence of drugs and alcohol in a group setting (but not necessarily drug dealing *per se*).

On the plus side, youth gangs provide a sense of loyalty, membership, identity and protection, and there may be financial benefits and opportunities for 'fun' as well. On the down side, imprisonment, gaining a bad reputation, increased difficulty in getting a 'legitimate' job or settling down with a family, being afraid and being consumed by hate for others may flow from involvement in gangs.

This book explores the nature and dynamics of the youth gang as a particular social phenomenon. The stories and narratives herein represent an amalgam of voices and experiences from around Australia, involving many different social and ethnic groups. It needs to be reiterated that this is basically a story unique in many respects to what is happening, specifically, within this country. While there are obvious commonalities with gang formations and gang activities in other places around the world, and there are shared similarities with regard to the economic, social and political positioning of gang members within their respective societies, the empirical reality described in this book is nonetheless distinctive. It is an Australian story.

The presentation is intended to reflect the commonality of specific gang experiences across the board, while being sensitive to particular differences that shape how different groups of young men experience their participation in gangs. As a whole, the book attempts to provide a sense of why young people form and join gangs, and what gangs as gangs actually do. Again, the key or universal feature of gangs is group violence. It is this that is at the centre of the relationship between youth gangs, masculinity and social respect.

2
Gangs and Identity

Introduction

Research into youth gangs is usually driven by three basic questions: do gangs exist, are they a problem, and if so, what should be done about them? Addressing these questions can, however, be a complicated and difficult task. Gangs research is fraught with problems, many of them stemming from how we define youth groups and how we interpret the various activities of those who hang around in groups.

The concept of 'gang' is highly contentious and controversial. On the one hand, there are researchers who argue that gangs, as such, exist, that they are a problem and that they must be studied in detail if prevention strategies are to be successfully employed. From this perspective an effective and appropriate response to gang issues requires a thorough assessment of local communities and neighbourhoods, and careful appraisal of the nature of the problem [1].

However, not everyone is convinced that the term 'gang' is appropriate or that gangs research is necessarily a good thing or socially progressive. For instance, commentators in the US and the UK have criticised both the concept and those who extensively base their research on the idea of 'gang' [2].

Much of the disputation regarding the existence and magnitude of the alleged gang problem hinges on key definitional parameters, principally the appropriate conceptualisation of youth collectivities – that is, youth in groups. Settling on culturally suitable distinctions to be drawn between the various youth-group formations is one of the fundamental precursors to the accurate quantification of gangs and gang-related incidents. Although a source of ongoing consternation, this definitional ambiguity is not unique to any one country. Indeed, debates over defining youth gangs are a crucial part of most academic discussions and critical media studies that deal with the gangs question. This is so for at least three reasons.

First, how we define 'youth gangs' determines the number and composition of what it is that we are talking about. Wide definitions (of 'youth', of 'gangs') gather more young people into the gangs' conceptual net; narrower ones offer a more exclusive conceptualisation that incorporates fewer young people. The varied spectrum of collective youth behaviour – from recreation and leisure groups, to peers, friendship circles and family – can be distorted to the extent that every connection between young people is interpreted as being due to, or generated by, gang identification. It all depends upon how 'gang' is defined in the first place.

Second, the naming process associated with youth gangs research also helps to shape how issues and social problems more generally are framed. This is the essence of the 'gangs talk' critique. This refers to the idea that talking about gangs in imprecise and generalising ways has a tendency to make everything a gang problem, thereby diminishing attention on fundamental issues, such as racism, poverty and social inequality [3]. Gangs may exist, but, if every social issue is framed in terms of gangs, the underlying social causes of conflict, criminality and marginality recede from the academic and political agenda. What is on the analytical menu therefore has major implications for public policy and political decision-making.

Third, the gang as a frame of analysis tends to be about group status and relationships to a group. This means that most gangs research is about collective behaviour and group engagements. Part of the limitation here is that very often the personal experience of life in a community is ignored or downplayed because of the overriding emphasis on 'the gang' as the central feature and organiser of a young person's life. Where individual biography fits into the gang scenario may be missed insofar as analysis favours the collective over the individual. Yet people live complex lives and experience many changes in the course of growing up (and, indeed, ageing generally). Gangs imply a relatively fixed social status; individual experience, however, is always dynamic and ever changing, and involves a multitude of different relationships with different people and different institutions at different times.

Identification of gangs

US research has concluded that a few general facts about gangs can be applied across assorted geographic, demographic and ethnic settings:

Gangs are diverse – They vary, for example, in ethnic composition, criminal activities, age of members, propensity towards violence and organisational stability.

Gangs change – They evolve due to direct factors (e.g., prevention, intervention, suppression efforts) and in response to indirect factors (e.g., demographic shifts, economic conditions, influence of the media).

Reactions to gangs vary – Some communities deny that they exist while others sensationalise them if one is identified; some communities establish task forces to address gang issues while others conduct assessments to determine the nature and scope of gang problems.

Effective responses are diverse – Communities have developed various responses to gangs, including prevention, intervention and suppression or enforcement.

The message here is that gangs research (and the development of anti-gang strategies) must begin with the premise that there is no one single model of 'gang' as such [4]. The great variability in youth-group formations precludes a reliance upon either stereotypes of youth gangs or narrow definitions of what constitutes a gang. The sensitivities required of gang scholars are captured in what is known as the 'Eurogang Paradox' – the denial that there are US-style street gangs in Europe, based on a 'typical' US gang, a model that is not at all typical of gangs in America [5]. In other words, reliance upon stereotypes to define gang life not only allows the denial of youth gangs but it misrepresents the actual diversity of gangs in the US.

For instance, US researchers have developed a range of gang typologies to describe diverse youth-group formations from the criminally instrumental to the purely recreational [6]. Moreover, Canadian, European, Australian, Nicaraguan and South African research has increasingly emphasised that gang formation is a social process involving complex forms of membership, transformation and disintegration (a point returned to in Chapter 5 when we discuss gangs and transnationalisation) [7]. Indeed, US research challenges popular media images based on traditional stereotypes, and it demonstrates, for example, that in many cases gangs are typically not highly organised, and that the gangs, drugs and violence connection applies more to adult gangs than to youth gangs.

Klein distinguishes between five different street-gang structures by comparing groups on the basis of:

- whether or not they have subgroups or internal cliques;
- their size in terms of the number of members;
- the age range of the membership;
- the duration or longevity of the gang;
- whether or not it is territorial;
- its crime versatility versus whether it specialises in particular kinds of crime.

The importance of this typology is that it indicates further the diversity of street-gang formations, and thus reinforces the fact that gang stereotypes do not match gang realities [8].

A feature of contemporary US gangs research is the general observation that the composition of youth gangs is changing and that there are large differences in how groups are structured and organised. Again, the emphasis is on the analysis and close examination of specific youth-group formations rather than making assumptions and presumptions about the character of youth gangs. This point is reinforced in South African research that argues that the obsession with gangs has not been backed up with a detailed description of what gangs are and what they mean to different people. The little research that has been done on gangs reveals only that the term has developed a special ambiguity, and that in the South African context the notion of gangs is plagued with stereotypes, false assumptions and half-truths [9].

Canadian discussions of gangs make much the same point:

It is difficult to speculate as to the extent to which gangs are present in Canada. Gangs are a confusing issue for Canadians. Information given by media, law enforcement and government sources often contradicts information given by theoreticians and statisticians. These contradictions arise from different groups and organizations attempting to control the gang situation, whether it be informally or formally. Therefore, general impressions of gangs are abstract and enigmatic, resulting in a concerned and fearful public [10].

Interestingly, it is the diversity and ambiguity surrounding gang formation that in its own way may create disquiet amongst general members of the public.

US-style gangs, as customarily defined in terms of being highly structured, organised and criminally motivated, are less prevalent in other countries, and particularly do not feature amongst teenager group formations as such. The typical way of describing US youth gangs is to provide a composite picture of distinguishing characteristics. These generally include:

- a self-formed, complex association of youths (aged 12–24 and predominantly male) united through mutual interest, the members of which (customarily numbering in excess of 25) maintain regular, ongoing contact;
- a formalised structure and organisation maintained through strong intergroup solidarity and loyalty;
- identifiable leadership and rules;
- distinctive geographic, territorial, ethnic and/or other forms of domain identification; may involve self-designated names and may be associated with specific symbols, such as distinctive articles of clothing, tattoos, hand-signals, vocabulary or graffiti tags;
- specific and purposive role rationale and group norms, including structured, continuous engagement in criminal conduct [11].

Whether and to what extent such gangs actually exist in the US is, of course, subject to debate. Big questions have also been asked as to whether similar types of gang formation have been transplanted to other national contexts, in particular the UK.

Miller's definition of youth gangs is considered one of the better ones: 'a self-formed association of peers, united by mutual interests, with identifiable leadership and internal organization, who act collectively or as individuals to achieve specific purposes, including the conduct of illegal activity and control of a particular territory, facility, or enterprise' [12]. This is meant to exclude motorcycle gangs, prison gangs, racial supremacists and other hate groups, and to exclude gangs whose membership is restricted to adults.

Another somewhat more flexible variation on this is provided by the Eurogang Network, which uses the following definition: 'A street gang (or problematic youth group) is any durable, street-oriented youth group whose involvement in illegal activity is part of their group identity' [13]. As various related research has also demonstrated, quite often the core illegal activity of most concern is street violence.

While there is no standardised definition of a gang, nevertheless there is some agreement on the basic elements as outlined above. Further to this, Maxson and Klein identify three criteria for defining a street gang that have implications for the development of suitable anti-gang strategies:

- community recognition of the group;
- the group's recognition of itself as a distinct group of adolescents or young adults;
- the group's involvement in enough illegal activities to get a consistent negative response from law enforcement and neighbourhood residents [14].

These criteria have been echoed in South African legislation, which provides a list of factors that are relevant for the identification of a gang member during prosecution and sentencing [15]. This includes:

- admits to criminal gang membership;
- is identified as a member of a criminal gang by a parent or guardian;
- resides in or frequents a particular criminal gang's area and adopts their style of dress, their use of hand signs, language or their tattoos, and associates with known members of a criminal gang;
- has been arrested more than once in the company of identified members of a criminal gang for offences which are consistent with usual criminal gang activity;
- is identified as a member of a criminal gang by physical evidence, such as photographs or other documentation.

In practice, the specific features of any particular youth-group formation will vary greatly. But if the group sees itself as a 'gang', and is perceived by others around it as a 'gang', primarily because of its illegal activities, then this constitutes the minimum baseline definition of a gang. But are all groups of young people gangs?

Research into youth gangs has to locate these specific kinds of group within the context of other types of youth-group formation. That is, it is important that distinctions be made between different sorts of group – which may include gangs, youth subcultures, friendship networks, school cohorts and sports teams. Similarly, the reasons for group formation and the typical focus of activities can provide insight into differences between groups – as with distinguishing between social-centred and criminal-centred activity [16]. Recent studies also describe diverse forms of group association amongst young people from diverse socio-ethnic backgrounds. This is explored further in subsequent chapters.

The issue of youth gangs has come to the fore in many jurisdictions worldwide, and the question of how best to respond to gang activities has generated considerable attention from academics, policy-makers and law-enforcement services in recent years. With this upsurge in interest, however, the often central place of race and ethnicity in gang members' identities, a phenomenon apparent in many different national contexts, has been acknowledged as well. Issues of group membership, formation and activity have to be analysed from the point of view of where members are coming from, as well as how 'outsiders' view the group.

Identification of gang members

There are, then, major difficulties in defining what a gang is. So too are there major problems in trying to identify who a gang member is and what might be their precise relationship to a particular youth-group formation. The issue here is not so much the presence of the group but a particular individual's involvement with that group. Group membership is largely a fluid process, with specific individuals having varying degrees of association over time.

Consider the following. A young person may occasionally associate with a gang but not be a member. A young person may participate in the activities of the gang once in a while but not be a member. A young person may desire to be a part of the gang but not actually become a member. A young person may say they are part of the same crowd, or gang, but not actually be a member of the relevant core group. A young person may have all the external trappings of a gang member (street-gang culture in the form of dress, posture, talking style) but not be a member of a gang.

Gang membership is not absolute or fixed but highly variable and changing. Indeed, there is often no clear dividing line between those who are in a gang and those who are not. My Australian research has found that group membership and friendship networks are perhaps best conceptualised as being highly variable – there are layers of belonging and connection that vary according to circumstances and activities (discussed in greater depth in Chapter 3).

Different ethnic groups collaborate or have alliances with other groups. They might share together in drug taking, making music or even fighting. In some instances the neighbourhood connection is stronger than ethnic identity as such, as when outsiders enter into the local area to have it out with a particular ethnic-minority group, and various ethnic groups combine together against the intruders. In other cases, the local gangs are part of larger ethnic networks and subgroups, incorporating large geographical areas and relationships across distances (including international boundaries). Being a member of a gang is generally a contingent process, one defined by specific activities, special relationships and specific networks at any particular time.

Gang membership also tends to be marked by different degrees of commitment and association. Any particular group tends to be loosely organised around a core group (the hard core or leaders), fringe members (who participate in gang-related activities on a less frequent basis) and 'wannabes' (those who aspire to be hard core members of the main group). Again, these categorisations are fluid and may not always apply to actual group formations. In general there is no set pattern of recruitment and membership; in our national research there was only one mention (out of hundreds of interviews) of a gang initiation ceremony. Otherwise, who belonged to what group and in what capacity tended to be highly variable depending upon the individual, and on the circumstances that might bring together groups of young people. People could drift in and out of particular youth formations, including those self-described by the young people as 'gangs'. For some it was a short-lived passing phase; for others it might constitute a longer-term commitment. Other relationships and networks, particularly those revolving around ethnic networks, were more permanent but not gang-centred as such.

Depending upon who is defining gang membership, according to what criteria, there may be disagreement over whether or not a particular individual is in fact a gang member. Variables that might be considered include symbols or symbolic behaviour that tie the person to a particular gang: self-admission of gang membership, association with known gang members, type of criminal behaviour, location or residence, police identification as a gang member, other informant identification as a gang member, and other institutional identification as a gang member. In the end, the issue of individual gang membership can be as contentious as defining particular youth-group formations as being gangs. In either case there are major areas of ambiguity and uncertainty. In both cases, as well, things have a tendency to change over time.

Gang membership is also shaped by how others outside immediate social networks perceive youth-group formations. Whether it be the media, politicians, law-enforcement officials or academics, the portrayal of certain groups of young people as gangs may well produce the very thing that is being described. In other words, most gangs are not that organised, but treating them as if they are has potentially serious social ramifications: 'Treating them like cohesive groups may create a self-fulfilling prophecy... It can provide the group with a common point of conflict as well as a label and identity, setting a self-fulfilling prophecy in motion' [17]. If a particular group is called a 'gang' enough times, then it may well transform into the very thing that it has been named. This is particularly relevant with regard to the so-called Gang of 49 in Adelaide. A group of 49 indigenous young people were basically lumped together into one social category, sensationally by the media ('gang') and administratively by the police ('Aboriginal'). Eventually the labelling process itself contributed to a 'real' social problem that government authorities felt compelled to address [18].

It is not only perception by others but self-perception that is crucial to the development of gang identity. Sydney research has found, for example, that some of the young men who were interviewed presented themselves as a gang in order to gain a measure of 'respect' [19]. The symbolic representation of themselves as members of a gang, however, was more at the level of overt performance (i.e., presenting an image of being tough and dangerous) than in relation to particular kinds of professional criminal activity. The point of claiming gang status was to affirm social presence, to ensure mutual protection and to compensate for a generally marginalised economic and social position. A slightly different example of this naming process is provided by the Glenorchy Mafia in Tasmania. Here, what was once a sports team for 'disadvantaged kids' that was jokingly referred to, by the young people themselves, as the Glenorchy Mafia evolved over time into that which was being mocked – namely, a publicly identified youth gang.

Significantly, research indicates that where young people themselves claim gang membership they tend to engage in substantially more anti-social and criminal behaviour than those who do not profess to be gang members [20]. Who you say you are thus has implications for what you do and with whom. Group identification is thus intertwined with group activity.

Graffiti: 'gangs' or 'crews'

What if you don't want to call yourself a gang but others do? The ambiguities of gangs and gang membership are illustrated by considering the nature and dynamics of graffiti gangs in Adelaide. Our research found that, frequently, members of specific groups, while describing their activities in gang-like terms, denied that they were a gang. They insisted that they don't call themselves a 'gang' and don't act like one. Instead, many respondents were emphatic in their use of the term 'crew'. Similar to a gang, they would occasionally get into fights with other groups but this was not central to the group's activities.

For example:

> Sometimes – if people are being fuck heads, but we don't go out and start fights. We'll bring trouble if trouble comes to us.
>
> (15-year-old young man, Adelaide)

This was confirmed by another young man who commented:

> Oh if you're talking about a gang in terms of that – no. But been with like involved with a bunch of people called a crew and yes I have got into a few fights with crews.
>
> (18-year-old young man, Adelaide)

Fighting sometimes did become bigger in the lives of the group, however, as explained by the same person.

> Because shit was going down on a regular basis and, you know, I was willing to be in it twice a week, but not every fucking day. My mates told me, you know, 'Oh it's only going to happen once in a while – once in a while – you'll be right.' Then it started getting a bit too heavy, you know, I don't have the mind for that shit.

Usually the fights were over territory. Different groups claimed ownership over particular parts of the city. They did this through use of 'tags' – unique slogans, symbols and ways of graffiti writing that are identified with specific individuals and specific groups.

> So we didn't like anyone spray painting or doing anything like that around our area and nobody was allowed to hurt anyone in our crew unless they were from our crew and if they did, we'd go and get them back. It's just generally we were known as fighters.
>
> (18-year-old young man, Adelaide)

Each territory was protected by force if need be, and this was conveyed to potential interlopers through graffiti warnings as well as by word of mouth. Gang tags were also used to stir up trouble with other groups. Group X would travel to the territory of Group Y and tag over their tags. Building respect for and within a group is also linked to doing good graffiti art – good pieces with characters and lots of colours. But this art likewise has to be protected:

> Like you get a bit territorial with graffiti and stuff. Like you go and pick – you have your own spots where you go along and do things. Like you've done them for like lots of years. Like we do pieces and stuff like down creeks and nobody can see it. So I guess it gets a bit territorial. Like if someone comes along and goes over it, like that's your space kinda thing, so you always go back over it again and sometimes fights occur and stuff like that.

> Big groups go on big missions kind of thing. Like go along with a lot of people and just all do like this huge wall and every single person will do a big piece on it. Like a big colourful piece like background and like we'll colour in some stuff or whatever on it, and like we'll get in trouble if you don't ask obviously, so you can get in a fair bit of trouble for it. Trespassing and damage of property and all sorts of stuff as well.
>
> (18-year-old young man, Adelaide)

Another young person observed:

> The trouble would often start as a result of graffiti related things. When a graffiti artist goes over somebody else's tag with their own tag, that's a sign of disrespect. So that can start a fight between gangs.
>
> (17-year-old young man, Adelaide)

The border between legitimate and illegal is a fine line. On the one hand, 'everyone' is seen to engage in graffiti, implying a universal type of activity amongst young people. On the other hand, there are definite skills involved that make it much more than just vandalism:

> Everybody does graffiti – like everybody... Umm, it's got a reputation and stuff. It's like got lots of good graffiti artists and people with lots of experience and, yeah, stuff like that. People who've travelled around the world and done graffiti professionally and not professionally and stuff like that. So yeah, people wanna join just to be more

like them. Like some people like have role models and things, so they wanna be like them, they wanna join.

(18-year-old young man, Adelaide)

Illegal – like graffiti is illegal, so probably all the time, but I don't know. But police call graffiti anti-social, but that's only because they don't want it to be socially acceptable, so everyone's gotta hide it because it's illegal. But really there's like a whole little underworld and it's pretty cool.

(17-year-old young man, Adelaide)

A combination of pride, group identity, sense of territory and honour means that rivalries exist and violence can escalate around who is tagging what.

There were territorial factors where if you started putting tags up or pieces like in a certain area, if there's a gang there that feels like this is our area then they'll start – I mean they'll put their tags over your piece, and that's how the wars get started between graffiti gangs and groups like that... There's a problem if another group tries to copy, you know, what you're doing and, you know, puts your tag up or something like that or whatever then that's an automatic bashing straight away. That's just the rules those graffiti gangs operate by is that if you do that sort of stuff, you can expect to get your head kicked in. So you've gotta get smart and better be careful about what you're doing and where you're going, whose toes you're going to tread on if you're in this area or whatever.

(18-year-old young man, Adelaide)

Fighting occurs but is this really gang fighting? Groups are rivals but is this really a sign of gang conflict? According to the participants, it is the crew that counts, and it is graffiti that is at the heart of the crew. Loyalty to the group and to the art is not construed as necessarily being a gang thing as such.

The personal makes the individual

Another basic premise of this chapter, in addition to the notion of complexity in defining gang membership, is that we need to go beyond the master status of 'gang member' to consider the varied aspects of each person's biography. As illustrated below, biographical accounts, in conjunction with social analysis of communities, demonstrate that people relate and interrelate in complex ways that go beyond simplistic stereotype. Life is full of contradictions and paradoxes, and the future is far less predictable than many conventional gang paradigms suggest.

The richness and complexity of life experience tends to get lost in research that focuses solely or primarily upon one particular group's activities. By drilling down deeper into individual experiences, it is possible as well to view these young people quite differently from the image of angry, aggressive young men blindly engaging in offensive behaviour because that is the group thing to do. More personalised case studies reveal complexity and ambiguity, not the one-dimensional thug or gangster of popular imagination.

Social identity has a series of interconnected objective and subjective features that taken together combine to create multiple and varied identities. We are never just who we say we are; we are always a creative project, a self-in-the-making. The complexities of social identity are illustrated in Figure 2.1, which provides insight into the diverse contributors to identity formation [21]. Importantly, the notion of social identity that is conveyed in this figure incorporates all of these elements simultaneously into the one individual. We are singular, and

---

Identity is:

Chosen: I am who I say I am – People have some choice in how they wish to construct their own ethnicity and identity – as Australian, as hyphenated Australian, as German/Irish descent (agency in choosing identity).

Bestowed: I am who others say I am – Certain stereotypes and ethnic markers are used to construct ethnicity and identity for people – as 'Middle Eastern', as ethnic gang member, as not-Australian (identities that entrench the sense of being Other).

Simultaneous: I am more than one identity at the same time – I can be Australian and Lebanese, Australian and Jewish, Australian and Spanish-speaking (bicultural and transnational identities).

Strategic: I am who I am depending upon the circumstances – I am Lebanese, Lebanese-Australian or Australian depending upon whether I am at home, with my friends, at school or overseas (hybrid identities).

Virtual: I am who I am as shaped by global telecommunications – I can support Manchester United Football club without ever going to England; I can be affected by worldwide portrayals of Muslims, Jews and Hindus (virtual communities; communities considered through the lens of sameness rather than variation in beliefs, practices and attitudes).

Figure 2.1 Complexities of social identity

collective; agents of our own fate and subject to external pressures. Like a chameleon, we change and morph into different people depending upon social context and empirical circumstance. We are local and global at the same time. We are one, we are many – but all of this takes place within our one singular being.

People make sense of their lives in complicated ways. We are all part of wider families and communities than simply those of our mates and colleagues. Consider, for example, the position of gangs within local communities:

- There are frequently close ties between gang members and other members of their community, whether through family, religious or cultural linkages.
- Gang members do not simply and solely engage in criminal activities, but in a range of conventional activities that bring them in close contact with other people in the local community.
- Gang membership (however loosely defined) may be a continuous feature of some communities and thus have a measure of traditional legitimacy attached to it.
- Gang-related activity may in fact tap into underground or criminal economies that are on the whole beneficial to many ordinary residents in poorer working-class neighbourhoods (in that they provide a source of income and purchasing power that allows money to circulate within community agencies and businesses).
- Gang membership may be viewed by adult members of a community as an important way in which to protect each other, and to maintain a particular social identity that is important to the community as a whole (visible expression of ethnic pride and strength).

There are, then, connections between social circumstances that give rise to gangs and the community relations that sustain them. Just as these connections are situational and depend upon historical as well as contemporary factors, so too the life of each individual within a gang is multidimensional. To illustrate this, we can briefly consider the stories of 'Mohammed' and of 'Tan', a couple of young men we interviewed in Sydney as part of the national youth gangs research.

Mohammad's story

At the time of the interview, Mohammad was 17 years old, a Muslim and Lebanese-background young man. He was very conscious of family and cultural ties:

The best thing about my area is that everyone there is just like me. We came from the same place, our parents have the same background and we all speak the same language, we're into the same things and we can – like we just know – we just know, you know, how we all feel and that. It's just like one big family over there. We all grew up together and like people from – it's just like a small part of Lebanon in Australia.

Mohammad was subjected to racism at school by one of his teachers, and generally felt that the 'Arabs' and the 'Islanders' were picked on and consciously excluded from student representative bodies. He also felt that the police were racist, especially since most of the time they intervened when nothing wrong was happening.

Anger at his own immediate situation was compounded by the hurt felt about his family's country of origin in the context of life in Australia. Mohammad commented on the treatment he received compared with other members of the community:

No one calling them 'wog'. No one telling them to go back to their country. You know like, you know, you look around and you see all these Aussie kids and they're happy on their skateboards and shit and with their mums and their dads and stuff giving them money and stuff and it's because they're in their country. You can't say nothing to them. But us we should – no matter how long not matter how long we're going to be here and no matter how much the government give us money we're always going to feel like we're outcasts...I reckon no matter how much money we have, we're never going to be happy, we're never going to feel accepted.

The sense of outrage and injustice translated into aggressive, violent behaviour. Yelling at people on the streets, picking fights with other young people in the district, stirring people up – these were all part of 'normal' group activities. The sense of differentness and alienation was heightened whenever the group went into other suburbs, especially beach suburbs such as Manly.

Being different heavily impacted upon the process of social belonging. It certainly pulled people together into extremely close bonds:

You've always got someone – someone's always got your back all the time – all the time. You're never in danger. Like I never feel afraid.

Like I can come to Bankstown any time of the day, any time of the year, by myself and I've lived in Bankstown all my life and I've never ever been robbed or harassed or, you know, in Bankstown because of the people I hang out with. You've always got someone to turn to. There's always someone to listen. You can say it's more like a family because we all look after each other. You know a few months ago one of us got ran over and every single one of us went to the hospital every day. Every single one of us went to the hospital every single day until he got out. When he got out at his house we visited him there. So it's like that.

The moral basis of the group's behaviour was partially revealed in answer to a question about the difference between bullying and gang activity. It is here, as well, that we see fluidity in terms of who can or cannot be included within the gang:

Bullying is for people that feel low and the only time they feel good is when they find someone weaker than them. Like we don't bully. We don't sit there and see someone looking at us and say: 'Oh lets go jump him 'cause he's looking at us.' We don't fuck – there is a few of us that go round jumping people for money and that, but I don't know, but we don't make it as like a hobby to just sit there at the station and look at people and just start bullying 'em and pushing 'em around. Actually we're more like a gangster – like there's a kid whose twenty-one. He's got Downs Syndrome. He hangs out with us even though he's not Lebanese. He's not Arab. I think he's an Aussie or something, yeah, but he hangs around with us and like we usually protect him from like if anyone ever makes fun of him like we're the ones that will stick up for him.

It is not only protecting the weak and vulnerable, as well as one's mates, that make Mohammad feel good. Other things do too:

Going to the Mosque a lot makes me feel good. I like to help out around the neighbourhood like if my mum needs something or my friends' mums need something or if their dads need help or anything. Like for example the bloke with me out there his dad is building a house down near Bankstown College and I always go down to help him out there for nothing. Yeah that makes me feel good.

Mohammad's story is one of loss and pain, pride and generosity. It is his story but it is also the story of his country, his neighbourhood, his friends. It is depressing, yet strangely exhilarating and hopeful. It shows the goodness interspersed with the harshness, and how the senseless can make sense at the level of the everyday.

Tan's story

Tan was 18 years old at the time of interview. He was born in Australia but has a Vietnamese background and speaks Vietnamese at home with his parents. He is a Roman Catholic.

Several years ago, Tan was involved in a criminal gang. Unusually, for this specific type of gang, it did not comprise just one ethnic background:

> When I was younger I kind of went off and did my stuff. Kind of got recruited into a gang pretty much...and it was funny because they were a different nationality to me. It's actually called the Hong Kong Gang, so a Chinese gang and I was pretty much the only Vietnamese person in that group at that time I think in a level that is pretty high. I was asked to learn a bit of Chinese and stuff, so we could relate sometimes and when there's problems you would know what's going on.

The gang made money by selling drugs, and by stealing and then selling items. Tan was recruited to help sell PlayStations that had been stolen from a warehouse. One of his roles was to facilitate the street-level distribution of stolen goods by finding people to buy the products that they sold, and to find places that were good for an illegal job. In his mid-teenage years, Tan joined the gang because he wanted friends, he wanted money and he wanted power. The group he was associated with was based in the city rather than in the local neighbourhood.

At the local level, however, he created his own group, which likewise had mixed racial and ethnic backgrounds:

> Two of them were Chinese and the other one was Australian. That was pretty funny. The reason why I wanted an Australian was because he was big and I thought size counted, so I recruited him. I think the rest were all Vietnamese.

The group was formed consciously and intentionally as a criminal gang. The membership thus reflected the connections and activities of that kind of group formation. Gang activities included group fighting. They also included extortion:

> you've got an area to look after. You walk down, you've got shops you can make money out of. It's just respect money they call it, so we don't destroy, you know, your shop or something. So you walk in and you tell the guy, look you know, you have to pay so much a month.

This was organised violence, at the local level, with ties across the city. The gang's activities also included robberies, credit-card fraud, procuring of passports and drug dealing. They even sold university degrees to overseas students.

In school, Tan experienced what he describes as a subtle form of racism from some of his teachers. For example, they would allow 'Australian' kids to eat freely in class but tell Tan and his fellow 'Asian' students off if they did it. He also commented on both how unfairly the Lebanese people were treated and yet how racist one Lebanese student was.

> it was funny because he's the one going around the school bullying everyone else and he's Lebanese. Just because people didn't treat him the way he wanted doesn't mean he had to go around treating everyone else like shit ... It was pretty interesting to see that. He was pretty racist for a while. I think now he's grown out of it and it's died down a bit, but yeah it was pretty bad at the time.

Tan has been involved in many violent incidents, including gang fights and single assaults on other youths. He was charged at one stage with 'assault with a deadly weapon' and other charges, but these were dismissed. His early attitude was that nothing really mattered, and that he could not care less about things since there was nothing to lose and nothing to gain. His life started to change due to the influence of his (now ex-) girlfriend.

> She got afraid of me getting hurt most of the time, so and I didn't want to see her being hurt. I kind of cared for her a lot. I think at that

time that was the only thing that I cared for – really, really cared for – so I listened to a lot of things she said.

She convinced me it's not worth dying over. You could die for your country, but not over that.

According to Tan, learning personal responsibility ultimately stemmed from his personal relationship and his desire to respect the wishes of his girlfriend.

After leaving the gang, Tan became involved in various youth volunteer activities in the local area. This was motivated by a desire to repair some of the harm he'd done as a gang member:

I think after I left the gang I thought: 'I've hurt too many people. It's time for me to give back to the community'. I also do a church youth group. I'm with them as well, so yeah it's something to give back for something I've taken out. I think it helps me feel better, sleep better I think during the night.

Redemption for Tan means taking personal responsibility to change one's life. It also means restoring the balance as much as possible.

Biography and being in between

A more in-depth and less gang-focussed examination of the lives of Mohammad and Tan reveals that young people going through extraordinary experiences find varying ways of coping with their particular social circumstances.

Listening to the stories of Mohammad and Tan allows us to better appreciate the temporal dimension of lived experience – the ways in which people and circumstances change over time. This is important, for as much as anything it precludes locking any individual into a preordained pathway based upon where they are in the here-and-now. The future is open and mutable, although the parameters of what is possible are structurally bounded by the weight of the past and the institutional opportunities of the present. The determinism of positivist risk-based trajectory analysis falls far short in anticipating or explaining the zigzags of real life experiences amongst individuals (see Chapter 9).

The limitations of conventional approaches to the problem of youth gangs, which tend to define people primarily and solely in terms of gang membership, are also apparent. Each of the young men in our case studies was a gang member, and yet much more than this. They were part of ethnic communities, of families, of school groups and of street scenes. Not all of their lives was spent 'in the gang'. Not all of their time was spent 'doing gang stuff'. Each young man, during the course of their interview, mentioned how scared they were of the violence, of the possibility of not having their close mates around them. They are strong and vulnerable at the same time.

Each of these young men likewise demonstrated the importance of generosity and 'giving' in their lives. The importance of the expenditure of various kinds of capital, as well as its accumulation, in the lives of young people is highlighted by Monica Barry [22]. By expenditure of capital she means that people want to expend – to give something to someone else – as part of feeling good about oneself and one's place in the wider community. Far from being always the taker (as implied in gang activities), there is impetus to also be the giver. Both Mohammad and Tan found contentment in giving up their time and energy as a volunteer for their mosque and church, respectively. They didn't have to do this – it was freely chosen and pleasurable activity for both of them. Good and bad rarely resides in the individual; it is constructed around practices, not people.

The pragmatic way in which groups are formed and exist is also an important theme. While ethnicity is the key marker of group formation (including youth gangs), this does not preclude interesting exceptions to this general rule. Mohammad spoke about the inclusion of an Anglo young man with Down's Syndrome in his group. Tan talked about his criminal gang being led by Chinese, and of his own personal group that included Chinese and Australian youth as well as Vietnamese. Racism in general (against Lebanese, against Vietnamese) does not always end in segregation and social division. Personal contacts and personal friendships, built up at school or on the street, for the purposes of the social or the criminal, provide a counterfoil to the tendency to see identity and activity as exclusively exercised through the lens of ethnicity. Moreover, a dislike of 'Australians' in general because of institutional and cultural privileging, and direct experiences of racism, is mediated by personal interactions of a more positive kind.

The common strengths in specific diversities are alluded to in other work that has examined the in-between status of ethnic-minority youth:

> While some young people very consciously claim their ethnic identity, they also link a more tolerant and open-minded attitude in their

association with diverse friendship networks. In this way, culturally diverse groups can give young people the ability to associate less problematically with a wider range of 'others', making cross-cultural connections and affiliations. While many of the young people who took part in our research have a sense of exclusion and rejection from mainstream society, for the most part they are not cynical about a commitment to values of tolerance, equality and diversity [23].

As this chapter has indicated, the exclusivity of some youth-group formations, such as gangs, implies a much smaller social canvass than that described in this quotation. Yet closer analysis reveals that group dynamics do not preclude a series of mutual interactions (e.g., between the Lebanese and the Samoan; between the Vietnamese and the Chinese) that may involve shared interests and shared social status in specific situations. Antagonism between Vietnamese and Chinese is forgotten in schoolyard and classroom situations that negatively affect both. Music and entertainment provide bridges between the Lebanese and Samoan who make fun for themselves in very similar ways, and who both feel to be outsiders to the mainstream.

Examination of personal biography also provides some indication of the shifting nature of relationships, of how people from diverse ethnic and social backgrounds come into and out of the lives of each individual. A sense of justice, fairness and generosity permeates the accounts of Mohammad and Tan, even in the midst of oppression, racism and social exclusion. These positive qualities are also intrinsically cross-cultural in nature. We understand and empathise with those who 'do good' by protecting the weak and vulnerable, and who volunteer their time to help others. This, too, is a platform upon which to build community solidarity and intercommunal peace.

Conclusion

We began this chapter by stating that defining gangs is always going to be highly contentious. As we work our way through the key elements of gang membership, the more complicated things become. Some of the complexities associated with gangs are further explored in Chapter 3. For now, suffice it to say that studying gangs is from start to finish a contested exercise.

As illustrated in the latter part of the chapter, we need an approach that allows for insights that show the dynamics of social relationships as they are constructed in the crucible of everyday choices, negotiations and actions. Who we are is, and always has been, a continuous process. The contours of this process are structurally influenced by matters pertaining to class, gender and ethnicity, but the process itself is marked by ambiguity and paradox as much as by broad propensities and continuities. Herein lies the possibility for positive social transformation, individually and collectively, in dealing with issues of systemic marginalisation and social inequality.

3
Groups and Networks

Introduction

This chapter starts with the recognition that young people in Australia spend a lot of time in the public domains of the street, regardless of social background. However, as construed by the mass media and in the statements of political leaders, youth activity on the streets is in many instances equated with gang behaviour. But do gangs as such really exist in Australia? Are they really the threat to society that media portrayals would have us believe?

The notion of gang can mean different things to different people. Imprecise definitions and perceptions of young people based on stereotypes, however, often feature prominently in media treatments of young people, and especially ethnic-minority youth (see Chapter 1).

How best to categorise people and experiences in ways that provide accurate and sensitive portrayals of social life is part of an ongoing conundrum for social research. This is especially evident in research and scholarship dealing with phenomena such as youth gangs [1]. Diverse social factors and networks bring young men and women together. In the Australian gangs research, it was observed that ethnicity (i.e., a distinct cultural identity) often forms the core of social relationships but then intersects with variables such as geography (e.g., specific locality), age (i.e., mainly teenagers but up to mid-20s), size (i.e., sheer number of people who congregate at any point in time), affiliation (i.e., with people from similar cultural backgrounds) and familiarity (i.e., of one's immediate neighbours, peers and acquaintances).

Gang formations and gang-related behaviour

Periodic media reports about the perceived proliferation and criminal or anti-social activities of youth gangs have long featured in press stories about young people in many parts of Australia – from Melbourne to Adelaide, Perth to Sydney. These reports are by no means new. Indeed, the idea of gangs has been associated over a lengthy period of time with various kinds of youth-group formations.

From the mid-eighteenth century to the end of that century, for example, much public concern was directed at the 'push larrikins' of Melbourne and Sydney (see Chapter 4). These were groups of young men (the groups were called 'pushes') who, through their appearance (e.g., wearing of pointed-toed boots) and behaviour (e.g., getting drunk, getting into fights), became easily identified as threats by the media, the police and the general public. The streets were the meeting places of the pushes and they had their origins in the poverty of their members. The push larrikins were born out of a very unsettled state of society, and they reflected the lack of amusements, recreational outlets, jobs and overall means of livelihood for these young people. Deviancy was grounded in the form of the gang.

By contrast, public consternation about young people in the mid-20th century revolved around the 'bodgies and widgies', young working-class men and women who were identifiable by their particular visual styles and leisure concerns [2]. The bodgies and widgies represented a new teenage culture, with an emphasis on fashion (long hair styles for the boys, gabardine skirts for the girls), street presence, dancing, and rock and roll music. From 1950 to 1959, the phenomenon of the bodgies and widgies captured the imagination of the media. These were working-class young people with jobs, and they were engaging in the first stirring of a distinctive teenage consumer-oriented culture. In doing so, they represented a threat to middle-class values and culture, and much of the media condemnation (and distortion) centred on alcohol use, sexual behaviour and family breakdown associated with the bodgies and widgies. Deviancy was linked to a new youth subculture.

Until recently there has been relatively little concerted research into the nature and dynamics of contemporary youth gangs in the Australian context. Much of the knowledge about youth groups, including gangs, has been based upon anecdotal information and popular media imagery derived from elsewhere, including and especially the US. Many disputes have taken place over the existence and magnitude of the alleged gang problem. This has been due mainly to problems in defining what a gang actually is.

The specific features of any particular youth-group formation will vary greatly. As discussed in Chapter 2, if the group sees itself as a gang and is perceived by others around it as a gang, primarily because of its illegal activities, then this constitutes the minimum baseline definition of a gang. But research into youth gangs has to locate these specific kinds of group within the context of other types of youth-group formation (see Chapter 2). As indicated in the earlier mention of the larrikins and the bodgies and widgies, groups may be defined in the media as deviant but not necessarily as a gang. Similarly, the reasons for group formation and the typical focus of activities can provide insight into differences between groups.

Gang-related behaviour

Enter the importance of making a distinction between gangs as such, and gang-related behaviour. The distinction arose in the course of our trying to figure out what was happening in the lives of young people who were interviewed as part of investigations into the dynamics of youth gangs. For example, our 1990s research on ethnic-minority youth in Melbourne found that group conflict, and especially street fights, were common across the sample group. Whatever the ambiguities of the term 'gang' amongst academics and young people themselves, membership of certain groups or collectivities was nevertheless associated with varying degrees of violence and illegal activity. To outsiders, such street activity could well be interpreted as a hallmark of gang membership and engagement. For insiders, however, group membership was often linked to a form of protection against racism and street violence rather than a violent outlet. For many there are major positive benefits to be derived from group participation with young people from similar class, ethnic and religious backgrounds.

Gang-related behaviour can initially be categorised in terms of types of activity (in another context, some of these activities have been associated with different types of gang) [3]. There are four types of activity:

Criminal – The main focus of the activity is directed at making money through illegal means (e.g., property theft and drug selling). This kind of activity may be sporadic and episodic, and it may not be central to a group's overall activity. Or it may involve complex relationships, techniques and skills, in essence a whole culture and highly organised division of labour within which profit-making occurs.

Conflict – The main feature is that of street fighting and where violence is associated with gaining social status and street reputation.

This kind of activity is marked by an emphasis on honour, personal integrity and territoriality (defending one's physical or community boundaries). Issues of self-esteem and identity, and constructions of masculinity and self-protection loom large in consideration of why conflicts occur and persist over time.

Retreat – The main activity is that of heavy drug use and generally a withdrawal from mainstream social interaction. Illegal activity mainly lies in the use of drugs as such, rather than in violence or other forms of anti-social activity. However, due to the drug use, property crimes and crimes of violence may result, often on an impulsive and senseless basis. The presence of drug users may create moral panic or disturb the sensibilities of other members of the public who are witness to them.

Street culture – The main characteristic is the adoption of specific gang-related cultural forms and the public presentation of gang-like attributes. The emphasis is on street gang culture, incorporating certain types of music, ways of dressing, hand signals, body ornaments (including tattoos), distinctive ways of speaking, graffiti and so on. It may be 'real' activity in the sense of reflecting actual group dynamics and formations. It may instead simply be a kind of mimicry, based upon media stereotypes and youth cultural fads.

An important feature of this description of different types of activity is that the activities actually pertain to young people in general rather than to youth gangs specifically. That is, young people may engage in one or more of the activities described, at different times and in different locations, to a varying extent depending upon social background and other factors. They may do so on their own or with a group, and involvement in particular activities may be for short or long periods. In other words, what is described here as gang-related activity does not equate with gang membership. Nor does gang membership necessarily translate into participation in these activities. For example, it has been observed that 'In some gangs, using drugs is an important means of gaining social status. In others, drug use is forbidden, especially if the gang is involved in selling them' [4]. In addition, it may be that individual members of a gang engage in specific types of illegal activity, such as selling drugs or homicide, but this may not be a function or outcome of the gang as a whole.

The visibility and group nature of much youth crime lend itself to gang explanations for juvenile offending. That is, most youth crime involve more than one person, is usually easier to detect and the activities of young people tend to be more public than those of other groups. However, the group nature of juvenile offending should not be confused with gang-related criminality as such. The vast majority of youth crime tends to be episodic, opportunistic and trivial in nature, and it either arises out of the spontaneous activities of social groups or is linked to a small number of chronic offenders who account for the bulk of juvenile crime [5]. While youth offending cannot be equated with gang activity, nevertheless, membership of a gang can play a major part in criminal engagement. US research, for example, has shown that there are significant differences between the criminal behaviour of youth gang members and non-gang, but similarly at risk, young people. It was found that gang membership increases the likelihood that members will commit serious and violent crime and the frequency with which they will do so. This is similar to findings of recent gang to non-gang comparative research in Australia [6]. In other words, gang membership does not explain juvenile offending in general but it can exacerbate it in practice.

Gang problems

A distinction can be drawn between gangs and gang-related behaviour. A further analytical point also needs to be made. That is, not all gang behaviour is necessarily criminal, illegal or 'bad'. Therefore one must distinguish between different kinds of gang behaviour. More importantly, the question can be asked: When do these gang behaviours become a problem?

The following elements have been identified as central to what constitutes a problem:

- A problem involves a group of harmful incidents [and thus a long-term solution to prevent its re-occurrence].
- The incidents that make up the problem must be similar in some way [on the basis of time or place, the people or behaviour involved, the social or physical environment within which it takes place].
- A problem must be of direct concern to the public [usually involving injury, or stolen or damaged property, or serious social and economic costs].[7]

In 1990s Melbourne gangs research, there was much confusion and ambiguity over the difference between gangs and groups. In each case, membership tended to revolve around similar interests (e.g., choice of music, sport and style of dress), similar appearance or ethnic identity (e.g., language, religion and culture) and the need for social belonging (e.g., friendship, support and protection). Group affiliation was sometimes perceived as the greatest reason why certain young people were singled out as being a gang and why particular conflicts occurred between different groups of young people.

In the end, if gangs as a problem are to be addressed, then a series of questions about gangs and gang-related behaviour generally need to be asked [8]:

- Do gangs exist in our community?
- How do we know they exist?
- How long have these gangs been in operation?
- Approximately how many youths are involved in these gangs?
- How are youths recruited into these gangs?
- What behaviours do these gangs engage in?
- What specific harm do these behaviours cause?
- Is someone being injured?
- Is something being stolen? If so, what?
- Is property being damaged?
- Could serious social or economic costs result from these behaviours?
- Who carries out these behaviours?
- What efforts, if any, have already been made to control gang membership or harmful activities?
- Are specific individuals, businesses or community groups complaining about gang activities? If so, what specific behaviours or activities are they reporting?
- Are there behaviours being carried out at certain times and places?

It is important to bear in mind the positive features of gangs for many young people (and, in some cases, for their parents and other family members). Gangs can provide support and security for vulnerable groups of young people. They can provide opportunities for status, group identity and excitement. They can provide a mechanism for young people to cope with oppressive environments, and represent one response or option to chronic marginalisation and social exclusion. All of these features point to the importance of peers and peer networks in the lives of young people, but they leave open the matter of the social content of youth-group formation. The problem is not with youth groups, as such; it is with what groups of youths do.

Interpreting how gangs change over time depends on two things: the concepts deployed to explain gang formation in the first place, and the empirical history of the group in question. Gangs may enjoy a short life span, or they may persist over time as quasi-institutionalised groups. If the latter, then it would appear that entrenched, longstanding cultural and socio-economic factors are determinate. If the former, then gang formation is more probably due to temporary peer-group dynamics, fluctuations in local regulatory situations or employment markets – in other words, trends and fashions that ebb and flow according to immediate circumstances.

Groups that persist over different generations of young people would appear to involve a transfer of some type of commonality within communities. To put it differently, the persistence of a gang or specific group identity can be explained in terms of, for example, sharing the same ethnic background and social experiences as earlier generations (e.g., Lebanese Australian youth). Or it may be the case that gangs of young people are linked to 'underclass' conditions, wherever and whenever these become evident, and that their persistence is best understood in the context of the wider political economy. Or it could be a combination of social and economic factors that pertain to specific groups or geographical areas. The persistence of gang formations has implications for intervention strategies insofar as gangs often occupy an ambiguous position within local communities and may, therefore, not be perceived as quite the threat that outsiders may deem them to be.

Although certain gangs may be seen as a more or less permanent fixture of some neighbourhoods, suggesting a basic continuity in gang life, the actual composition and activities of each gang formation needs to be examined closely and empirically. That is, the character of particular gang formations will be different depending upon who the current members are. As Moore observes, new cliques or gangs may start up every few years, each with their own name and separate identity. They may identify with previous gangs or cliques that have gone before them, yet they are autonomous from previous generations [9]. Having gangs in a neighbourhood over time does not therefore equate to the same gang persisting over time. Each group of young people constructs the kind of group formation dictated by its times and circumstances, while drawing upon past examples to guide them in this process.

An analysis of the life course of locally based gangs is vital to understanding membership patterns and preferred activities. For instance, one can ask whether or not gang membership is 'inherited'? Do young teenagers join certain groups because of siblings and/or other relations being associated with these groups? What role do family ties have in both the persistence of gangs and gang membership over time? What impact does this 'cultural tradition' have on gang processes and the possibility of breaking the pattern? How does one become an ex-gang member? What social processes entrench gang status and gang membership over time (e.g., imprisonment and release of gang leaders back into the same community)? These are important practical questions, especially given that there is evidence that as gangs mature, the criminal involvement of their members grows more serious [10]. The longer and more established the gang, the more likely it will engage in higher levels of violence and criminal activity.

Much of the public concern over youth gangs in Australia seems to be driven by images of 'colour gangs' in the US. Close examination of the Australian social landscape, however, makes it hard to substantiate the presence of such gangs in this country. Nevertheless, the presence of large groups of young people on the street, or young people dressed in particular ways or with particular group affiliations, appears to have fostered the idea that Australia, too, has a gang problem.

This is especially so in relation to the activities and perceptions of ethnic-minority youth. Indeed, in recent years the hype and sensationalised treatment of youth gangs have tended to have an increasingly racialised character. That is, the media have emphasised the 'racial' background of alleged gang members, and thereby fostered the perception that, for instance, 'young Lebanese' or 'young Vietnamese' equals 'gang member'. The extra 'visibility' of youth ethnic-minority people (relative to the Anglo 'norm') feeds the media moral panic over youth gangs, as well as bolstering a racist stereotyping based upon physical appearance (and including such things as language, clothes and skin colour). In fact, media images and treatments of ethnic-minority young people are generally very negative. It is frequently the case as well that particular events are seized upon by the media to reinforce the 'ethnic' character of deviancy and criminality in ways which stigmatise the wider community.

The image of gangs is a powerful one in terms of public perceptions and has engendered varying kinds of social reactions. For example, the social status and public perception of young people in groups very much influences the regulation of public space. Many groups of young people, some of whom might be labelled 'gangs', for instance, tend to hang out in places like shopping centres. To a certain extent, much of the concern about gangs is really a misunderstanding of the nature of youth subcultures, of how young people naturally associate with each other in groups, and of the material opportunities open to them to circulate and do things in particular places. In most cases, however, the presence of identifiable groups is not the precursor to activity which is going to menace the community as a whole.

We also have to be aware of how young people mobilise gang symbols and imagery as a form of 'huff and puff', a way to make themselves seem bigger and badder than they really are. Gang images and mimicry can themselves be used as a form of self-protection [11]. Adopting a name for the group may be part of this posturing. However, naming processes may contribute to group transformations over time, accruing a reputation and generating negative social reaction. Groups thus can change over time, as can individual participation in a group.

Gang characteristics

By and large it can be concluded that most bands of young people on the streets of Australia are not gangs but groups. A review of specific gangs research over the past 30 years confirms some of the ambiguities surrounding this designation.

Melbourne Study 1980s

A 1980s study of youth gangs in Melbourne, for example, found that while some characteristics of these groups mirrored the media images (e.g., the masculine nature of youth gangs, their preferred 'hang outs' and shared identity markers, such as shoes or clothes), the overall rationale for the groups' formation was simply one of social connection, not crime.

In their study, Aumair and Warren cited five key characteristics of youth gangs [12]. These include:

- overwhelming male involvement, which in turn reinforced certain 'masculine' traits in the group setting (e.g., fighting prowess, sexual conquest, substance use and minor criminal acts);
- high public visibility, given the lack of money and therefore a reliance on free public spaces for recreational purposes;

- an outward display of collective identity, in the form of the wearing of similar styles of clothing, adopting a common name for the group and so on;
- organisation principally for social reasons, and consequently low rates of criminal activity, as indicated in the absence of formalised gang rules and a social rationale for gathering together, rather than a criminal objective;
- differences between public perceptions of the 'gang problem' and the real nature of the problem, as illustrated by the fact that most criminal activity seemed to be inwardly focused, involving one-on-one fights and substance abuse.

Much of the criminality exhibited by youth gangs, therefore, is inward-looking and linked to self-destructive behaviour, such as substance abuse, binge drinking and the like. The popular perception is that gangs seek to violate the personal integrity and private property of the public in general; closer investigation reveals the insular nature of much of their activity.

As users of public space, ethnic-minority youth are particularly visible due to ethnic markers, such as physical appearance and language, and because they often congregate in numbers. Whether these groups of young people constitute gangs, as such, is a matter of systematic research and careful interpretation. Several studies in recent decades have examined so-called ethnic youth gangs in various Australian cities.

Adelaide Study 1980s

Due to media concerns about street kids and loutish behaviour on the part of some young people in the inner city, a study was undertaken in the late 1980s to investigate the potential and actual needs of young Italo-Australians who frequent Adelaide city streets [13]. It found that groups of young men, united around their common Italian heritage, did meet regularly, both in the suburbs and in specific 'Italian' areas of the inner city. The groups essentially formed on a social basis, with 'hanging around' an activity in its own right shared by group members.

The study found that periodically there were fights between the Italo-Australian young men and other groups. Conflicts tended to be based upon ethnic identification, and to involve the 'Italians', the 'Greeks' and the 'Australians'. Sometimes the Italians and Greeks would find solidarity with each other in their common difference with the Anglo-Australians. It was the 'wogs' versus the 'Aussies'.

Fights tended to occur due to taunts and jeers between groups of young people. For the Italo-Australian young men, this often took the form of racist discourse that attacked their legitimacy as Australian citizens and residents ('they call us Wogs and they say go back to Italy'). Group behaviour and group protection reinforces the cohesion and identity of the group as a whole. Thus:

> Rivalry and physical conflicts with other racially based groups reinforces their identity both as Italians and as 'macho men'. In this context, especially as victors in the fight, they can turn their status as 'wogs' from a point of derision to something of which they can be proud [14].

The themes of social connection, identify formation, collective protection and active resistance to racist provocation surfaced in other recent studies as well.

Melbourne Study 1990s

Our Melbourne study of ethnic youth gangs in the mid-1990s consisted of interviews with young Vietnamese, Somali, Latin American, Pacific Islander, Turkish and Anglo-Australian young people [15]. It found that membership of a defined group tended to revolve around similar interests (e.g., choice of music, sport and style of dress), similar appearance or ethnic identity (e.g., language, religion and culture) and the need for social belonging (e.g., friendship, support and protection). Group affiliation was simultaneously perceived as the greatest reason why certain young people were singled out as being members of a gang. This identification process was in turn associated with hassles by authority figures, such as the police and private security guards, and conflicts between different groups of young people on the street or at school.

To some extent the media image of youth gangs does have an empirical reference point. That is, many young people do hang out together, in groups, on the street. And, as is the case with most young people, periodic offending and illegal behaviour does occur. But this type of activity tended to be a by-product of group interaction rather than a rationale for group formation. Nevertheless, the identification of certain young people as members of this group or that group was also tied to real tensions and problems at the level of intergroup relations amongst the young people.

For instance, the study found that street fighting and school-based fights were a fairly common occurrence. The specific reasons for the fighting were varied. Racism and treating people with disrespect were crucial elements in the explanation. Likewise, so was the sense of ownership and belonging associated with particular local areas and membership of particular social groups. Social status for these young people is thus something that is both contested and defended, and this in turn is generally tied to one's identification with certain people and places.

Sydney Study 1990s

Another study of ethnic-minority youth, particularly in relation to the issue of gang-related behaviour, was undertaken in Sydney's western suburbs in the 1990s [16]. The research involved interviews with Lebanese young people and other community members, as well as media and policy analysis. It found that a major problem was the 'racialised' reporting of crime when the media dealt specifically with 'Lebanese' youth. Ethnic identifiers are used in relation to some groups but not others (e.g., Anglo-Celtic Australians). Moreover, the 'explanations' for such 'ethnic crime' tends to pathologise the group, as if there is something intrinsically bad about being Lebanese or, more generally, Middle Eastern.

The study pointed out that the groups that exhibit the highest rates of imprisonment, including, for example, the Lebanese, Vietnamese and Turkish, also have the highest unemployment rates. Put simply, the issue of social exclusion appears to be central to any explanation of youth offending involving particularly disadvantaged groups. Marginalisation was also central to explaining the perception of widespread involvement in youth gangs amongst Lebanese youth. Even so, the main forms of association amongst Lebanese young people were first and foremost friendship groups. These groups also functioned as a defence against experiences of racism and exclusion from the cultural mainstream.

The Sydney study found that there was an intersection of masculinity, ethnicity and class – in such a way as to affirm social presence, to ensure mutual protection and to compensate for a generally marginalised economic and social position:

> This performance of the 'gang' functions in several ways: it provides a venue for cultural maintenance, community and identity; and at the same time provides the protection of strength in numbers in the face of physical threats by other youth, and harassment by police and other adults… Central to their partial negotiation of their experience of racialisation, they affirm a masculine and 'ethnic' identity of toughness, danger and respect [17].

Assertion of gang membership can thus be interpreted as attempts by the young men to 'valorise' their lives and empower themselves in the face of outside hostility, disrespect and social marginalisation.

Gangs, ethnicity and social identity

Australian gang studies have largely concluded that the rationale for most youth formations is primarily 'fun' (i.e., as part of a social network) rather than 'business' (i.e., as part of a criminal network). Nevertheless, while the purpose for a group forming tends to be social, rather than criminal, each type of group may, to a lesser or greater extent, engage in illegal activity, fights or drug use. This, however, is not driven by the agenda of the group as such, nor is it particularly unusual for Australian teenagers and young adults generally. Much of what happens on the street is contingent upon specific circumstances and events. Fighting, for example, is a general feature of (male) street life but it arises due to different causes and involves different individuals and groups, depending upon specific conditions.

One of the key findings of Australian research is that ethnic background and identity are often equated with gang membership. In the end, however, the issue is less one of gangs *per se* than one of social identity and the frictions associated with group interactions based on ethnic stereotypes.

Ethnicity is central to group formation and to the gang phenomenon in contemporary Australia. This is so both at the level of popular image – as reflected in media fixations with 'ethnic youth gangs' – and with regard to the social activities of large groups of (mainly) young men at the local neighbourhood level. Who you are, in terms of social identity, is largely determined by ethnic and class background, and gender. Who you hang around with is likewise shaped by ethnicity, amongst other social factors. Whether or not you are considered a member of a gang is partly a matter of perception (and, indeed, whose perception). It also very much depends upon the extent of engagement in group activities that are illegal and/or seriously anti-social. Violence is a major shaping factor in the genesis of youth gangs. It is also a major defining feature of the activities of these groups.

The link between ethnicity and violence is at the heart of the gang phenomenon in Australia (see Chapters 7 and 8). That is, group identity, group formation and group activity that are specifically associated with gangs tend to be founded upon and reinforced by physical and verbal conflicts between rival groups of young people.

Gang membership is heavily tied in with group violence. However, this violence is manifest within a wider context of social marginalisation and exclusion based upon class and ethnicity. Antagonisms on the street – between groups of young ethnic-minority youth and authority figures, such as the police, and between diverse groups of young people – are constantly reinforced by negative stereotyping, media moral panics and the day-to-day racism experienced by these young people.

The durability of gang formation is influenced by ongoing violence, generally in public spaces, that is collective in nature and that involves serious assault. It is this intertwining of ethnicity and violence in the lives of young men from particular ethnic-minority backgrounds that makes for the constitution of street gangs in the Eurogang sense – a durable, street-oriented youth group whose own identity includes involvement in illegal activity. Nevertheless, there are complexities here that need to be unravelled. Violence is ubiquitous amongst young ethnic-minority men, yet not everyone is regarded by others or by themselves as gang members. To put it differently, racism and racist violence are basic features of life for certain ethnic minorities. It is this, in turn, that provides the ground for the emergence of specific group formations in which street violence, as such, becomes a central defining feature.

As we have seen above, gangs research in Australia over the last few decades has pointed to the importance of ethnicity in how gangs are socially constructed in places such as Sydney, Melbourne and Adelaide. This research has been of a qualitative nature, generally involving interviews and observation as key techniques of data collection. The research has also been sensitive to the impact of diverse immigration histories and experiences on different ethnic-minority youth. In addition, it has tended to frame issues in terms of community relationships as a whole rather than specific individuals or particular groups abstracted from their local community context.

By and large, media 'moral panics' have been directed at ethnic minorities in Australian cities, although the specific minority group has varied depending upon location and time period. For example, in Sydney today the 'folk devil' of concern tends to be Muslim and Arabic youth, whereas in the 1970s it was young people from Italian and Greek backgrounds. In Melbourne and Perth it is 'Asian' young people who feature in the newspaper headlines and around whom gangs discourse is wrapped. Gang descriptors have generally been linked to specific waves of immigration, as new groups have settled in Australia in significant numbers (e.g., Mediterranean migrants in the 1960s and 1970s; South East Asian migrants in the late 1970s and early 1980s; Muslim and

Arabic migrants in the 1990s; African migrants in the 1990s and 2000s) [18]. Gang descriptors have also been based upon specific types of crime which are linked in the public eye with particular immigrant groups (e.g., drugs with Asians; terrorism with Muslims).

Whether or not the tag of 'gang' is warranted is subject to dispute; yet the perception and image of the gang is, with very few exceptions, racialised through its associations with specific minority groups. The negative perceptions of these youths also play a part in generating varying forms of resistance on their part, including the use of violence, as a means to bolster group solidarity and enhance personal self-esteem. How this resistance occurs is nevertheless contingent upon both local context and the specific ethnic group in question (see Chapter 4). The remainder of this chapter explores how young people define who they are by considering how different groups engage in the world around them.

As part of the national youth gangs research, we interviewed 50 young people in the Bankstown area of Sydney. The interviews were arranged and carried out by local youth and community workers, who had been briefed on the process and interview schedule. Those interviewed either identified as being a gang member or were perceived by others to be a gang member. Three main groups of young people were interviewed: Lebanese (Australians), Samoan (Australians) and Vietnamese (Australians). The sample also included a couple of migrant youth from Fiji and Jamaica. Five young women were interviewed as part of the sample but, while associating with gangs, none identified themselves as a gang member. The stories of each main group provide interesting insights into gang formation, group identity, and ethnicity and violence. While most public and academic attention has been solely on young Lebanese people, the stories of other young people in the same neighbourhood add further complexity and richness to our understanding of gangs and gang-related behaviour.

Friends and enemies

To understand gang formation and gang activities, we first need to appreciate the nature of group dynamics in the local area. Gang members are simultaneously members of particular gangs and of diverse social groups, and there is some overlap between the two. How different groups relate to each other has implications for how gangs are formed, the nature of gang membership and the kinds of violence associated with different gangs. Group membership hinges upon shared ethnicity, language and culture. It also very much depends upon locale, age and activities. Each group of young people more or less said that 'anyone' could be a member of their group. However, in practice, membership was highly selective and exclusive to their particular ethnic group. In part, this simply reflects family connections and basic things such as speaking the same language – both literally and figuratively in relation to religion, origins and shared understandings of manners, honour and relationships.

While the primary group connection is to one's specific ethnic group, there are other connections that are also significant. Some of these are based upon activities and some on simple geography. For example, the Samoan and Lebanese young people generally shared an interest in rap music. Rapping together was okay and was one activity that was generally inclusive of people regardless of ethnic background.

Living in the same area also was meaningful, even if the young people did not hang around together in the same groups. Many of the youths commented on the negative 'bad' reputation of the area, yet most were proud to live there and wished to remain there in the future. Identity was in fact often constructed both in terms of ethnicity and in terms of locality.

The FOB's [Fresh Off the Boat] and the Lebos like they've come together around Bankstown...smoke weed with the Lebos. And help us in fights...but it's mostly them that bring the trouble. Like they always call us to come and help 'em and that. Against other Lebos and the – Asians.

(Samoan-Australian young man, Sydney)

Living in an area of relative economic disadvantage and high levels of unemployment also meant that group membership had specific class dimensions that cut across ethnic belonging.

To belong to our group you're either an Arab or an Islander, you know, you can't belong – you've gotta be from here. From Bankstown. You can't be one of them rich Arabs that live up that way in, you know, their fathers and brothers they buy them cars and stuff. We don't hang out with them much with them pretty boys that, you know, spend all their time running after girls and stuff. You can't be a, pardon me, wuss.

(Lebanese-Australian young man)

Social difference and social belonging was not constructed only in terms of material advantage; there were fairly strong antagonisms expressed by the Lebanese and Samoan young people against Asian young people, although there was relatively little contact, including gang fights, between the groups. The latter category includes, amongst others, Vietnamese and Chinese young people. The problem here often begins at school. Time and again the Lebanese and Samoan young people talked about racist teachers and being treated in a discriminatory way by others at school. By contrast, they thought that Asians were favoured by teachers. They were also conscious that Asians tended to do better academically than themselves. Their own negative experiences of schooling tended to manifest in bullying behaviour against and dislike of Asian students.

Each group tended to have particular 'enemies' and potential allies. In some cases these were one and the same. For example, generally speaking the Vietnamese did not particularly like the Chinese (reflecting antagonisms stemming from longstanding conflicts between the countries of origin). Yet, on occasion, for example at school, the two groups would get along, due in no small part to being lumped together as Asians and being subjected to racism by others. On the other hand, the category 'Islanders' includes an array of nationalities, yet most of the Samoans interviewed were very antagonistic towards Tongan young people. This was reflected in gang talk and gang gear – the Bloods (Samoans) wore red, the Crips (Tongans) wore blue and other Islanders (e.g., a Fijian young man in our sample) were caught in between conflicting loyalties.

Ethnicity was largely seen as establishing the boundary of membership, whether with regard to a social group or to a gang. The ways in which friends and enemies are socially constructed at the local neighbourhood level, and with respect to ethnicity generally, provide the first filters in the sifting out of who is 'eligible' and who is not for specific gang membership.

Nonetheless, group membership and friendship networks involve many different points of belonging and connection, which vary according to circumstances and activities. The variables that constituted the basis for making social connections are presented in Table 3.1.

As indicated in the table, there were a variety of connections between the young people beyond that of ethnicity as such [19]. 'Affiliations' are based upon certain given shared circumstances, which tend to be outside the young person's immediate control, that bring people together. Social connection is also related to 'attractors', based upon choice and

Table 3.1 Connecting to and as a group

Affiliations (Connection through given circumstances)	Attractors (Connection through choice/preference)
Local area	group activity
School	size of group
Ethnic communities	criminality
Religion	violence
Class background	music
Male bonding	drugs
Friends	acquaintances
Family	masculine display

preferences (e.g., in relation to music and sport), that likewise facilitate shared activity amongst individuals.

Living in an area of relative economic disadvantage and high levels of unemployment also meant that group membership had specific class dimensions that cut across ethnic belonging. Distinctions were drawn between 'the rich', who were privileged, and those young people who were perceived to be stronger because they had to do things the tough way.

Specific activities were associated with specific types of group formation. For example, fighting was definitely a 'male thing'. However, hanging out, rapping and music-making allowed for inclusion of young women into the scene. Criminal acts, such as armed robbery and assault, as well as group fights, were pretty much the domain of the young men, however. Masculinity was very much constructed in terms of toughness and being manly through aggressive physicality. It also included notions of loyalty to the group and to each other, to courage and fearlessness, and to mutual protection.

Group membership and friendship networks involve many different points of belonging and connection, which vary according to circumstances and activities. Many of the young people who were interviewed had friends from other ethnic backgrounds. They were all familiar with the other groups who lived in their neighbourhood. Different groups would collaborate or have alliances with each other, particularly the Samoan and Lebanese, depending upon what was happening in the neighbourhood at the time. They might share in drug taking (e.g., smoking cannabis), music-making (e.g., rapping) or even fighting (e.g., combining against a third force). In some instances, the neighbourhood connection was stronger than ethnic identity as such, as when outsiders from a similar group (e.g., an outside Lebanese gang) entered into the shared geographical area in order to battle it out with local Lebanese youth.

In other cases, as with the Samoan young people, the local gangs were part of larger ethnic networks and subgroups, incorporating large geographical areas and relationships across distances. For example, there were connections across the city (i.e., different groups of Bloods which sometimes had additional local names as well), as well as across the Tasman Sea (i.e., back to New Zealand, from where many families had migrated).

In the end, while group membership is exclusive, individual friendship is not, and groups can combine in varying ways to protect territory, reputation and specific individuals. Most of the young people who were interviewed had an active part in fighting and other kinds of anti-social behaviour. Most could be labelled a gang member. All of them said that first and foremost, it was important to be part of their particular group – which in this case inevitably referred to specific ethnic-background youth formations.

Specific gangs as defined by Eurogang standards do exist (i.e., durable criminally oriented groups), but they emerge from and are blended with youth groups identified by certain social descriptors (i.e., relating to ethnicity, illegal activity such as cannabis use, rap music, antagonism toward other groups, etc.). This makes it hard at times to distinguish the street gang from the non-gang group, particularly from an outsider's perspective. Violence and illegality tend to feature in each type of group's behaviour and activity. However, when someone says, 'I am a gang member', this is meaningful from the point of view of the type and extent of violence in which they engage. Thus, group identity is still crucial to the key focus of group activity.

Other group dynamics

In addition to class, ethnicity and gender, there are several other variables that came to our attention in the course of the national youth gangs study. One of the most important was the size of the group at any point in time.

Size does matter

Our respondents tended to describe themselves as gang members or as being involved in gang activities when the group was large. Large groups were often involved in large conflicts, and planned fights were invariably defined as gang fights. Distinctions were made between groups of youths (e.g., four mates looking for excitement) and youth gangs (e.g., grouped violence over time). The former is ubiquitous amongst the young male population; the latter signals a more organised and self-conscious appropriation of gang status. The latter was also tied into the periodic escalation of 'revenge' conflicts in which large groups of young men clash on the basis of well-defined gang identities (usually associated with territory).

The use of new technologies (e.g., SMS and mobile phones) serves to enhance swarming – that is, the rapid coming together of young men en masse – again usually for the purposes of fighting. As an Adelaide young person said,

> We'll just get on the phone if we need backup and that, so then the size will increase greatly. People just come... Like within half an hour, we can have all seventy-three people meet in Victoria Street for a brawl.
>
> (18-year-old young man, Adelaide)

Ethnic-minority status was sometimes the key defining characteristic of those who found instant protection amongst their peers precisely because of their ethnic background. However, the identification of ethnic group with gang, while it offers the promise of protection for all, also makes everyone within that category a potential target. Moreover, different ethnic-minority groups have different reputations when it comes to vulnerability. For example, in places like Melbourne or Sydney, Indians were viewed as more vulnerable to victimisation than the more seemingly tough groups, such as Samoan or Lebanese young people.

Size also seemed to be relevant when it comes to who was committing which types of crime, and the basis upon which different layers of the gang would come together as gang members. This is indicated in Table 3.2, which shows that variations in the size of group and status of membership influence the nature of the engagement in criminal or illegal activity.

It was not only the size of the group that shaped group activities and individual engagement in particular activities; age was significant as well.

Age matters too

One of the striking things about the national research project was the age diversity within and between different groups. For example, in

Table 3.2 Group characteristics and criminal engagement

Size of group	Type of crime
small (2–5 persons)	armed robbery
	drug dealing
medium (<15 persons)	opportunistic street assaults
	drug use
large (>15 persons)	group violence against other gangs
	gate crashing
Status of membership	**Engagement in crime**
leadership core	all types, including volume crime (drugs, drug dealing and theft) and serious crime (interpersonal and group violence)
general membership	large group violence
	poly-drug use
wannabe and peripheral	only very large group violence
	some drug and alcohol use

relation to a graffiti group in Adelaide, we were told that there were 80–90 members, and that the youngest was 14 and the oldest 29. Diverse ages were linked to diverse activities and diverse status within each particular youth-group formation. The type of crime, violence and illegal activity engaged in depended, in part, upon the age of the person. In many cases the youngest members were related to older members, and in some instances fathers and grandfathers had been involved previously in similar gangs. The core members tended to be late teens and early 20s, with wannabes being younger and ex-members being older.

Age is important to the process of moving into and out of a gang. Gang involvement is a social process and 'growing out' of the gang is simultaneously 'growing up' for many of the young people involved. At the front end, however, there is often a sense of hero worship amongst the wannabes in relation to older members. In some situations, a stint in prison or juvenile detention brings with it important 'street cred' and reinforces rather than diminishes hero status amongst members. Younger members are socialised into the life of the gang by being asked to do certain things as suited to their age. As they mature physically, fighting becomes more central to their participation.

There was also evidence of the exploitation of younger members by older gang members for specific types of crime. Young people were susceptible to bribes – the offer of alcohol, drugs and sex – in return for undertaking certain activities. They could be built into the revenue stream of those gangs that were evolving into more conventional criminal organisations – for example, by participating in drug running and fencing of goods. For older gang members who have never worked and who have no prospect of ever having a formal job, the gang structure provides a platform towards life-long criminal engagement. In this kind of situation, younger members can be instrumentally used as a source of profit and power as the older gang members move into their 20s and 30s.

The matter of age also counts when it comes to how age-based peer groups transform into age-related gang groups. Leisure activities in school and in the neighbourhood, including rugby and other sports, can bring young people together in ways that help to forge strong personal bonds. The durable collection of connected individuals may take the form of increasingly anti-social activity depending upon local factors and specific trigger events. For example, group fights may occur periodically, and may solidify identity in terms of territory and activity. What happens during the school years may also prepare a pathway into more serious crime as well. This may see the maturation of individuals through 'youth' crime (e.g., intimidation on trains) to 'adult' crime (e.g., drugs and violence).

Conclusion

The lesson to be drawn from the research which has been carried out so far in Australia is that most often the gang is simply a group of like-minded young people who enjoy each other's company, and who share support and life experiences in common. The street will continue to be a key refuge for young people in general, and groups of young people will continue to have fun – and to occasionally 'muck around' – as they have done for many decades and, indeed, centuries. But the precise character of these groups, and the specific activities in which they engage, depends as much as anything on the availability of community resources and the level of social respect accorded to young people, regardless of specific background.

There are nonetheless some groups that could fit the description of gang. The dynamics of these groups were contingent upon factors such as class and ethnic composition, preferred social (including criminal and illegal) activities, numbers of young people drawn into the orbit of the gang (and when and why) and age profile. Gang participation and identification in Australia has tended to be a 'guy thing', although some young women do participate on the fringes of male gangs as girlfriends. Still there are cases where young women call their group a gang, and engage in violent conflicts with other groups of young women, although this is relatively rare in the overall scheme of things (see Chapter 10).

When it comes to Australian youth gangs, there is little evidence from around the country of formal rules or leadership structures as such. Two or three key or core leaders would seem to organically emerge from a neighbourhood, school, community or family. There seemed to be fluid entry into and exit from the various youth-group formations, including self-described gangs. There was a definite pyramid structure when it came to age, crimes, level of engagement and identification with 'gang'. As part of this, a core group generally exists and sometimes this group persists in criminal and anti-social behaviour. Group activities ebb and flow according to the presence of a core group. Finally, there was a pattern which saw the escalation of 'normal' youthful conflicts due to the gang intervention (e.g., for gang members, violence is expected and fun, plus there was ready access to weapons, numbers and peer support).

4
Fluidity and Continuity

Introduction

A key criticism of contemporary gangs research is that gang analysis (or, as some describe it, 'gang talk') blurs the distinction between youth, street gangs and organised crime. In so doing such research also entrenches a racialised understanding of gang: the term has increasingly become equated with black, minority ethnic and immigrant young men. Gangs research is thus seen to apply to particular ethnic-minority groups in any specific society, and as part of this to simultaneously exclude majority youth from the label. Moreover, it is the pathology of the labelled group which is frequently seen as the problem (and thus the focus for police and other interventions), rather than systemic marginalisation and changes in political economy. It is the latter that positions different population groups unequally in society, and that feeds both a process of criminalisation of the disadvantaged and the moral panics that accompany this.

This chapter provides an analysis of historical, cultural and transnational aspects of how youth gangs are framed as a social phenomenon in Australia. The class framing of gangs is evident both in the working-class backgrounds and the socially disadvantaged positions of gang members, as well as in the historical and contemporary signs and symbols of 'gangness'. For example, the push larrikins of the late nineteenth century had distinctive modes of dress and behaviour that made them stand out as essentially working class and troublemakers. Such social dynamics resonate today in the form of the global circulation of gang images that are appropriated differently in diverse national settings but that nonetheless provide distinctive social markers (see Chapter 5).

The racialisation of gang discourse is evident in contemporary portrayals of 'ethnic youth gangs' and in the ways in which ethnic-minority young people are positioned within the Australian social fabric. Although racism stems from different historical bases (namely, colonialism and immigration), it is people of colour and those from non-mainstream ethnic and religious backgrounds who are most likely to feature in public discourse about gangs, and to be subjected to police profiling. The transformation of social difference into social deviance is achieved not solely through the actions of the young but in and through the social reactions generated by mainstream society, supported by the interventions of the state.

From street Arabs to push larrikins

To discern the nature and dynamics of youth gangs, analysis needs to consider patterns of activity as shaped by class position and class relations. Class situation is linked to specific types of criminality [1]. Thus, where one is located in the class structure will influence the kinds of social activity engaged in, the propensity to engage in such activity and the intensity of that involvement. It will also shape the perceptions of other classes regarding specific class-related activity and, of course, whether activity will be identified by the state as criminal, and whether it will be policed or punished.

The criminalisation industries of the state and the media reflect concern about subsistence criminality and the visible street presence of the working classes, especially beyond the boundaries of their particular suburbs. On the one hand, deprived individuals, families and communities tend to organise their own means and forms of subsistence and enjoyment. They will especially do so under circumstances in which they are excluded from desirable areas in which to live and separated from opportunities to find paid work. Moreover, even if work is there to be had, illegality may be far more rewarding, secure and satisfying as a source of income than the insecurities and exploitations of precarious employment in the formal sectors of the economy [2]. On top of this, while in the longer term crime may not pay particularly well compared with the wages offered by full-time employment, it does hold the promise of quick money in lump sums – something that is especially attractive to young people who have little experience of regular employment income.

On the other hand, the ideological representation of the poor and underprivileged as an irresponsible 'underclass' is built into the policy apparatus of the state in relation to both welfare and criminal justice. Unemployment and resistance to enforced participation in exploitive workplace situations are reduced to 'bad attitudes' and 'bad families'. Those individuals who manipulate and 'rip off' the welfare system are touted as 'typical' of welfare recipients, the message being that few of these people can really be trusted. The response therefore is to impose varying forms of mutual obligation on the poor – below poverty-line benefits and inadequate services in return for work search obligations and the imposition of training and employment programmes (which, in turn, often fail to address or compensate for the fundamental social inadequacies of mainstream education and paid employment). For those who do not play the game, there is exclusion from state support. Of these, some will make a living through alternative means, only to be faced with further state coercion – in the form of increased policing, harsher sentencing and greater use of imprisonment.

The crux of state intervention – especially for those nation-states that have highly restricted social welfare supports if any at all – is how best to manage the problem of disadvantaged groups (their presence within and migration beyond their suburban borders, and their activities), rather than to deal with the specific social and economic issues that underlie disadvantage. This is because to eradicate disadvantage would require action to reverse the polarisations in wealth and income, and thus to pit the state directly in opposition to dominant class interests. The focus on the poor themselves as the problem has long been evident in policy and legislative measure (witness the history of the Poor Laws in England). It is also seen in the ongoing contestations over public space involving working-class hooligans and, of course, youth gangs.

Youth gangs and working-class street life

For example, children and youth of the working classes in the nineteenth century were implicated in a succession of moral panics relating to their activities and presence on the street. From around the mid-1800s onwards, most major cities in the Western world witnessed the emergence of, and moral panics over, groups of young people on the street. Variously branded – from street Arabs in London, to hoodlums in San Francisco, to larrikins in Melbourne – the banding together of large groups of young men was essentially linked to urbanisation and industrialisation [3]. Social formations of this type were the child of the Industrial Revolution, an event that placed great masses of people together into urban conglomerations for the purposes of manufacture and trade.

The male body was integral to working-class life – in the factory, the mines, the sports field, the army – and likewise in leisure pursuits. Solidarity on the working-class street was constructed through physical strength and the 'muscle' that could be mobilised. Whether employed or unemployed, social status and individual reputation was constructed through aggressive physicality. For disadvantaged street-present youth, this was even more important as a marker of strength and manhood, especially if no work was available to them. Much the same kind of emphasis on the male working-class body as a source of social status continues today (see Chapter 8).

The discourses used to describe and explain the disadvantaged, the social outcast and the non-respectable poor have varied greatly over time and in terms of emphasis. Certainly in the 1800s there was great public concern in places such as England and Wales over the 'dangerous' and the 'perishing' classes. The former were seen as intrinsically threatening, the so-called criminal elements of society. The latter consisted of the poor and the destitute, but who nevertheless aspired to be part of the respectable working classes. In describing the dangerous classes, distinctions were drawn between categories of people on the basis of social position and moral situation.

Some commentators of the mid-nineteenth century divided humanity into two broad races, using language such as 'the nomadic' and 'the civilised' to suggest fundamental difference [4]. It is but a small step to see the nomad as the street Arab – that transient person for whom the street itself constitutes home. The 1840s was in fact replete with descriptions of 'predatory hordes' of young people on the street, who appear to almost belong to another race, which in the context of British imperial power opens the door to peculiar forms of naming the Other:

> And perhaps it goes without saying that so un-civilised, un-Christian and un-English were these young thieves and rascals that there were known flatly and uniformly in this era as 'street Arabs', 'English Kaffirs' and 'Hottentots' [5].

Importantly, then, terms such as 'street Arab' connote not only difference but foreignness. In the English context, it is interesting that terms such as this, and indeed, the term 'hooligan', have been equated with 'un-British' as being alien to the values and temperament of the ordinary Englishman. This is so, even though a systematic history of street life and youth conflict demonstrates that such activity is entirely endemic to the UK and not a foreign import at all [6].

It was in Sydney and Melbourne in the 1880s that the Australian youth group formations known as the larrikins were most prominent and visible, although these were also of concern in places such as Brisbane [7]. The larrikins tended to have a distinctive form of dress, featuring hard black hats, bell-bottomed trousers, high-heeled and pointy boots, colourful scarves and collarless shirts, although the descriptions of men and women tended to be highly exaggerated in media reports of the day. By the 1880s, many of the larrikins (and their female partners, the 'larrikinesses' or 'donahs') were organising into 'pushes' – that is, gangs. These sometimes had initiation ceremonies, and some appeared to be organisationally highly structured.

The crucial thing about the push larrikins, however, was their street presence. They basically socialised and lived in the streets of the working-class neighbourhoods of Melbourne and Sydney. The street was their home-away-from-home. And no wonder. Most came from poor backgrounds and crowded, uncomfortable housing. There was no other place to socialise but the public spheres of the street and the park. For these young people the street was multifunctional, a movement route as well as an entertainment venue [8]. For some the street was also a source of income, through the informal economy of the black market, through prostitution (including very young girls, some under the age of 10), and through robbery and theft. Such public spaces were simultaneously communal and commercial, lively and a source of livelihood. For the working-class youth, they offered something for everyone.

Most larrikin activity was essentially harmless and trivial, notwithstanding injuries and even occasionally deaths arising from street fights and that sort of thing. Their biggest crime, it appears, was to insult the 'respectable' and the 'rich' with whom they interacted on the street. There was a long tradition of this. The Cabbage Tree Mob of the 1840s, for example, gained notoriety for its harassment of upper-class Sydney residents: 'The group's activities were generally limited to the delivery of insulting or offensive remarks to wealthier passers-by, and the occasional knocking off of the symbol of high status, the tall black hat' [9]. The push larrikins revelled in their sartorial appearance, as it expressed who they were and created a sense of shared identity. They also had loads of fun in hanging around on street corners and making suggestive remarks to passers-by. Sometimes these remarks were abusive, and sometimes they were accompanied by physical intimidation and assaults. More often than not they were highly objectionable, as they were intended precisely to offend the more 'respectable' members of the society. The comportment and attitudes were, from the beginning, designed to upset as well as to empower.

Interestingly, the other key target of the larrikins was the Chinese, with whom they often shared the same poor and dilapidated neighbourhoods. White Australia was, to some extent, built from the ground up as well as the top down. Throughout much of the 1800s, places such as Sydney remained overwhelmingly white and British. This was reflected in the politics of the street insofar as larrikinism as a social phenomenon was essentially constructed in class terms. The 'us' and 'them' tended to be focussed around poor working-class lads versus the bourgeois middle classes and the rich, with the Chinese implicated in the Othering process as much as anything by their proximity to the larrikin homes.

Extensive negative media treatment of larrikins and larrikinism from the 1880s to the turn of the century saw concerted attempts to curtail their activities [10]. According to Murray, the term 'larrikin' was to gain official status in the records of crime in 1883. In relation to an assault and robbery, the description of the wanted youths stated that they are of 'larrikin appearance'. Once established, the term then morphed into a new kind of fixed status: the larrikin. Thus, as Murray describes it, a new kind of social identity was formed:

> Until then a man's occupational defined him, or his nationality. The cosmopolitanism of Sydney reveals itself in the pages [of the police reports]: Scotsman, Irishman, Syrian, Lascar, Portugese, American black, Jamaican, Aborigine, Frenchman. The occupations are as diverse: stonemason, gentleman, card-sharper, spieler, cabman, seaman, servant, butcher. A gamut of class and activity. But now a new occupation appears: larrikins. No longer do the culprits have 'the appearance of'; they are simply what they are: larrikins [11].

The identification of larrikins as an offender category was further transposed into the notion of 'larrikin-type offences'. The New South Wales Legislative Assembly was to publish a report entitled 'Police Reports Respecting Disturbances Between the Military and a Certain Section of the Public known as "Pushes"' in 1890 in which data were presented for arrests for selected offences related to larrikinism [12]. The offences included:

- riotous behaviour;
- assault police;
- common assault;
- obscene or indecent language;
- injure property (vandalism).

Finnane describes a series of police files from the 1890s to the 1930s in Brisbane that were classified originally by police under the heading of 'larrikinism' or sometimes 'larrikinism and pushes' [13]. They included complaints about stone throwing, obscene language, insulting women and girls and fighting.

As the history of hooliganism tells us, such behaviour is far from unique to larrikins or to this particular period in time [14]. But the association between larrikins, larrikinism and specific types of offence allows for an even greater sense of class-based targeting and labelling. It actively facilitates and justifies official interventions that are highly distinctive, discrete and discriminatory.

The push larrikins are generally studied as a social phenomenon directly related to the notion of street gangs. Youth gangs are almost by definition implicated in violence (see Chapter 7). The concept of swarming is generally less relevant in relation to gang violence as such, except where large congregations of young men (and some young women) band together for the express purpose of opposing the police or fighting another group. Periodically, gang members amassed in numbers, and their engagement in street fights included organised battles as well as spur-of-the-moment conflicts. Yet, some of the most memorable events involving gangs, such as the push larrikins, stem from spontaneous gatherings that evolved into violent events.

Boxing Day 1884 saw a riot at Bondi Beach [15]. The picknickers were in plentiful supply but so too were the larrikin pushes. Fuelled by alcohol and a dispute over rights to the same girl, it was not long before an affray turned into a riot. When the police arrived, it was to them that the crowd turned. The police then became the enemy, and several suffered injury after being chased down the beach by a large group of larrikins. But this was not the end of it:

> The hot day, meanwhile, was inflaming others with the demon too, and as the whole of Bondi was now in uproar, many private fights broke out, with some contenders not knowing why they fought and others probably giving it the religious twist of the Orange and the Green [16].

The specificity of the first fight thus engendered chaotic outbursts involving a wide variety and large number of participants. The presence of many people in one place – the formation of crowds – can shape group behaviour depending upon the purpose of the crowd formation. In some crowd situations, mob-like behaviour may emerge insofar as being in a crowd seems to offer the opportunity to 'lose one's mind', and thereby to lose the normal social controls that guide decent human interaction [17]. The so-called mob mentality describes the situation in which the crowd dictates general behaviour over and beyond the individual. The larrikin propensity to violence was in effect one trigger to wider mob violence around them.

The phenomenon of push larrikinism was variously explained by contemporaries of the day. Some pointed to the affluence of the age and said that the pushes were borne out of the prosperity of the labouring classes – life was too easy and too good, and shortened working days meant more time out on the streets. Others suggested that it was the warmer weather of Sydney climes that was so conducive to outdoor activity. The absence of recreational opportunities was noted, as was the problem of drunkenness. The influence of the news media in amplifying the excitement and stimulating emulative behaviour was put forward as well [18]. Less often mentioned were economic causes, urban degeneration or simply the traditions of working-class leisure. In many cases, causation was simply reduced to a matter of bad people doing inappropriate things. At any rate, by the start of the new century, the moral panics over the larrikin pushes had died down, and the media and political agendas turned to other matters – the construction of the (white) nation.

Moral panics surrounding the push larrikins tended to be framed in terms of class rather than race. This can be interpreted in several interconnected ways. First, much of the behaviour of the larrikins was intentionally offensive to the 'respectable' and better-off sections of the citizenry, as well as to authority figures such as the police. This is not new, nor has it diminished today if one considers the case of particularly disadvantaged working-class neighbourhoods [19]. The clear divide in this instance is class-based differences in situation and outlook based upon different resources, traditions and cultures.

This was also a period that saw the emergence of social distinctions between the 'rough' and the 'respectable' within the working-class itself [20]. The idea of public propriety was increasingly linked not just to middle-class notions of morality and lawful behaviour but to the aspirations and changing materials circumstances of the emergent labour aristocracy of skilled workers. Those who were most subject to state attention, in the form of concerted police intervention, were those youths associated with the 'rough' end of town. Young people perceived to be hard-working and gainfully employed were not seen as problematic or as warranting the same kind of negative treatment, even though their street behaviour may in fact have been in many respects the same as that of the identified larrikin. This situation has echoes of contemporary discussions and perceptions of the behaviour of the underclass relative to the working-class mainstream.

Second, the period of the rise of the push larrikins also saw the material consolidation of the White Australia policy. This was manifest in legislation against Chinese immigration, and in extensive attacks upon Chinese people in the streets, the media and in political circles. Given that the composition of the pushes was white and working-class, their activities were not racialised, except to the extent that the term larrikin itself is sometimes seen to originate in the words of an Irish police officer. The larrikin was not necessarily seen to be foreign in the same way that the English depicted the street Arab. Perhaps for this reason the term, today, also resonates positively as a home-grown Australian phenomenon that is to some extent celebrated in popular culture.

Third, as Finch describes at length, the 'larrikin outrages' were constructed at a time when the bourgeoisie were reconstructing the form and purposes of the city:

> Working-class youth experienced the streets of their cities and towns as multifunctional streets – that is, as places for socialising as well as for travelling from one place to another. The moral panic about larrikins was not due to a change in the behaviour of working-class youths but, rather, to a change in bourgeois notions about what the street was for. The combined fear of the revolutionary potential of the multifunctional street combined with the new importance of the orderly footpath in commercial activity and spectacle-based consumerism created the folk devil of larrikins [21].

Hence, it was not only the attitudes of the larrikins towards the upper classes that highlighted the class divisions of the society but the efforts of the upper classes to materially reconfigure urban space itself. As Cohen also observes, changes in the nature and perception of street culture were also accomplished through the efforts of sections of the working class itself [22]. Respectability was integral to the public politics of the trade union and the Labour Party. Through these institutions, major transformations in working-class culture in general were to occur.

Arabs on the streets and youth gangs

Some 100 years or so later, the character of the street has changed, and so has the nature of the moral panics over street-present youth.

In high-immigration countries, such as Australia, today, ethnicity is seen to be central to group formation and more generally to the gang phenomenon. This is so both at the level of popular image – as reflected in media fixations with ethnic youth gangs – and with regard to the social activities of large groups of (mainly) young men at the local neighbourhood level. Who you are, in terms of social identity, is largely determined by ethnic and class background, and gender. Who you hang around with is likewise shaped by ethnicity, amongst other social factors (see Chapter 3).

The fusion of class and ethnic dynamics with regard to the street is frequently manifest in the form of class-based and race-based policies that have direct and indirect negative consequences for ethnic minorities. This is spelled out in some detail in Wilson's analysis of why African-Americans are disproportionately over-represented amongst the jobless in the US, and Wacquant's analysis of the ghetto as a racially defined social and economic space [23]. A crucial factor in high levels of unemployment and poverty is the location of many black Americans in segregated ghettos, a process exacerbated by selected government policies and programmes. Similar concentrations of ethnic-minority groups in heavily disadvantaged areas is apparent in Sydney with regard to the Lebanese communities [24]. Likewise, in Germany, segregation based upon class and ethnicity has been identified as a major problem, with prevailing policies only making things worse. Heitmeyer comments that,

> Not surprisingly, when the traditional forms of social recognition through work and mainstream social institutions become increasingly inaccessible, new forms of recognition are sought. Ethnic encapsulation provides a problematic solution to social recognition because it frequently involves cultures of violence [25].

Resurgent interest in street gangs and youth groups in North America, Europe and Australia (see Chapters 1 and 2) provides some indication of the consequences of inadequate and inappropriate policy 'answers' to the underclass problem. As indicated in this research, and as graphically demonstrated in events such as the Paris street riots of 2005, young people of ethnic-minority background have become a major source of consternation across the Western world. The same is true in Australia as it is elsewhere.

For example, young people in the western suburbs of Sydney, particularly areas such as Bankstown and Lakemba, have featured prominently in media reports and academic studies in recent years [26]. From the media and politicians' point of view, young Muslim men – of 'Middle Eastern appearance' – have become the *bête noir* of sensationalised reportage and political intolerance [27]. From rape gangs to terrorists, the public discourse has vilified Lebanese (Australian) young men in particular. This has been occurring for a number of years, at least back to the time of the first Gulf War in the early 1990s. Lebanese young Australians are the 'larrikins' of modern day Sydney 'outrages'. Their groups are equivalent to the gang 'pushes' that were deemed so threatening to Sydneysiders of yesteryear. As we shall see, however, the folk devils of today are also more than simply larrikins – they are 'foreign'.

The public presence and visibility of Lebanese young people forms part of the reason why they have become so prominent in media-driven moral panics. Lebanese Australians have established residence in great numbers in suburbs such as Bankstown. Given their overall socio-economic situation, they now constitute the new 'dangerous classes' of late capitalism and are perceived as a breeding ground for criminality, immorality and social deviance. Young people hang out in parks and on the street. They engage with rap music, as producers and consumers. They drive around in convoys of cars seeking thrills and excitement. They gather together to socialise – and to fight. They use public space to entertain and to be entertained. In our interviews with young people in the suburb, the largest ethnic-minority group was identified as the Lebanese. It was this group that was also seen as the most aggressive, in school and on the street, and to instigate fights the most often. Its members were considered cocky and arrogant, even by friends and allies (e.g., Samoan-background young men who live in the same area). Violence of this sort is very much tied up with group identity and group protection (see Chapters 7 and 8). To the outsider, however, it simply appears threatening, intimidating, aggressive and rude. It reinforces the differences between 'them' and 'us'.

Public denigration and negative generalisation about the entire Lebanese community has been reinforced by specific events in which individual members of the community have committed crimes. A social process has occurred over a number of years in which social difference has been transformed into social deviance. Even though most of the young men in the area were born in Australia or have been here since early childhood, they are treated as outsiders. Already subject to economic disadvantage and social marginalisation, a generation of young people has grown up in a social atmosphere that is very hostile to their culture, to their community, to their religion and to their very presence.

A particular problem for young people in western Sydney, for example, is the racialised reporting of crime when the media deal specifically with 'Lebanese' youth. Ethnic identifiers are used in relation to some groups but not others (e.g., Anglo-Celtic Australians). Moreover, the 'explanations' for such 'ethnic crime' tends to pathologise on a group basis, as though there is something intrinsically 'bad' or 'deviant' about being Lebanese or more generally Middle Eastern. Such explanations also suggest that the origins of the criminality stem from outside Australia and are related to immigration and 'foreign' ideas and cultures, rather than being linked to social and economic inequalities within the country. Racialisation of this kind has a major impact upon public perceptions of the people and the issues, and on how state agencies such as the police respond to these perceptions [28].

There are important contextual factors that shape the specific content of this racialisation process. The post-Second World War era witnessed the integration of many new population groups into the Australian social and cultural mosaic, albeit under terms mainly set by the dominant white Anglo majority [29]. This process has generally been characterised by a period of various public oppositions to the new settlers in the first instance, followed by a gradual transformation of the Other into the 'ordinary'. One might consider here, for example, the social history of the Greek and Italian, and their place in Australian society today. The experience has been different, however, for recent Muslim and Arabic immigrants, at least within the Sydney context. In this instance, the transition has been troubling, it is in a constant state of flux and it has not yet been completed. The settling-in process has been interrupted and distorted by overseas events – such as the Gulf wars and particular terrorist attacks (New York, Washington, London, Madrid and Bali) – and by issues surrounding the wearing of the hijab and burka that have negatively impacted upon the place and status of the Muslim in wider Australian society and fuelled fear of the Other at several levels.

The outcome of this Othering process has been captured in systematic academic study of these young people and their neighbourhoods. For example, as discussed in Chapter 3, Collins and associates observe that for many young people the way to overcome marginalisation and alienation is to find other ways to affirm their social presence – namely, to form or join a gang [30]. From this vantage point, gang membership is significant not because of presumed criminality but because it provides a means to empower the young men in the face of outside hostility, disrespect and vilification.

Young men from this part of Sydney also featured prominently in the Australian beach riots of December 2005. These occurred at Cronulla beach in south Sydney, the nearest beach suburb to these neighbourhoods. The event saw several thousand people rioting, in the process damaging property and violently attacking anyone who had a Middle Eastern appearance. Many participants wrapped themselves in Australian flags. Many, too, participated in shouting out the highly offensive words 'Fuck the Lebos' in unison, as a common theme to the aggression. The next day saw reprisal attacks. Dozens of carloads of people from the community that had been targeted the previous day retaliated by engaging in similarly 'random' violence throughout the beachside suburbs. The point is that there exist highly volatile relations between 'Lebanese' and other young people across major parts of the city. This negativity has been brewing for a number of years, in part fostered by the territorial segregation of particular groups into racialised patterns of disadvantage [31]. Where you belong is increasingly socially constructed in relation to specific 'ethnic locales' – areas defined by particular combinations of economic, social and cultural characteristics.

What recent studies and recent events have demonstrated is the potential for extreme aggression and mass violence stemming from profoundly oppressive social circumstances. Racism permeates the lives of many of the young Muslim and/or Arab men, as it does other ethnic-minority groups in Sydney and elsewhere [32]. Coupled with economic, social and political marginalisation, it is no wonder that violence of varying kinds features prominently in their lives. The central paradox for these young people, however, is that the more they try to defend themselves, the more likely they are to be targets. The more they resort to membership of street groups and engagement in fighting to assert themselves, the more they will be treated as outsiders and as deviant [33].

Not surprisingly, some of the young men present themselves in a gang precisely in order to gain a measure of respect. The symbolic representation of themselves as members of a gang, however, was more at the level of overt performance than in relation to particular kinds of professional criminal activity. One of the ironies of media representations of gangs is that it makes membership of such a group appear even more attractive than otherwise might be the case.

Riots describe a situation in which large numbers of people seem to spontaneously engage in unlawful, anti-social and violent behaviour. Recent riots in the Australian setting have seen hundreds of people take to the streets – generally directing their anger at property such as cars, and to authority figures such as the police [34]. The trigger for the Cronulla riots was a punch-up involving young men from Middle Eastern backgrounds and off-duty Anglo surf lifesavers at the beach the week before. However, the media frequently plays a major role in reflexively creating violent events by publicising them in advance, sensationalising them when they occur and exaggerating the enormity of particular events relative to 'the Australian way of life' – hence the stimulation and provocation to violence is to some extent inspired by the mass media itself. This is exactly what occurred in the case of the Cronulla events [35].

Indeed, the Sydney media did a lot to foster the idea that 'trouble' would take place on the weekend in question. Not surprisingly, lots of 'troublemakers' showed up expecting precisely the very thing that was being warned against. At least a portion of the crowd were actively looking for violence. It was on the agenda from the outset. For these young men, the attraction was the violence, not solely the public issues surrounding the beach as such. The point is that the advance notice that there would be a crowd gathering at the beach opened up the possibility for violence to take place. The crowd became the social vehicle through which the desired collective violence could ensue.

However, the violence that occurred was not socially neutral. It was targeted at the Lebanese and others of Middle Eastern appearance. As with the push larrikins of olden days, ultimately the riot was blamed on Lebanese youth. Whoever engaged in violence ('the hot day...was inflaming others with the demon too') was less problematic than the source or inspiration for the violence – the Middle Eastern gangs. If not for their presence, if not for their actions, there would have been no Cronulla riots. So went the script for the continuing moral panic about 'the Lebanese'. It was their 'way of life', their values and morals, their actions and behaviour, their religion that, yet again, was publicly scrutinised, vilified and mythologised.

What this particular event signified was a strong and very particular racialisation of street life, including and especially with regard to group conflict. Interestingly, it was the demise of the White Australia platform in the late 1960s (in practice) and 1970s (in policy) that opened the door for ever more extensive immigration from non-UK-background people. This period of ostensibly non-discriminatory immigration has been accompanied by certain distinctive social processes of social inclusion and social exclusion that are not only forged at the level of broad societal resources and structural disadvantage. Nor are they just constituted through ideological and political processes of separation and differentiation. Exclusion and inclusion are 'made' in the crucible of the everyday, in the mundane activities and relationships of young people as they negotiate their daily lives.

The presence of young Lebanese people in collectivities, on the street, doing things has been shaped by a range of socio-economic, spatial and cultural factors. Moral panics surrounding these young people have, from the very beginning, been framed in ethnic rather than class terms. Just as the street Arab connoted 'un-British', so too the Arab on the street today signifies 'un-Australian'. In a fashion similar to the description of larrikinism as an offence, there is an implicit offence category in the New South Wales police description, people of 'Middle Eastern appearance' (it is notable that this is the only jurisdiction in the country that uses such ethnic descriptors in public descriptions of alleged offenders). In part this 'offence' stems from the actions of a few young men, which were then transposed into the community as a whole. Specifically, a series of gang rapes by young Muslim men in Sydney during the late 1990s and early 2000s led to a media frenzy over the alleged 'unassimilable' attitudes of Muslim/Arab men towards women. Thus, in one fell swoop, all Muslim/Arab men were tarred with the same criminal brush.

The association of Middle Eastern or Muslim with 'terrorist' is yet another image of evil that spans the group as a whole [36]. The establishment of a specific Middle Eastern 'gangs squad' within the New South Wales police further reinforces the idea that somehow these particular young men, and these particular communities, are different and more troublesome than other young men and other communities within the state. All of this serves to reproduce the fiction that somehow the Middle Eastern gang is a product of immigration, an import to our shores, rather than a social phenomenon created and sustained by rampant media vilification, and social and economic disenfranchisement.

Conclusion

This chapter has provided a description of two groups in Australian history that have variously captured the public imagination and been at the centre of moral panic in their respective time periods. The push larrikins were known as louts (and perhaps, today, legends) who accosted people on the streets and who, by their very presence, asserted their own particular social identity. Their fun, however, was not the fun of the respectable or the ruling classes. Accordingly, they were castigated, put under surveillance and arrested. The changing nature of the street, and of class relations, would no longer allow the larrikins – the 'rough' end of the working class – to do what they had done before in the public spaces of the city.

A century later it is the so-called Middle Eastern gangs of Sydney that are featured in moral panics about street-present young people. Like the push larrikins, these youth likewise take to the streets. It is here where they, too, are most visible. They, too, are notable for their appearance. And they, too, have managed to create their own category of 'offence' for which they are named. This time, however, the Lebanese youth is considered a foreigner as well as an outsider. This is so even though history tells us that, like the street Arab and the larrikin, contemporary youth are products of their own time, their own neighbourhoods and their own circumstances. They are 'made in Australia'.

5
Gangs and the Transnational

Introduction

As noted in Chapter 4, in recent years and in a number of countries, the processes of marginalisation and criminalisation have been imbued with a distinctive racial or ethnic character. Ethnic minorities, people of colour and immigrants have become socially defined through the language of gangs, and have steadily been subjected to coercive rather than enabling forms of state intervention. The aim here is to consider the gang phenomenon in an international context, and specifically to discuss the nature of gangs through the analytical lens of transnationalisation. The term 'transnationalisation', as used here, refers to an approach that attempts to distil common and convergent elements amongst gangs from many different national contexts, as well as to identify points of difference and divergence.

The chapter begins with a brief acknowledgement of the burgeoning literature on youth gangs, particularly in Europe, and of the tensions and disagreements that have emerged amongst those engaged in the study of youth-group formations. As part of this discussion, a brief summary of key propositions pertaining to gangs, based upon a general reading of youth gang literature, is provided.

The chapter then provides an extended discussion of key themes that may help us to understand the similarities and differences in gang formation around the world. It is necessarily speculative and exploratory in nature due, in no small part, to the breadth and diversity of gang formations (and gangs research) and the complexity of the phenomenon at hand. Although generalisation is complicated, and in some senses inadequate, it is important to recognise broad international themes that constantly appear and reappear in the research literature as they provide the conceptual platform upon which our understandings of youth gangs might be enhanced.

Transnational study of gangs

Institutionally, the growing importance attached to gangs research within academic circles is reflected in the formation of the Eurogang Research Network, which enjoys participation from over 20 different countries, including leading gang researchers from the US. In a similar vein, the number of publications dedicated to the gang topic in recent years attests to the continuing and consolidating interest in youth gangs in various countries and continental regions – for example, the US, the UK, Australia, Europe, Africa and, more generally, on the global stage [1].

A number of key themes and contentions typify the research literature, such as: gangs exist, in many different forms; gangs constitute a problem that is growing (although to whom they are a problem is itself subject to debate); gangs are spreading across regions (both urban and rural) and across nation-state borders; gangs stem from, and represent, significant social changes within different national contexts (particularly shifting economic regimes and changing immigration patterns); gangs demand varying but integrated responses from both national and local state agencies and related authorities (although whether they are, or should be, the targets or the beneficiaries of state intervention is likewise open to debate).

Key propositions about gangs

The lived realities of those young people who identify with gangs are invariably complicated. Given this, it is not surprising that researchers who try to interpret what is going on in their lives sometimes find it difficult to get things right, particularly since most research involves quantitative surveys or a 'dip-in dip-out' interview approach, rather than extended quality (and ethnographically robust) time spent with gang members. On top of this, gangs research and the development of appropriate anti-gang (or pro-youth) strategies are beset by persistent problems and definitional disputes. They are also made more complex due to the ambiguities and paradoxes of youth group behaviour generally (as indicated in Chapters 2 and 3).

Despite these limitations, key issues surrounding the analysis of gangs can be summarised in the form of a series of basic propositions. These are based upon research from many different countries and draw upon

US, Canadian, European, English, Australian and South African studies, amongst other writers working in the area. These propositions are relevant to and underpin subsequent discussion of transnational gangs as a specific concept [2].

Proposition 1 – Research has increasingly emphasised that gang formation is a social process involving complex forms of membership, transformation and disintegration.

Proposition 2 – The composition of youth gangs is ever-changing and there are significant differences both in how groups are structured and organised and in how different organisations, agencies and researchers describe the situation. As stated, the very term 'gang' – and the means by which its identity/ies is/are defined, framed and understood internally and externally – is complicated and pitted with ambiguity.

Proposition 3 – Gangs are primarily expressions of identity, and identity itself is shaped by multiple intersecting factors, including community recognition of the group as a gang, the group's recognition of itself as a distinct group, and the group's involvement in enough illegal activities to attract consistent negative responses from law enforcement officials and local people.

Proposition 4 – Just as there are problems in defining what a gang is, so too there are major difficulties in trying to establish who a gang member is. Group membership is a fluid process and, over time, specific individuals have varying degrees and types of association with groups and/or gangs.

Proposition 5 – Even where a gang can be determined to exist, gang membership is not absolute or fixed since it is highly variable and changing, and there is often no clear dividing line between those who are in a gang and those who are not – there are layers of belonging and connection that vary according to circumstances and activities.

Proposition 6 – Many young people who do not identify with gangs may nevertheless engage in gang-like behaviour, such as criminal activity, street fights, drug use and wearing gang-type clothing. Gang-related behaviour is not the same as gang membership. Nor do all gangs engage in the full range of gang-like behaviour.

Proposition 7 – Not all gang behaviour is necessarily criminal, illegal or 'bad' since a lot of what young people do is simply to hang out together. Much of the time the gang is not a problem for nearby residents, for other young people or for its members.

Proposition 8 – Where young people claim gang membership, they tend to engage in substantially more anti-social and criminal behaviour than those who do not profess to be gang members. Thus who young people say they are has implications for what they do and who they do it with. Group identification is intertwined with group activity.

Proposition 9 – Gang membership is heavily tied in with group violence. However, this violence is manifest within a wider context of social marginalisation and exclusion invariably based upon ethnicity and class. Antagonism on the street – between groups of young ethnic-minority youth and authority figures, such as the police, and between diverse groups of young people – is constantly reinforced by negative stereotyping, media moral panics and the day-to-day racism experienced by the young people.

Transnational gangs as a specific phenomenon

An initial distinction can be made between a global perspective on gangs and the notion of a transnational gang. Hagedorn, for instance, describes three key differences between 'traditional' (American) criminology, and a more global and alternative form of social analysis. Specifically, he argues that traditional criminology views gangs as temporary adolescent departures from the mainstream, basically an American social form that is a by-product of industrialisation and urbanisation, and a youthful by-product of social disorganisation and not primarily as racial or ethnic organisations. By contrast – and based upon ethnographies and cases studies from many different parts of the world – an alternative vision of gangs is based upon three key observations:

- While most gangs are unsupervised teenage peer groups, many others have become institutionalised within ghettos, barrios and favelas across the world.
- Gangs are found all over the world, responding to and reflecting the changing socio-economic and political conditions of globalising cities.
- Gangs are 'social actors' whose identities are formed by ethnic, racial and/or religious oppression; through participation in the underground economy; and through particular constructions of gender [3].

Importantly, and as will be further discussed below, a global analysis of gangs can demonstrate certain common features amongst groups, regardless of locality, and indeed the sharing of ideas and images across borders becomes part of this process. But the local gang is not the same as the transnational gang.

The transnational gang can be seen to have several distinctive features that differentiate it from other types of gang formation:

> Various definitions have cited one or more of the following character-istics in defining a transnational gang: (1) such gangs are criminally active and operational in more than one country; (2) criminal activ-ities committed by gang members in one country are planned, directed, and controlled by gang leaders in another country; (3) such gangs tend to be mobile and adapt to new areas; and (4) the crim-inal activities of such gangs tend to be sophisticated and transcend borders.

In essence, the transnational gang is seen as a group formation that operates across boundaries and borders and not simply within them [4]. Such gang formations have been studied in several different ways.

For example, the transnational gang has been portrayed as repre-senting a different stage of overall gang progression. So called first-generation gangs are seen to be turf-oriented and localised, while second-generation gangs are seen to have a market rather than turf ori-entation and to be drug-centred. Third-generation gangs are said to have goals of power or financial acquisition and a set of fully evolved politi-cal aims, and they may embrace terrorism to achieve their goals [5]. Not surprisingly, this type of analysis stems from, and is closely linked to, national security understandings of gangs. Indeed, since the events of 9/11 there has been a steady fusion of criminal and national security issues, and public sector responses [6]. Moreover, the multiple ways in which groups of young men are arming themselves and inserting them-selves into local political economic structures means that 'war lords' in places such as Somalia do represent certain empirical realities that are hard to ignore.

However, it is perhaps too easy to conflate different types of social formation into the one unitary category – gang. Life is not this simple. Nor is there a simple or linear progression through the three identified stages of transnational gangs. Rather, the actual world of gangs is marked by multiple sorts of group formation, many different types of association of armed young men, and constantly changing group and operational dynamics. This makes the question of definition even more problematic. As Hagedorn notes,

> As today's gangs proliferate, they often morph into ethnic mili-tias, drug posses, vigilantes, mercenaries, political parties, or even

religious police. Gangs and similar alienated and angry groups are a fundamental and long-term characteristic of the global era [7].

There is no set structure, no predictable or evolutionary stage. Indeed, while gangs are ubiquitous – they are everywhere – they are simultaneously local and unique. Each has to be understood on its own terms, and in its own backyard.

Having said this, it remains the case that transnational gangs exist, the origins and development of which are also highly contentious. Perhaps the most notorious of the transnational gangs in the world today stem from a period of forced deportations from the US whereby street gang members in Los Angeles and elsewhere were arrested and deported to El Salvador, from where their families originated. Back 'home' (even though many had never lived there), such gang members associated with ex-guerrilla fighters and ex-soldiers who had turned to crime in the absence of employment [8]. The net result has been the phenomenon of the MS-13 and 18th Street Gangs in a revolving door movement of people between parts of Latin America (particularly El Salvador and Mexico) and the US. The transnational gang has, in effect, been made in the crucible of restrictive immigration policy and punitive criminal justice regimes.

What global gang study demonstrates is the methodological significance of historical appreciation, and the importance of place and socio-economic contextualisation. Specific historical and material conditions – including shifting migration patterns; economic polarisation and social inequality; war and drought; varying capacities and changing willingness of nation-states to provide essential services; and entrenched racism – shape how particular groups form and develop. Similarly, the threat (or opportunities for social change) posed by gangs is differentially conceptualised and portrayed depending upon local political context: from an emphasis on perceived criminality and threats to national security, through to their potential to stand at the forefront of significant societal reform. It is through global, comparative and historical analyses, therefore, that differences in the origin, formation and development of gangs on the one hand, and state and civil society responses on the other, are best understood.

The following discussions elaborate on some of these observations by considering how they relate to broad processes of social change. In essence, we turn our gaze from discrete factors and specific trends to the more general patterns that underpin the formation of, and responses to, youth gangs. This involves taking a bird's-eye view of young people and youth gangs, and the kinds of social world that most influence their life experiences and life chances.

Commonalities and differences

While considerable variation in gang formation exists at the empirical level – type, size, structure and composition – important points of both commonality and difference warrant further explication. These, in turn, relate to broad social processes of a worldwide nature that shape what happens at the local level.

Commonalities

As noted by many youth gang and youth studies researchers, the phenomenon of gangs is closely linked to social exclusion. The systemic and structural exclusion of identifiable categories and classes of people from the mainstream institutions of society – most notably the institutions of formal paid work and education – is linked to wider processes of social change.

In particular, globalisation has directly impacted upon and fed into the manner in which many young people are being repositioned in their respective societies [9]. Fundamental shifts in the international political economy (in the form of the activities, and dominance, of transnational corporations), combined with the pervasive influence of microchip technologies (in the form of new communications, especially the Internet), underpin profound social, economic and cultural changes across the globe. Increased urbanisation, social inequality, concentrations of poverty and dependency upon the wage are creating major hardships for families in cities, particularly when labour markets fail to accommodate and absorb the movement of people into the urban centres or provide employment for those who remain living in rural areas. Meanwhile, the free flow of images of material consumption, opportunity, wealth and street culture impact on those subject to the pressures and deprivations of modern life.

Social exclusion – particularly as it applies to the gang phenomenon – is manifest in three general tendencies:

Marginalisation – Identifiable constituencies of young people are systematically excluded from mainstream institutions and are compelled to seek alternative forms of social capital (e.g., social networks, friendship groups and institutional links) and to engage in alternative means of gaining access to societal resources (e.g., food and shelter).

Criminalisation – The same young people become targets for concerted and systematic state intervention of a coercive nature. They are constructed in both the public eye and within the state apparatus as inherently and exclusively problematic to the social order, thus necessitating determined and forceful modes of intervention.

Racialisation – In many countries, the processes of marginalisation and criminalisation are imbued with a distinctive racial or ethnic character, such that ethnic minorities, people of colour and immigrants become defined essentially as gangs, and thereby subject to coercive and corrective, rather than enabling and supportive, forms of state intervention.

These are by no means startling revelations. Critical criminology has long observed that class division and social inequality are fundamental to understanding the nature of particular forms of 'criminality' and the criminalising responses of the state [10].

The processes of marginalisation are related to the presence of reserve armies of labour (particularly women and migrants, and especially guest workers), the creation of surplus populations (e.g., the long-term unemployed), and the pauperisation of both the working poor and the welfare poor. Those subjected to immiseration include the unemployed who are destitute due to the nature of local labour markets, minorities who are excluded due to social factors such as race, ethnicity or religion, and those who are poor because of age, disability or divorce. All of these are systemic social processes. As Wacquant observes with regard to one specific form that marginalisation takes, 'a ghetto is not simply a topographic entity or an aggregation of poor families and individuals but an institutional form, a historically determinate, spatially based concatenation of mechanisms of ethnoracial closure and control' [11]. In other words, at a communal level, these things do not happen by chance, nor are they colour blind. Constructions of racialisation and the impact of racism are particularly salient.

Present conflicts and societal disjunctures – depending upon country and region – also have to be historically contextualised and understood with reference to imperialist traditions. Consider for a moment the implications of the colonial era for understanding contemporary Europe:

Due to the special relationship between the colonizers and the colonized, citizens were often free to travel between the European nation and the ex-colony. Many of these groups stayed in the colony nation, for example, England (e.g., India, Pakistan, and West-Indies), France (e.g., Algeria, Morocco, and Senegal), Portugal (e.g., Brazil and Angola), and The Netherlands (e.g., Indonesia and Surinam) have a large – and growing – number of inhabitants with roots in their former colonies [12].

Colonialism is at one and the same time the maker of both difference and of deviance. The ethnic presence is both numerical minority and 'other' – the colonial subject. Racism is built into the fabric of much European tradition, history and citizenship, just as slavery is ingrained within American traditions. It follows that gang formations across different national contexts are historically embedded within long and complex legacies of colonial relations.

Differences

While general similarities are apparent across the many and diverse gang formations worldwide, there are, nevertheless, important differences. At a systems level of explanation, this is perhaps best explained in terms of differences in the institutionalisation of welfare. The means by which societal resources are communally shared, or not shared, has a big impact on human behaviour, including the behaviour of identifiable groups of young people.

In countries that have well-developed welfare state apparatus – universal provision in education, welfare, child care, income support, parenting benefits and so on – levels of social solidarity and social trust tend to be high. Conversely, for countries with less developed or poorly structured welfare systems, the opposite normally applies. Here the focus on individualism – and associated concepts related to personal responsibility and personal accountability – translates into lower levels of trust and less concern about the welfare of others [13]. Fewer welfare safeguards and more tightly rationed (or denied) access to economic and social support, together with greater reliance upon individual initiative, enterprise and free markets, make life and the competition for resources more demanding and altogether more difficult.

The general global trend vis-à-vis welfare provision has signalled the steady retreat, if not erosion, of the agencies and benefits of the welfare state *per se*. This has occurred under the cover of neoliberal reform, the ideological emphasis on individual rather than collective responsibility for welfare, and the institutionalisation of cuts in welfare spending, user-pays schemes and a 'mixed economy' approach within which the free market expands and state provision contracts. As Hagedorn also points out, in many nation-states there is no universal welfare to be cut in the first place, since the social and economic infrastructure is historically chronically weak [14].

With regard to gang formations and associated phenomena, the provision of state welfare, or not, impacts upon and shapes core social relations and conditions, including the following:

Level of violence – In the most social democratic societies, where welfare provision is freely available, gang violence tends to be less intense, less deadly and less severe than elsewhere, where welfare entitlements are more limited or are simply not available [15]. Institutional welfare provision moderates violence to the extent that extremes of poverty are mediated by some form of material support. Life often remains hard but it is less desperate when such support is available.

Motivation for gang membership – While all gangs involve some sense of identity and identification, often associated with ethnicity, the rationales underpinning gang membership vary (at least in part) due to economic (read 'welfare') circumstances. The reason for becoming part of a gang often includes an accumulation logic (gaining access to valued economic resources) and/or it might rest on affiliation (being part of a group and engaging in processes of social belonging). Each is influenced, to a greater or lesser extent, by the nature of wider educational and employment opportunities and welfare settlements.

Evolving community–gang relationships – Gangs evolve, form, dissolve and reform over time. Some are embedded in local communities and have intergenerational roots; others are more transient and fluid. The precise function, role and/or place of a gang within a community is partly a reflection of what it signifies over time, and the kinds of everyday relationship that gang members have with the wider community (including non-gang-related activity). Pressures bearing down on gang members due to the impact of neoliberal ideology, policy and practice will change the character of the gang–community relationship.

There are many additional differences between gangs, including the role and engagement of young women in gang affairs, and gang structure and organisation (embracing entry and exit rituals and processes). Such differences require further detailed exploration, taking account of cultural, local, regional, national and international patterns, and the nature and impact of global trends in specific places and on particular demographic groups.

Transferences and identities

A core aspect of gang discourse that traverses borders and boundaries is moral panic. In many countries, moral outrage is frequently created and/or stoked by the media in ways that both demonise particular groups of young people and/or brand them as gangs [16]. In turn, youth gangs are frequently portrayed as dangerous, deviant and destructive, and such media-constructed images are intertwined with political and public responses that call forth repressive measures and collective revulsion.

Transferences from place to place

Media negativity towards (and fascination with) gangs involves the international circulation of particular ideas and images. Moral panic is not exclusively limited to a discreet one-off episode, nor are specific events necessarily separated from each other in mass-media discourse. Indeed, as Poynting and associates convincingly argue, the means by which any identifiable group is persistently presented and conceptualised as a 'folk devil' stems from the ways in which discourses are assembled over time and serve to reinforce key messages and stereotypes [17].

In this way, the mass media are key to social constructions of ethnicity and social differences that transcend national borders. As stated, much popular understanding of youth gangs in North America, Europe and Australia is heavily racialised. In large part this stems from how the media presents and reports on particular ethnic groups, with contemporary media images of minority communities in different national contexts being generally negative (e.g., the Lebanese in Australia, North Africans in Italy, West Indians in England). This is especially the case with respect to recent immigrants and people of colour. Equally, particular events are often seized upon by the media to reinforce the ethnic character of deviancy and criminality in ways which stigmatise whole communities [18]. As the experience in the US indicates, immigration is frequently associated with the gang phenomenon. For example, the four major periods of gang presence in the US – the 1890s, 1920s, 1960s and 1990s – were all linked to significant social changes, including increased immigration [19].

Beyond moral panic, however, not all groups respond in the same way to similar material pressures and popular media images. There are two key issues here which are of particular interest. The first relates to how certain ethnic and cultural groups are more likely to form gangs than others, and why this might be the case. For example, van Gemert's research on Moroccan and Turkish immigrant youth in Amsterdam found that compared with Turkish youth, Moroccan boys and young men are significantly over-represented in police statistics, and the majority of gang members are reported to be Moroccan [20]. Here are two identifiable groups of immigrants with significant differences in how they appear to be settling in to the host country. Explaining this difference requires nuanced community studies rather than a homogenised 'gang approach'.

Yet the differences between Turkish and Moroccan youth are far less obvious than those that exist between these identifiable groups and mainstream Dutch young people. Both ethnic-minority groups are disproportionately represented in the criminal justice system, and both are regularly subjected to anti-Islamic vilification, which is reinforced and reproduced in the Dutch media. Stories about misbehaving Moroccan young people feature particularly strongly:

> Although the stories are typically overblown, the trouble of Moroccan youth is now accepted as social fact. Terms that refer to this such as street terrorism, beach terrorism and street terror have become commonplace, invariably in relation to Moroccan youngsters [21].

Intense and negative media attention has been accompanied by coercive state-based intervention, leading to deteriorating police–youth relations that, in turn, further reinforce the image of Moroccan young men as antisocial. All of these factors contribute to the identification of these particular young men as gang members.

A second issue pertains to how gang style and gang images are localised in their re-representation and reconstruction. To put it differently, young people might appropriate 'universal' images and yet transform them into unique forms and practices within their immediate milieu:

> Despite the similarity in names and gang style, there are important differences between Crips in the USA and Crips in The Netherlands. The latter are far less organized, are not organized

around drug sales, are not territorial, and engage in much lower levels of violence. In other words, European Crips have more in common with Crip gang style and affectation than organization or behaviour [22].

Here we have a case of ostensibly similar gang images, symbols and culture that in reality are quite different.

Continuing along the same lines, the names 'Bloods' and 'Crips' are also used in New Zealand and Australia, where they essentially comprise ethnic markers: the Bloods refer to Samoan young people, the Crips to Tongan young people [23]. The colours each group wears (Bloods, red, Samoan; Crips, blue, Tongan) are immediate and striking signs of ethnic, and indeed original island, origin. The relationship with the US Bloods and Crips is tenuous, and the terms have basically been appropriated less as a gang identifier and more as local descriptions of ethnicity. Gang styles and associated cultural forms (e.g., hip hop), therefore, are culturally transmitted but not necessarily culturally emulated. For example, the Australian hip hop scene is dominated by ethnic-minority young people whose voices are distinctly (immigrant) Australian and whose cultural content/message is likewise unique to their circumstances [24]. Similarly, indigenous rappers in Australia have appropriated the form but use different language (sometimes literally a different language) to express what matters to them in their particular cultural universe [25].

Whatever the similarities and differences, the uniformly problematic images associated with gangs tend to impact negatively. In other words, the social consequences of moral panics typically include ostracising and penalising identifiable youth groups – especially migrant and ethnic-minority youth – on the basis of their presumed immoral and threatening behaviour, often by implementing legislation and stepped-up police interventions to prevent or prohibit street presence and certain types of activity. In this sense, the notion of 'transference' refers to the way in which certain people, ideas and images are conveyed from one place to another. From the point of view of moral panics over gangs, this usually includes popular representations of stereotypical gang characteristics (e.g., the colour gangs of the US Hollywood ilk) that frequently fail to capture and/or accurately represent nuanced differences. The dissemination of such matter has been enhanced by the advent of the Internet and associated technologies, such as *Facebook* and *YouTube*. Often what is conveyed is simply wrong or just plain racist. At the sharp end of this phenomenon, linkages between a social identity and national security are forged, in particular ways such as the recent (2010) case involving images of 'Muslim gangs in Australia' being posted on the Internet by a private US national security activist group. Furthermore, myths and images of this kind may also be picked up and perpetrated via 'legitimate' or 'respectable' Internet exchanges, such as the e-mail information list of the Eurogang Research Network, which reproduced this particular 'story' without any analytical or critical comment.

Such representations tend not only to induce panic, fear and anxiety but also to impact worldwide on the ways in which young people see themselves and their activities; how they behave and make sense of their lives. Paradoxically, at this level, the gang image is not necessarily seen as 'bad' but rather as something to aspire to or emulate; the gangs moral panic itself can serve to amplify the excitement attached to the label. For marginalised and often criminalised young people, transgression can be very appealing, especially as it both inverts the negativity of the label (being instead a sought-after status) and reinforces notoriety (since it feeds back into the very thing that is popularly detested). Street credibility and peer respect is fashioned out of precisely the process that most turns the state against the young people in question – the appearance of gang affiliation.

Ironically, depending upon the jurisdiction, anti-gang strategies can materially feed processes of identity formation and group consolidation. As mentioned earlier, this is most evident in the US, where gang members in Los Angeles have been deported to El Salvador. The result of this has been the formation of US-style gangs in El Salvador and the subsequent flow back into the US of gang members returning to their original 'home' [26]. Thus coercive interventions can sustain and provide a feedback loop into the very problems presumably activating state action in the first place.

While most gangs exhibit a very restricted presence by engaging in activities predominantly at the local area level, the flow of people and ideas across borders (e.g., Maori and Samoan young people migrating with their families to Australia) adds a transnational character to what occurs at the local level. So, too, the Internet, and the many gang sites associated with it, provides a ready forum for transfer of information, images, ideas and attitudes. The latter is particularly significant insofar as what is being conveyed includes the usual hyper-masculinity trappings but also affective attributes such as the sense of anger and injustice at being 'on the margins'. Gang membership becomes an important part of social connection and social belonging at many different levels.

Globalisation and identity

Social identity forms a key aspect in understanding gang formation, gang activity and gang membership. Identity is multilayered and complex (see Chapter 2). For the present purposes, it is important to note that much gang identification is forged through international as well as local contexts. All young people today are growing up in a world characterised by phenomena such as globalisation, neoliberal political economy, war and consumerism. The specificity of personal being, however, is shaped not only by epochal and global features but also by the mundane experiences of family, friends, neighbourhood, school and community [27]. The global may shape the local, but it is on the streets and in the suburbs that the particularities of social life are constructed and made manifest. This is why different gang formations take on such different substantive shapes and characters.

Several recent edited volumes, for instance, have each in their own way affirmed the complicated intersections between the ongoing projects of the 'self' (constructions of personal identity), the importance of specific local contexts (material resources and social histories), and wider global social, economic and cultural processes (globalisation) as these pertain to youth gangs [28]. Group formations such as gangs are located in particular spaces at particular times and are engaged in particular kinds of activities. The collective and the personal – in terms of identities and wellbeing – are fused in the praxis of group formation and group dynamics. Furthermore, research has demonstrated that the complexities of social life frequently pivot around ethnicity and ethnic identity, which, as stated, are themselves dynamic, historical and multidimensional. Indeed, family and ethnic ties are especially vital to analyse in the case of transnational gangs. For example, New Zealand Maori and other Pacific Islanders have close family links across the Pacific region (especially into Australia, but in countries such as the US as well). Ideas and activities are transferred both through direct family relationships (in the form of visits, and via migration) and through Internet sites that resonate with or are developed by members of the community across different times and spaces.

To understand both the fluidity and the solidity of identity, we need to comprehend actual migrations and migration processes, including ongoing links to historical homelands and ethnic traditions amongst certain migrant and established groups. But we also need to grasp both general ethnic identifications and the importance of territorial cross-ethnic alliances at the local level. This has been described via the notion of 'defensive localism', in which gangs fight to protect territory [29]. In protecting territory, however, ethnicity and locality combine in ways that sometimes privilege ethnicity, and sometimes territory – depending upon who the protagonists are, and who is defined as an outsider at any given moment [30].

Conclusion

This chapter has provided a broad overview of what can be described as the transnational nature of youth gangs. Such transnationalisation incorporates several key elements. Analytically, processes of social exclusion, welfare institutionalisation and moral panic – and the particular concepts and social processes that pertain to each of these – are vital. There are various commonalities and differences in gang formation that flow from, and are consequences of, the social positioning of young people in any particular society.

Equally, within the global political economy, transference processes – which in this instance include the movement of images, ideas and people from one place to another – are also key. Such processes enable members of youth groups to develop and inhabit different symbolic and cultural universes at the same time through the magic of modern communications systems and technologies. Yet, when all is said and done, gangs are ultimately defined by and tied to localised material conditions and welfare settlements.

Social, economic and political exclusion, with consequently severely retarded life chances (vis-à-vis the mainstream), propels many young people into gang activity. Globally, it is structural issues relating to inequality, poverty, unemployment and injustice that are at the heart of gang formation and gang activity. That said, as with the case of specific gang formations, the 'gang problem' will vary greatly from location to location. There are profound dangers in treating all such groups in the same way, particularly where this leads to social (and frequently racist) profiling, stigmatisation and pathologisation, and opens the door to criminalisation and inappropriate coercive state interventions. As Hagedorn emphasises,

The complex world we live in is not made up of neatly defined groups, some criminal, some political, some cultural. The world of gangs comprises flexible forms of armed groups, some changing from gang to militia to criminal syndicate to political party, or some existing as all types simultaneously [31].

Gang life is inherently changeable and complex.

6
Indigenous Gangs and Family

Introduction

One of the themes of this book is that social identity is multilayered and complex. It is shaped by many different factors and forces, and it is ultimately tied to specific local contexts and material circumstances. For gang members, this complexity is no less true than for non-gang members. They, too, are influenced by historical and global processes and they, too, find their individual and collective identity in the crucible of lived experience within specific communities and families. Social belonging is vital to both identity and personal vitality. The family, as broadly defined, is at the centre of this process for young people [1].

The role of gangs as a sort of 'family' has been noted in the youth gangs literature. Sometimes this is framed in terms of the gang as a substitute or replacement family for young people whose families of origin do not provide adequate resources or secure affective relationships. The gang is seen as separate from the family of origin, even where its functions appear to take on that of the family *per se*.

What happens, however, if the gang is simultaneously, and literally, one's family? That is, what if the family and the gang are basically one-and-the-same? Certainly the evidence from the Australian youth gangs research seems to point in precisely this direction (see Chapters 2 and 3). Most of the young people we have spoken with over the years have brothers and uncles and fathers and cousins with whom they share intimate family ties. For those in youth gangs the broad tendency is to also share in gang membership with relatives as well as friends.

This chapter is premised upon three basic propositions. These are:

- that the gang performs a family-like role for gang members, regardless of specific social composition, particularly when it comes to

material support, emotional refuge, psychological wellbeing, physical
protection and social belonging;
- that in some cases, particularly with regard to ethnic-minority youth,
the gang mainly comprises family members and/or members from a
distinctive and frequently tight-knit community, which means that
there already exist strong filial bonds within the context of gang
formation;
- that in the case of indigenous young people, the gang and family
connection is unique insofar as the colonial experience reinforces an
Othering process that is distinctive and specific to this group.

When it comes to the latter instance, consideration of the close inter-
connection between family and gang is important for several reasons.
It is important first because by understanding this connection we can
better appreciate the social determinants of gang formation and the reasons why the gang becomes so central within some young people's lives.
Second, the development of anti-gang strategies that do not reflect, and
respect, family considerations are bound not only to fail but also to
reproduce the worst aspects of oppressive colonial rule.

Many of the causes of indigenous gang formation and mobilisation
are inextricably linked to the systematic dispossession of indigenous
people and their ongoing subjugation within a non-indigenous criminal justice system. The breaking up of families has been central to these
processes, historically and in the contemporary time period. The social
consequences have been devastating for indigenous people, including
young people.

Growing up indigenous

The experiences of indigenous peoples have been fundamentally shaped
by colonialist processes, and yet their experiences are variable due to
the diverse social worlds that they inhabit [2]. As with youth in general,
there is great variability in indigenous communities, and the indigenous
population as a whole is heterogeneous across many different dimensions. What unites the many is the shared experiences of injustice,
inequality and oppression at the hands of a colonial state, an experience
that continues to the present day [3].

Today the Aboriginal and Torres Strait Islander population – the
indigenous peoples of Australia – is estimated to be about 2.4 per cent
of the total Australian population. The indigenous population is relatively young compared with the non-indigenous population. In 2001,

39 per cent of indigenous people were under 15 years of age, compared with 20 per cent of non-indigenous people. In 2002, just over half of indigenous people aged 15 years or over reported that they identified with a clan, tribal or language group, and 21 per cent spoke an indigenous language [4].

Since the initial British invasion of 1788, the indigenous peoples of Australia have been subjected to myriad interventions, exclusions and social controls. This is not simply a historical legacy; it is part of the fabric of everyday life for many indigenous people today. Colonialism has had a severe impact on indigenous cultures and ways of life, as have the continuing effects of discriminatory policies and practices on indigenous life chances within mainstream social institutions. The dislocations and social marginalisation associated with colonialism have had particular ramifications for indigenous young people. It is worth noting that, historically, and in particular, young indigenous women were prone to policies that were intended to separate them from their families and communities, and that constituted a form of cultural and physical genocide. More recently it has been argued that rather than breaking up communities on the basis of a welfare or protectionist rationale, the same thing is occurring through the systematic 'criminalisation' of young indigenous people, although the main target now is young men [5].

Young indigenous people are very conscious of the dynamics of racism and policing in particular. Interviews with young indigenous people in Darwin and Alice Springs in the late 1990s made this very clear [6]. When asked about the things that most influence the way other people view them when they were hanging out in public spaces, the young people most frequently mentioned racism, stereotypes of young people and the fact that many older people did not seem to like young people hanging around together in groups. It would appear that the feelings of exclusion and undue harassment experienced by many of these young people were the result of negative reactions to them based on a combination of indigenous status, colour of their skin, age and class position. Typical comments from them included:

> Being black, people think you are going to commit a crime.
>
> (young man)

> Where old people are they stare at us if we're sitting there as if we have no right to sit there, treat us bad and serve us last. We still go out but...
>
> (young woman)

Darker skin makes them think we're troublemakers. Some other people just stare at us, some keep walking, some look dirty daggers at us.

(young woman)

I hate going down the shops. They [shop owners] always saying, 'Oh, you been shoplifting.' Everyone gets always accused of shoplifting round here. You can't window shop and browse. You can't even price something. You got to walk in there with the money and buy it there and then.

(young woman)

The position of young indigenous people in Australian society makes them very vulnerable to overpolicing and exclusionary practices. It also makes them angry [7].

Nevertheless, popular images and representations of indigenous young people tend to overemphasise criminal activities and substance abuse while ignoring the significant proportion of young people not implicated or engaged in these activities [8]. Other distorted or one-sided representations are apparent as well. There is, for example, the underlying assumption that all indigenous young people, regardless of family background, have similar issues and life chances. This assumption leads to little appreciation of social differences within the indigenous population, apart from those that separate the indigenous and the nonindigenous. The former are evident with regard to class, gender and ethnic differences within communities (e.g., tribal and family associations, as well as language), which manifest themselves in diverse ways, depending upon immediate social context.

Indigenous gang experiences

This section is based upon interviews with indigenous young people that were carried out in the early to mid-2000s as part of the national youth gangs study. This involved interviews with young people in each capital city who self-identified as being gang members, or who were identified by 'gatekeepers', such as youth and community workers, as being perceived to be and engaged in gang activities. Among the overall sample there were indigenous respondents in Canberra ($n = 13$), Hobart ($n = 4$), Perth ($n = 7$) and Darwin ($n = 7$). Although the total number were relatively small (only 31 individuals), the responses were remarkably similar. This was so regardless of city, and regardless of the specific background of the young person (e.g., in one city, the key source of respondents was young people serving time in a youth detention centre). A series of key themes presented themselves across the sample.

'Black fellas hang out with black fellas'

Not all of the young people who were interviewed for this study hung out with immediate family members. But family ties and identification as indigenous were central to their social networks and self-identity. Many of the young people came from chaotic and unstable family situations, and a number had been 'kicked out of house'. Their friendship group comprised similarly placed other indigenous youth. For one young Canberra woman, her mother was not to be trusted ('because I was pregnant and my mum told everyone'), but she could trust her sisters, who in turn she talked about as being like mothers to her. In this instance it was other family members from the same household who provided the main support.

For most of these indigenous young people, the sense of family connection was central to group identity and formation. One group – the Barclay Murder Squad in Darwin – had its name made up by the respondent's uncle. Only family members could belong, and no young kids or people from other countries were allowed in. Similarly, other respondents in Darwin spoke about how they stayed in the gang because it was made up of family and friends whom they had grown up with. The theme that local gangs are criminal groups based on family emerged strongly.

A Perth young man spoke at length about how his fellow group members were mainly his cousins. Family in an indigenous context generally refers to extended family rather than just the immediate nuclear family. Another young person from Perth observed that there are big groups and little groups that hang out together:

> whenever we meet all together that's just like on the weekend, but the ones that hang out would probably be cousins mostly and like people that live right next to them. They just go over to their house after school or whatever . . . there's a group that's related to each other and they probably hang out with each other the most. Like they're always with each other, but the whole – all of us always see each other, but some of them just because they go back to their auntie's house or whatever.
>
> (15-year-old young man)

By contrast, the question of indigenous identity is fraught with ambi-guity in places like Hobart (due to the peculiar colonial history of the state). This leads to complicated identity politics at the level of everyday relations. One respondent identified himself as being a bit of a 'black fella' and alluded to the fact that he has black identity in his family her-itage. He had at one stage been bashed, and his father had in a separate incident been stabbed, by other known members of the same gang. The perpetrators in this instance were described as 'my cousins that I don't like to claim as cousins, but they are. You can't help that can you, it's family.' Family ties come in different guises, and not every black fella identifies publicly as being indigenous. And, as this story indicates, not all 'family' relationships are close knit and friendly.

'If we wasn't Aboriginal, they would treat us like gold'

The social injuries of racism, prejudice and discrimination were appar-ent across the board. This is a profoundly disturbing and traumatic experience for many of the young people interviewed. A young woman in Canberra said:

> They even called me 'black dog' and I don't like being called black dog. That's how come I got kicked out of L High because people kept calling me black dog and shit... teachers treat me like I'm different compared to white people... And it really hurts [is upset and almost crying]... We had two white people in our group, but the others treat me like – like we were nothing 'cause we're Aboriginal and because the way life has grown is because Aboriginals are worth nothing, but white people are worth something. So we had hardly any white peo-ple for friends... Teachers treat me and my sister different because we're Aboriginal. That's the only reason. If we wasn't Aboriginal, they would treat us like gold.
>
> (15-year-old young woman)

Racism was in many cases a unifying experience, if for no other rea-son than that fights and conflicts were based upon race and ethnic background. One 18-year-old Canberra man told us that 'Yeah, we're always fighting with most other people in school 'cause we're just dark – outcasts compared to them.' This reinforces an outsider identity, while at the same time forging stronger links internal to the group, such that 'black fellas hang out with black fellas' (another 18-year-old young Canberra man).

Fighting, especially at school, was generally between white and black, and in some cases between Aborigines and 'wogs' (ethnic-minority youth from Italian, Greek or other Mediterranean backgrounds). In other words, fights were generally described as occurring between different races and people from different social backgrounds. Interestingly, a specific source of irritation and a trigger to violence was when someone would taunt another by saying something about their mum or dad. Protecting family includes responding to verbal abuse as well as other forms of threat:

> yeah we've got out area. If anyone comes through just pissing us off, we usually bash 'em, fight 'em, stuff like that.

What came through in the interviews was a strong sense of local territory. This was intertwined with family identity. In Darwin, for example, there seemed to be a clear pack mentality with strong family ties. A lot of the respondents' friendship groups and gang-related activity are with family members and people who are from the same area. In fact, the only extensive social contact they seemed to have was with members of their group. The gang is basically their family and friends from the local area. This was a familiar refrain in most of the Australian youth gangs research that was carried out, and it applies across diverse communities and locales (see Chapter 3).

In each of the cities where the interviews took place, the young people had specific local areas that they identified with and 'owned'. Large groups would gather at particular places, especially at weekends, and these were claimed as their own local territory. In Canberra it was noted that one group protected its territory by hanging around and 'giving it' to anyone who is a smart arse in their area. 'They just know that we're ready to fight – yeah and they'll get it', said one young man.

A racial identity was simultaneously bound up, therefore, with a sense of territory. Cultural identity – one's identification as being indigenous – was grounded by being located within a defined geographical space. A gang defends this territory. One Canberra young man described a gang as follows:

> Umm, just a group of friends, illegal activity, just territory – stuff like that. Just – yeah – cultural identity and stuff like that . . . umm, yeah we've got our area. Just [name of suburb]. If anyone comes through just pissing us off, we usually bash 'em, fight 'em, stuff like that.
>
> (18-year-old young man)

The notion of a place being 'our territory' was common across the sample group.

For some, the gang was akin to a clan, a big family, which is bound together by geography. Familiarity with one's territory means fierce protection of possible outside disruption to that territory. As one young man put it, a sense of territoriality best defines what a gang is:

> 'cause you've gotta look after your neighbourhood. You can't just let, umm, how can I put it? A stray come along. It's like having a nice beautiful garden right, and all it takes is one weed to come up and the next thing you know, the whole garden's gone 'cause you got one weed.
>
> (24-year-old Adelaide young man)

Interestingly, the sense of territory can also serve to divide indigenous youth from each other. One Darwin person who was in detention at the time of their interview could not wait until his release because his particular gang was in the minority inside the detention centre: 'In here, you haven't got any backup. There's Casuarina boys in here and there's only two Palmerston boys.' Protecting territory thus also demands a certain weight of numbers when young people are taken out of their home spaces and put into neutral places:

> it doesn't matter who they are or what race they are. We don't discriminate.

Gang membership is sometimes open, yet nonetheless contingent. For instance, in some groups, race is a defining feature of membership. As one Canberra youth stated unequivocally, 'White people can't belong to our group.' However, invocation of this criterion was not always the case for exclusion. Another young Canberra man spoke about what members of his group had in common, and the group included 'outsiders' (in this case referring to white young people):

> Loud, disruptive, criminalistic minds, ethnic backgrounds – we're all Aboriginal. There's a couple of outsiders that are also part of the crew and, you know, they just don't give a shit and they don't point the finger whether you're black, white, yellow or purple... They're just good to chill back and have a drink with.
>
> (18-year-old young man)

Territory, non-racist attitudes and not being a 'wuss' (i.e., conformist, and someone who does not like to party) are what combine to allow some membership association with a group regardless of racial and ethnic background. Similar observations were made in Darwin where, although one group comprised mainly indigenous men, other ethnicities were welcome; they just had to live in the local suburb.

The majority within each group were indigenous. But, as one Canberra youth stated, social belonging also involves various other social dimensions that allow for non-indigenous participation:

> We all like to charge. We all like footy – and sports as well. All like the same sort of music…Oh black music and stuff. R&B and that…it doesn't matter who they are or what race they are. We don't discriminate.
>
> (18-year-old young man)

Yet the same young person was to further comment on which people were more likely to join groups or gangs than other people: 'Oh a lot of people – like Aboriginals come down and they usually just join our group and stuff, like this year 'cause there's more Aboriginal people coming down…Yeah families are close together.' As in a Darwin interview, it seems that the primary phenomenon is that indigenous people hang out together, but this is not necessarily exclusive and can involve white people as well.

A bottom line does exist, however, when it comes to who is allowed to hang around with whom. It is not only about having a good time or protecting one's mates when it comes to fighting; it is about general attitudes towards difference and to the Other. As one Perth gang member stated,

> Racist people can't belong to our group. I don't mean just racist talk like 'cause like most of us are Aboriginal in our group. Like we don't like people who are racist to any group.
>
> (18-year-old young man)

The hurtfulness of racism goes much deeper than just the question of membership of a group, however. A Canberra youth had this to say:

> teachers were racist 'cause I may be white, but I've got Aboriginal in me and, yeah, I had a lot of shit thrown at me because of that. But I also threw a lot of shit back at people for giving it to me.

Not so much in verbal, but as in little bits of violence here and there... People throwing shit at me, it was mainly verbal, a couple of times physical. But mainly when people threw verbal shit about me – about racist remarks – I'm not going to mention 'cause they're pretty derogatory and it's just fucking ridiculous, you know, we're all the same fucking colour, we all have to fucking live in this world, so why can't we all just get along? I'm not racist – the way I see it I'm not racist. I just hate everyone.

(18-year-old young man)

Another Canberra youth commented on who he likes to hang out with and why in the following terms: 'cause we understand each other and we're always there to help each other. It's mainly Aboriginals, but my girlfriend, she's a wog and I've got another mate whose Australian – like white Australian.' In the end, this same young man chose to hang around with a smaller circle of friends:

Well I stopped like hanging around my Aboriginal mates 'cause they're just getting into too much trouble and I wanna start – I'm just with my girlfriend and, yeah, just chilling round with her and her friends... The Aboriginal boys, they all drink and, yeah, just carry on being dickheads and, yeah, that's pretty much it. Just walk around and get themselves into trouble.

(19-year-old young man)

Explaining and responding to the gangs/family nexus

To understand fully the issues and conflicts pertaining to indigenous young people's relationship with the criminal justice system, it is essential to acknowledge the continuing legacy and present realities of colonialism in the lives of indigenous people [9]. So, to also understand the attractions and dynamics of gang formation for indigenous young people, it is vital to put the relationship between gang and 'family' into social context. Accordingly, the next section discusses three interrelated issues, relating to family, criminal justice and social identity.

Questions of family

The negative impact of constant state intervention into the families and communities of indigenous peoples cannot be underestimated. The Stolen Generations Inquiry estimated that between one in ten and one in three Aboriginal children, depending on the period and location, were removed from their families between 1910 and 1970. Most indigenous families have thus been affected by this phenomenon [10]. The earlier policies of forced removals continue to have contemporary effects, as summarised by Cunneen and White:

> Twice as many Indigenous people who were removed as children reported being arrested; those who were removed reported significantly poorer health (NISATSIC 1997:15). Almost one in ten boys and just over one in ten girls reported that they were sexually abused in children's institutions; one in ten boys and three in ten girls reported they were sexually abused in a foster placement (NISATSIC 1997:163). There has also been a range of complex trauma-related psychological and psychiatric effects that have been intergenerational. These relate to issues such as parenting skills, unresolved grief and trauma, violence, depression, mental illness, and other behavioural problems. A survey by the Aboriginal Legal Service in Western Australia of 483 Aboriginal people who had been forcibly removed found that a third had also had their children removed (NISATSIC 1997: 226). Indigenous children are still significantly overrepresented in contact with welfare agencies. Nationally, around 20 per cent of children in care are Indigenous. A significant proportion of such children are placed with non-Indigenous families, which is particularly the case for those in long-term foster care [11].

The nature of state intervention – whether for welfare or criminalisation purposes – has had a profound effect on indigenous ways of life; their relationship to authority figures, such as the police; and the experiences of young indigenous people as they grow up in a (post)colonial context.

With regard to gang issues, the family is central. The relationship is at times complex and somewhat ambiguous, with several different dimensions. Depending upon the circumstances,

- family members are actual gang members
  or
- gang members are seen as family
  or
- family have very negative influences on the young person leading them to engage in a criminal/anti-social lifestyle because of a dysfunctional family background of neglect or abuse.

For some gang members, all three of the above apply.

One legacy of colonialism has been heightened levels of intrafamily conflict, including child sexual abuse [12]. The issue of indigenous family violence is prominent today in Australia and has led to massive state intervention in places like the Northern Territory. Our concern here is not with the nature of the intervention, nor with the documentation of family violence; rather, it is simply to say that such violence necessarily has a major impact on young indigenous people who witness and/or are on the receiving end of the violence.

Compounding the stresses of dispossession and marginalisation on many indigenous families and communities has been the removal of children from indigenous households. This has already been alluded to above. To these observations, however, we can add that for many of those who were removed from their parents, the role of parenting has subsequently been quite foreign, and in many cases individuals have also suffered from lack of communal support in childrearing [13]. This can lead to instances of neglectful parenting, abusive relationships and poor role modelling.

The nature and quality of parenting is thus partly shaped by the nature and dynamics of family formation as determined by oppressive state policies and interventions. For young people, this can have major repercussions in terms of upbringing and modes of conflict resolution. Bear in mind as well that there are huge pressures on indigenous children growing up in what is still a very racist social climate.

Questions of criminal justice

There is a close relationship between social marginalisation (incorporating racial discrimination and economic and social exclusion) and criminalisation (which constitutes one type of state response to marginalisation). Extensive research has been undertaken in recent years on the over-representation of indigenous peoples in the criminal justice system, research that has provided considerable evidence of over-representation in most jurisdictions, and particularly at the most punitive end of the system – in detention centres [14].

A recent report found that Aboriginal and Torres Strait Islander (indigenous) young people were hugely over-represented among those who are subject to juvenile justice supervision [15]. The statistical story is striking:

• Although only around 3 per cent of the total Australian population and 5 per cent of Australians aged 10–17 years are Aboriginal and Torres Strait Islanders, over a third (36 per cent) of those who had supervision in 2006–2007 were indigenous young people. In several states and territories there were more indigenous young people under supervision than non-indigenous young people (particularly in those locales where there are higher proportions of indigenous young people, such as Western Australia and the Northern Territory).

- Over a third of those in community-based supervision on an average day in 2006–2007 and nearly half of those in detention were indigenous young people. For example, of the 941 young people in detention, either on pre-sentence or sentenced detention, 410 were indigenous men compared with 437 non-indigenous males (18 unknown status), and 33 were indigenous women compared with 41 non-indigenous females (2 unknown status). Thus the over-representation increases the further one goes towards the harshest parts of the juvenile justice system.
- Of those aged 10–17 years, indigenous young people were nearly 14 times as likely to have supervision in 2006–2007 as non-indigenous young people. Indigenous young people under supervision are also more likely to be younger than non-indigenous young people and they are more likely to have entered supervision for the first time at a younger age. For example, for young people aged 10 to 15, 61 per cent of the average daily population in detention were indigenous, but the proportion decreased to 17 per cent for those aged 18 and older. Moreover, a greater proportion of females aged 10–13 years than males were indigenous.

These patterns continue a historical trend that criminologists have noted for quite some time. For the present purposes I want to consider some of the cultural and social consequences for indigenous young people, given the high rates of incarceration in particular.

First, prison is not a strange place to many indigenous young people. High rates of incarceration for both young and older members of their communities means that contact with the criminal justice system is routine and expected rather than unusual and foreign. Bad blood between authority figures is historically grounded, and is still played out today in contemporary social relations. This has a major impact on how young indigenous people see themselves. It also has significant implications for the labelling of indigenous young people in the public domains of the streets, malls and parklands.

Second, for some young indigenous people, prison is a place you want to go to. It can be a rite of passage for some young people [16]. Importantly, especially given the statistics on youth detention, in prison, indigenous people are frequently in the majority, and at the very least are represented in large numbers. They are the strong ones. They also learn the language of the prison and the detention centre. Such language can be both alien and attractive to the young people on the outside. This, in turn, can contribute towards a gang culture and gang mentality amongst some indigenous young people.

Questions of social identity

A major issue facing many indigenous young people is who, precisely, they are. This is by no means an easy question to answer. Recent musings on the nature of indigeneity and, indeed, identity generally have provided striking illustrations of the incredible complexities of defining who we are. Paradies points out that many indigenous people are simultaneously non-indigenous – they have European and Asian ancestry as well as Aboriginal and Torres Strait Islander ancestry. Furthermore, about half of all indigenous people in committed relationships have a non-indigenous partner. Yet, as Paradies observes, 'despite this heterogeneity in the Indigenous community, asserting a multi-racial Indigenous identity is neither common nor straightforward because racial loyalty demands that anomalous individuals choose to be either exclusively Indigenous or exclusively non-Indigenous' [17]. Further to this, however, as the youth gangs research indicates, many indigenous youth have their social identity thrust upon them, in the sense that they experience racism precisely because they are perceived to be indigenous. Racism at one and the same time reinforces a master status: social identity is partly a matter of how others treat us.

For those who do identify and who are identified as indigenous, the social world may be filled with complex expectations and, in some cases, violence. Study of young indigenous people in urban centres has shown that many feel uncomfortable with their status, especially after seeing how their parents were treated by non-indigenous people, and so the streets and crime become an alternative measure of who they are and the meaning of success [18]. Other research has demonstrated that the harder authorities push, and the more vilified they are by members of the general public, the more likely marginalised young indigenous people are to engage in activities such as chroming or paint sniffing [19]. In some instances, a gang identity is externally imposed upon them (as with the 'Gang of 49' in Adelaide), a phenomenon that may be unfair but that nonetheless has far-reaching social consequences.

For young people in remote communities, the response to marginalisation, unemployment and social devalorisation has included more than self-medication such as petrol sniffing. The small town of Wadeye in a remote area of the Northern Territory, for example, made national headlines in 2004 due to the emergence of a new kind of gang culture [20]. Hundreds of adults and younger children were forced to flee the town because of the high levels of violence perpetrated by members of groups with names such as Judas Priest and the Evil Warriors: houses were trashed and elders ignored. The fusion of contemporary music with extreme alienation with group violence shows that identity is diversely and oppositionally constructed within indigeneity as well as in relation to the non-indigenous.

The emergence of large-scale intergroup fighting between multiple extended families has also been reported in places such as Tennant Creek in the Northern Territory. In part this is due to the fact that there are groups residing in one community but from different geographic origins. Here again we hear stories of male youth gangs, such as the Bad Boys and the Eastsiders, and events such as Aussie Rules football carnivals, which reinforce team rivalry and provide an outlet for intergroup conflict [21].

Disapproval of their dress, manner, speech and other behaviour by members of the general public can foster continued and renewed antisocial behaviour on the part of some indigenous young people [22]. But this spiral of amplification has its starting point in the original marginalisation of these particular young indigenous people. In-fighting of the kind witnessed in Wadeye could be analysed in terms of masculinity, territoriality and other conventional gangs research concepts but, fundamentally, the deviance is grounded in the material conditions and cultural realities of the specific young people involved. Without addressing these kinds of factor in either case, no amount of coercive intervention will succeed in putting out the fires of frustration, suppressed anger, humiliation and separation.

Revisiting gangs and the family

As this chapter has illustrated through a discussion of indigenous youth gang members, there are complexities surrounding concepts of, and relationships between, family and gangs. Colonialism has profoundly affected how indigenous young people navigate their social spaces, including those of the family. The picture is complicated when it comes to other groups of young people as well.

Consider, for example, that the development of Lebanese youth gangs in Western Sydney has been interpreted by the young people themselves as fundamentally a family-building project. For instance, on the one hand, what unites them is the persecution and insults suffered by their families at the hands of outsiders. As one young person told us, 'If you insult one of us, then you insult our brother, and if you insult our brother, you insult our father, our mother, and put shame on our whole family.' On the other hand, part of the family ethos is to protect each other. This extends to situations where one of the family may be stopped by the police, thus requiring back-up by other family members [23].

Family obligations, therefore, may reinforce particular social identities and social practices that, to those who are ignorant of the local context (e.g., racist abuse or police maltreatment), may appear to reflect anti-social tendencies. It is but a small step to move from the criminalisation of specific individuals (based upon alleged gang membership and involvement) to portraying whole communities as being gang-like.

On the other hand, one dilemma of the 'gangs as family' phenomenon is that this can become reified in ways that present the gang as a desirable social form over and above other types of relating. For example, in New Zealand, some commentators have argued that in the case of Maori, gang associations are regarded as positive affiliations because Maori are assumed to be a collectivist people. For other offenders, gang affiliations are judged negatively and regarded as being indicative of an individual's anti-social behaviour. This type of thinking – one that equates gangs with Maori culture – can in fact entrench what is, for all its strengths, a mode of belonging that is based upon offending and anti-social behaviour. Furthermore, it fails to address the socio-economic deprivation and other related factors that are the main contributors to offending [24].

A positive response to gangs is possible, but it has to simultaneously challenge the basis of the gang mentality while respecting the importance of group connections. For instance, gang interventions involving indigenous people themselves as responders have involved a combination of reassertion of indigenous elder authority (e.g., cultural protocols), and extension of resources (e.g., schooling, jobs and housing) that enhance the social capital of young people in these communities. Gangs are not condoned, nor are individual gang members excused – they are responded to by whole-of-community approaches.

This chapter has explored the relationship between gangs and families, particularly as this relates to indigenous young people. Interviews with indigenous young people who describe themselves or who have been described by key informants as gang members demonstrate a series of overlapping issues in their lives. These include:

• The identity politics of the everyday is manifest in close communal and family ties among indigenous youth gang members – indigenous youth hang out with indigenous youth, sometimes by choice, some-times by the simple contingency of living near family members.

- Systematic discrimination and racism is a feature of everyday life for indigenous youth – social harm and humiliation is a daily experience that unites indigenous young people and thereby shapes self-esteem, and individual and collective identity.
- Specific locations are subject to intense forms of territorialism – defence of oneself and one's group is intertwined with claiming own-ership of defined geographical areas, and this reinforces a shared gang identity based on more than family affiliation.
- Racism is countered by both strong family ties and strong anti-racist sentiment – group membership is about shared experiences, shared feelings, shared familial links and shared attitudes, which can sometimes accommodate the non-indigenous.

Most if not all of these social dimensions are simultaneously contextu-alised by the pervasive influence and continuing intrusions of colonial relationships. These relationships are manifest in discriminatory polic-ing and inequalities in criminal justice, persistent inadequacies in wel-fare and educational provision, and diminished work and life chances for indigenous people relative to their non-indigenous counterparts.

Breaking up the gang, under these circumstances, is about breaking up the family. Yet, as this chapter has argued, it is the prior break-up of indigenous families, and the dispossession of indigenous peoples from their 'country', that has created a volatile and at times dysfunc-tional situation for many young indigenous people. In response, the gang can simultaneously perform the functions of a supportive family while actually being family in social composition. In the face of a hostile environment, one characterised by racism and extremes of social, eco-nomic and political marginalisation, the gang is thus both a network of emotional and material support and an important outlet for aggression and resistance. Imprisonment, itself, feeds this function and process of identity consolidation.

A reconstitution of the gang as family in a more positive and less anti-social direction, therefore, demands a shift in vision away from seeing the gang as the main problem. The answer lies in constructing a political vision that is socially progressive and that is inclusive of indigenous people. Dealing with racism is at the core of this process, as is addressing the continuing legacies of colonial rule.

7
Provocations and Punch-Ups

Introduction

The hallmark of gangs is violence. Gangs are in some ways best defined as groups of young men who regularly engage in acts of violence that range from the more trivial to the lethal. While much dispute exists over gang definitions, there is no arguing the fact that male violence and violence amongst males is ubiquitous – it is everywhere and anywhere where groups of boys and young men gather and hang out.

There is also evidence – especially in US research – that girls and young women occasionally engage in violent behaviour, are active members within some gangs and occasionally form their own gangs [1]. However, the degree, seriousness and prevalence of these activities and associations are much less than in the case of their male counterparts. Indeed, aside from indigenous young women, the work undertaken on youth gangs in Australia has revealed relatively little female participation in either gang life or gang-like behaviour. This observation will be taken up for further discussion in Chapter 10.

This chapter explores the contours of gang violence from the point of view of violence that occurs on the street, within the gang, and in comparison with non-gang members. We want to try to understand the attractions of violence among young men, as well as the dynamics and rituals that accompany violence. Violence does not take place in a vacuum. Accordingly, we also want to determine what it is about the social location of young people, and wider cultural contexts, that make violence so prevalent among young men generally and gang members specifically.

The World Health Organisation has defined violence as encompassing a variety of elements. It is

The intentional use of physical force or power, threatened or actual, against oneself, another person, or against a group or community, that either results in or has a high likelihood of resulting in injury, death, psychological harm, maldevelopment or deprivation [2].

This definition is inclusive of acts of both commission and omission (including, for example, acts of neglect), and acts that do not necessarily lead to injury, disability or death but that do involve harm. Importantly, the definition relates fundamentally to the health and wellbeing of individuals, regardless of cultural context (or cultural legitimacy given to enacting the harm). The violence exhibited by gangs and gang members certainly threatens the health and wellbeing of individuals, especially since in many instances it involves weapons (see below as well as Chapter 8).

A key feature of gang violence is that it is group violence. Violence in general, however, is not unusual in Australian society. Violence is, in fact, quite normal. It is manifest sociologically among young working-class men in particular and culturally in the form of general entertainment (e.g., most Hollywood, Hong Kong and Bollywood movies), as well as specific events that are premised from first to last upon violence occurring (e.g., cage fighting). Not all group violence is gang violence [3]. This is demonstrated in the violence associated with riots and mob fights, where in most instances the protagonists are not members of gangs. Gate crashers at parties may engage in group violence but not be members of gangs. Youth crime may likewise involve the use of weapons, but this does not necessarily equate to gang criminality. As with an analysis of gangs and gang-related behaviour, gang violence has to be analysed in the light of parallel processes, dynamics and participation that superficially mirror gang activity but cannot be equated with it.

It is fitting therefore that we begin this chapter with stories from gang members about what it is they do and how they do it. As we shall see, some types of violence are 'fun' and the thought of violence itself can be very attractive. The dynamics of violence indicate many different variations, group processes and rules of engagement. They also seem to show a trend towards lethal violence.

Experiences of violence

As with much street violence and domestic violence, there is frequently a close association between fighting, alcohol and drug use. Getting drunk and/or stoned is often a prelude to a night of fighting, on all sides.

> When our group goes out together, umm, those guys that we're fighting with are just so drunk, they just don't know who they're sparking with and get pulverised, or they just completely back off 'cause they see who we've got with us.
>
> (19-year-old young man, Canberra)

> there's all these pissed guys like starting fights and that and then it's just basically an all in brawl and they pull out trolley poles and pieces of wood and that.
>
> (15-year-old young man, Canberra)

But getting drunk is only part of the picture. Many of the young men involved in gangs are angry young men. They have big chips on their shoulders, and alcohol only fuels the aggression that is already there.

> We went out into the city pissed. It's mainly when we were out in the city pissed 'cause if we're round the city pissed, we're out to cause trouble. We're out to fucking – we're angry – someone's fucked us around or someone's ripped us off and we're angry. We don't want to sit and chill anymore. We just wanna get pissed and fucking start a fight. Walk past someone and take his hat and see if he wants to start something.
>
> (21-year-old young man, Sydney)

When asked why they fight, the usual replies make reference to things such as 'the four or five people in my group because they just love fighting' and to situational triggers such as 'say if we're doing something and someone death stares us, we'll get up and pat 'em'. One Hobart respondent simply said that is was 'pretty much *testosterone*' mixed in with a combination of badmouthing and 'being boys' types of things:

> Yeah, just usually some – like a dirty look or someone's trying to chat up the wrong girl and stuff like that, or a common one is they owe money and they haven't paid for it.
>
> (21-year-old young man, Hobart)

The reasons for fighting vary, however, depending upon location and circumstance. School-related fights, for example, can have a degree of formality:

We have this thing called like Fight Club, whenever two people are arguing or like seriously hate each other. Everyone else just makes 'em fight with each other.

(14-year-old young man, Canberra)

While pitched at the level of one-on-one, the event is nevertheless collective in nature, involving organisers and bystanders.

Most gang fights involve some kind of rivalry. Typically this involves territory:

Then well our group goes over there and tells them like – asks them why they're here, what they're doing here – then they get pissed off and we go into a fight.

(19-year-old young man, Canberra)

it's a thing if we hear that our enemy is up the street, we'll gather and we'll go looking for 'em like to make sure they don't – they don't disrespect our turf.

(19-year-old young man, Canberra)

Other reasons for fighting include competition in relation to graffiti, street racing and drug dealing, and conflicts over girls in the neighbourhood and for girlfriends. A big part of fighting relates to group identity and group perceptions:

On clubbing nights like Friday and Saturday you see it happen a lot between the Wogs and the Asians. It happens all the time. The Wogs are all one big group. Like they're all brotherhoods and stuff like that. They're all together, same with the Asians. There's always a lot – you know they're family or a relative in some way.

(19-year-old young man, Canberra)

If we're out in the city or something and a group that don't like us – like, you know, Australian born or whatever – they don't like the way we look and we don't like the way they look and so the fights happen.

(21-year-old young man, Melbourne)

For many gang members the fighting is experienced as random, yet constant:

It's very random. They might not – they don't like you because of the way you dress or the way you look or just because you looked at 'em, so they'll just go at you straight away or they'll just wait until they can get you so they don't get into trouble 'cause they're smart people.

(17-year-old young man, Canberra)

Fighting can be planned and groups can arrange to meet at prearranged venues and times. However, one gang member pointed out that increasingly the fights are more spontaneous and automatic in nature:

I remember back when I was growing up groups would meet places and have a fight. Today no group would meet nowhere. It's just if you see the other person on the street you give 'em a kicking. You know what I mean? You don't actually go with your group and they come with their group and you have a fight. It's not like that no more. No one comes to fights like that. If you see him on the street you've got him. If he sees you he's got you. So that's how it's changed.

(19-year-old young man, Melbourne)

For gang members there are huge group obligations to fight:

The old saying is 'you scratch my back, I'll scratch yours.' It all works like that. You know your group of people and they see what they can do. If you're ever in trouble, they're always there. They'll just back you up 100 per cent no matter what. We're like a big family – but yeah, basically we all just stick together.

(17-year-old young man, Canberra)

You've gotta have trust amongst your friends. There's usually not that much in a gang. There's not a lot of trust, but if you have trust and if you have a bit of power and if you're popular – that makes a gang.

(17-year-old young man, Melbourne)

Good fighters are seen as essential to group protection. Not surprisingly, then, good fighting is also equated with gang membership. Proving your worth in a fight is an important part of gang initiation:

It depends on how good a fighter you are. It depends on just the general image you put across ... If you look like you're looking over your shoulder constantly or doing any kind of shit like that, constantly worried then they won't – they won't even bother with you. But if you look like you've got a purpose and you know what you're doing – travelling – it's kinda like when you know you wanna go somewhere and you just don't look at anyone, just look at where you're going and you just go straight ahead kind of thing – I mean with people like that you get in easy.

(17-year-old young man, Canberra)

If you're in a gang and a fight starts from another gang, then it's just like two tribes trying to make a name for themselves – just to see if you can fight. That's what most people do if you're a newcomer into the gang – 'Go and smash that c***, then we'll see if you can fight.'

(15-year-old young man, Canberra)

The escalating use of weapons has changed the youth gang fight landscape in a number of ways. For a start, the level of harm has simultaneously risen with increased weapons use:

See these days when you go to fight, someone has a weapon. We'll argue first and see if he puts down a weapon. If he does, then it's weapons and my main – I've had a few weapon fights. I've been stabbed in this arm with a screwdriver. I've been stabbed in the gut.

(17-year-old young man, Canberra)

Yeah well I think things are changing these days. As in people used to fight – just fight – like if someone is angry – all right fight, you know, it's not a big deal. But these days people seem to take out weapons like knives and stupid, stupid, stupid things like that and throw rocks at people's heads and stuff like that.

(17-year-old young man, Melbourne)

Back in the day, they used to meet on the cricket field and they used to punch on 'til the last one was standing. That's what they used to do, but not no more. She's all fucking knives, guns, fucking you name it.

(19-year-old young man, Hobart)

It's a bit more dangerous these days than what it used to be, like there's fucking more weapons and shit. A few fuck heads have got their hands on guns and that. . . . fucking back when I was fucking twelve or thirteen, you know, you'd punch up with some c***. Now you've gotta worry about what they're going to pull out – fucking shit like fucking knives.

(15-year-old young man, Hobart)

Weapons include a variety of items, including baseball and cricket bats, poles from supermarket trollies, knives, tomahawks, curtain rods, machetes and chains.

The 'rules of engagement' for gang fights also appears to be changing. Traditionally there were unwritten rules that guided how young men fought each other. For example, this is captured in the expression 'don't hit a man when he is down'. Issues of fairness, and violence that is proportionate to the situation, have been undermined by increasing weapon use:

> Like people used to fight mostly with their fist. Now they fight with – like 'I don't need my muscle like 'cause I've got weapons' – and they're much more easier to get hold of so.
>
> (14-year-old young woman, Perth)

> I think a lot of people are now carrying knives and a lot of people probably think it's okay, and a lot of people are more focussed on, umm, not fighting honourably but more just staying alive. So yeah, I reckon it's changed. I think it's gone from, umm, people just, you know, getting a bit involved to people taking out knives and weapons for the sake of fighting.
>
> (16-year-old young man, Perth)

It is not only weapons use, however, that is changing the dynamics of group conflict. An escalation in numbers of combatants can also change the nature of the fighting:

> Well, our group only believes in one on one. We don't believe in double spanking, just fight one, but if someone else jumps in, then the whole group's just going to jump on them. If one other person from the opposite jumps in, the whole group will jump in.
>
> (17-year-old young woman, Canberra)

> Oh it starts off one on one, then it ends up four on one, then it ends up ten onto four and so on and gets bigger and bigger.
>
> (19-year-old young man, Hobart)

One result of these developments is that there are no apparent set rules. For some gang members this is a disconcerting development:

> No one fights fair anymore. Weapons brought out. Two tag teaming. I prefer a dead set good old fashioned fight just one on one. Let 'em

go till they beat the shit out of each other. No stomping though – just maybe a kick in the ribs or something like that.

(20-year-old young man, Hobart)

People, especially round this area can't be fucked being decent and having morals and fighting one on one anymore. They like to fight in groups, go around mobbing people. Some of the big boys – the old school boys – they'd just stand up and fucking wipe them out, teach 'em a lesson.

(20-year-old young man, Perth)

Interestingly, according to one gang member in Adelaide, there have been moves to reinstate some semblance of rules of engagement for groups in conflict with each other:

Umm yeah, it's a lot more organised now sort of. Like there's a rule now where you don't bash another group member like five onto one or something, like the numbers have to be fair yeah.

(17-year-old young man, Adelaide)

A Canberra youth stated that he and his mates don't like it when someone pulls a weapon on unarmed people, especially when they were at school. Those who did not abide by the street code would be made to pay by the rest of his group:

Oh some people would run in the bush and grab a fat stick – a chunky stick and start waving that around, but normally you'd get fucking nearly ten people on the bloke just pounding him on the ground, grabbing the stick, getting him up, kicking him in the head a couple of times and say 'fight fair mate'.

(18-year-old young man, Canberra)

The rules of engagement are to some degree situational in nature. That is, they depend upon location (e.g., school or the street), who is involved in conflict (known protagonists, such as at school, or strangers from another neighbourhood), and variables such as age and access to weapons:

Yeah it's got a lot tougher... Well years ago, everyone would fight one on one, you know, fist to fist and now you've got all these fucking teeny boppers running around trying to fucking stick you with knife. And then when you bash the shit out of 'em 'cause they pulled a knife on you, you're the one that gets in trouble 'cause you assaulted 'em and they can sue you.

(21-year-old young man, Canberra)

In other cases the rules of engagement refer to rules among group members as such:

> The rule is you can't bring trouble back to like other members because it's not right. Like one time a long time ago, my mate was getting chased by another group and he ran into his mate's house who was in my group. Later that night, the other group come back to my mate's house and threw bricks through his windows and like kicked in the front door, wanted him to come outside and it wasn't even his – they were looking for the guy that ran in there, not the guy that actually lives there. So yeah, just you can't bring nothing back to anybody else's house or, you know.

(18-year-old young man, Adelaide)

How you fight (with fists or with other weapons) is also connected to conceptions of manliness. More generally, the interpretation of violence is defined in terms of specific rules of engagement that help those engaged in it to make sense of it [4]. These rules refer to violence within the gang, such as initiation and fights between gang members, as well as external violence. For example, gang-related violence is often guided by rituals of restraint when a gang member fights another member of the same gang, whereas outsiders are more likely to suffer from a no-holds-barred approach. Gang responses to, and engagement in, violence are thus typically defined by the situation, not by the characteristics of the perpetrators as such.

In some cases there is the perception at the street level that some types of violence are not really violence. For example, a fair fight is not violence, but 'Violence occurs when the rules are broken. Violence is that which is unpleasant and morally non-defensible, like attacking smaller guys, using weapons, stamping on somebody who is lying down or putting your foot in somebody's face' [5]. In Oslo, Norway, then, the rules not only guide behaviour but also guide interpretation. Back in Australia, however, things are less clear cut.

Ambiguities or lack of explicit or implicit rules of engagement can in themselves lead to extreme violence insofar as 'anything goes', at considerable cost to everyone involved:

They wanna tell me to jump on someone's head, I was the first one to jump up and fucking stomp on that c***'s head. That's why I got out of that life. I'm not like that anymore. I had all that anger. I got rid of it all. It's gone now man. I just wanted to chill, but now it's all starting to come back.

(21-year-old young man, Canberra)

Fucking every week there's a fucking big blue and fucking half of us are still in hospital 'cause of cuts and shit, and it's like it's ridiculous, we always end up fucking in hospital – broken legs and shit.

(21-year-old young man, Canberra)

The nature of the youth violence described here is very much influenced by the fact that all of these young people were all self-identified members of youth gangs.

Gang versus non-gang violence

Indeed, one of the key findings of our Perth schools-based research is that gang culture is, indeed, largely a culture of violence. To understand this we have to appreciate both the nature of gang membership and the nature of gang-related violence. Our work has consistently found that there are significant differences between those young people who identify as being gang members and those who do not. Table 7.1 outlines the key differences across a range of relevant dimensions [6].

The Perth research also indicated that while many young people in school experience and/or witness conflict of some type, the nature of the violence differs greatly depending upon whether or not one is a gang member. This is illustrated in Table 7.2 [7].

What the interviews that were carried out around the country qualitatively indicated, and the Perth survey quantitatively demonstrated, is that gang violence is much more volatile, harmful and extensive than other kinds of youth violence. The potential exception to this is bullying, which, like gang violence, has received tremendous academic, public and political attention in recent years. However, as argued shortly, it is important to distinguish bullying from gang violence *per se*, while nonetheless acknowledging a relationship between the two forms of social harm.

Gang violence and bullying

For the present purposes the term 'bullying' refers to behaviour characterised by a distinct type of repeated aggression and a systematic

Table 7.1   Dimensions of gang and non-gang membership

Dimensions	Gang member	Non-gang member
Formation	large groups, includes older members	small to medium-sized, peer-based on age
Activities	criminal, anti-social	social, recreational
Locations	street-based, city, parks, licensed premises	privately based (own and others homes), commercial outlets (malls), beaches
Basis of membership	status, protection, illegal activities	friendship, belonging, group-based activities
Gender composition	male	mixed gender
Conflicts and violence	intensive and extensive experience of violence, as both perpetrator and victim	spontaneous and sporadic experience of violence, as both perpetrator and victim
Drugs	poly-drug use, regular and recent use, hard drugs,	experimental, sporadic use, soft drugs
Experience of school	social isolation, exclusion, low commitment, high truancy, outside problems, drug use	socially connected with school community, enjoy school, do well at school

abuse of power. In essence, bullying is about the exercise of power that simultaneously makes a social statement about the worthlessness of the victim [8]. A strong connecting point between youth gangs and bullying is the focus on violence (variously described, but that includes physical through to psychological aspects), and the risks and actual harms to individuals stemming from gang and bullying behaviour. When it comes to youth gangs and bullying there are two key questions of particular interest: Is there a causal association between participation in bullying and participation in youth gangs? And, does bullying take place within youth gangs?

Bullying has major effects on perpetrators, victims and observers. Moreover, those who bully may themselves be on the receiving end of bullying, at school, at home or on the street. The consequence of bullying lies in individuals changing their personal behaviour, from avoiding certain places at certain times of the day, through to becoming more aggressive and lashing out at those around them. Bullying can involve one-on-one confrontations or groups that pick on specific individuals and/or social groups. The dynamics of bullying are structural, situational and individual in that they involve social

Table 7.2 Dimensions of gang and non-gang violence

Dimensions	Gang member	Non-gang member
Group dynamics	violence and conflict tend to involve groups	violence and conflict tend to be individually based
Motivation	revenge, ongoing dislike, protection of territory, influence of drugs	spur of the moment, ongoing dislike
Location	outside and inside school, street locations	primarily inside school, institutional locations
Frequency	recent, regular and often, and involving ongoing group conflicts	occasional and sporadic
Intensity	multiple experiences of victimisation and as perpetrators, with large degree of violence exhibited	infrequent experiences as victim or perpetrator, and low level of violence exhibited
Weapon use	large proportion of weapon ownership, and use	small proportion of weapon ownership, and use
Injuries	frequent experience of injuries, such as wounds, with majority of respondents experiencing an injury	low incidence of injuries, and injuries relatively minor when experienced
Relationship to drugs	poly-drug use and extensive use of drugs linked to violence, also tied to drug dealing	alcohol linked to violence

differences between participants (e.g., ethnic or class differences), interactional factors, such as the presence or absence of observers (including guardians) and personal dispositions (e.g., propensity toward aggression). It is the complexities that surround bullying that can lead researchers to conflate bullying and gang behaviour.

For young people, engagement in bullying or gaining protection from the threat of physical violence may be important motivations for joining a gang. For instance, when considering the effects of bullying at school in relation to gang-related behaviour, research has found that bullying is a strong predictor of anti-social behaviour and development; that self-reported bullying at a younger age (14 years) increases the likelihood of violent convictions between ages 15 and 20 and self-reported violence at age 15–18; and that school bullies are much more prone than non-involved students to later offending [9]. Being a bully means being used to violence. It also means associating violence with everyday activities, including those experienced as pleasurable or fun, as well as those denoting street status.

Conversely, it has also been shown that repeated exposure to being bullied can undermine the health and wellbeing of vulnerable students, and harassment frequently has its roots in social prejudice (e.g., gay students, those from ethnic minorities) [10]. Being bullied at school is significantly associated with being bullied outside school. It is notable that in New South Wales between 2005 and 2009, there was an upward trend in the rate of recorded assault incidents between school-age children on government school premises during school hours, generally involving two students of the same gender (generally boys), aged between 13 and 15 years [11]. Such violence begets violence, especially when combined with structural inequalities and social differentiation. It has been observed that 'from the perspective of a marginalized individual living in a marginalized community who has suffered considerable personal trauma, the gang can be an effective mechanism for supporting violent aggression in what appear to be irrational ways' [12]. Personal tragedies, including being victimised, can affect children and young people in ways that put them on a trajectory towards gang involvement.

Interestingly, English research has found that a bigger proportion of young people are more worried about being physically attacked than bullied, hence implying that occasional violence, including group violence ,is ever-present and all-pervasive in schools [13]. This has also been found to be the case in our Perth youth gangs research, which found high incidences of both school-based gang violence and individual non-gang violence. At a formal definitional level, bullying refers to repeated behaviours that involve a range of physical and non-physical harms, but that are targeted at the same individual. Some of the gangs research shows that students are concerned about not only this kind of targeted, specific violence (i.e., what we usually think of as bullying) but also the more randomised forms of violence where you are never quite sure who is going to attack you and for what reasons. For example, the Perth research showed that there was a lot of violence involving non-gang students, usually of a one-to-one kind, as well as group-based violence linked to youth gangs. The triggers to violence are often situational (e.g., accidental bumping) as well as occasionally linked to intentional bullying. Overall, the extent of violence was of considerable concern to students and contributed to a general anxiety about being physically attacked.

While there are sound reasons to accept that bullying may help to propel some young people into gangs – either for protection or for enjoyment – the activities of youth gangs are not reducible to bullying-type behaviour as such. This is because of the specific character of youth gang violence. Thus, for example, US research has found that 'youth gang-related violence mainly emanates from inter-gang rivalries, turf protection and expansion, and interpersonal disputes or "beefs" ' [14]. This dovetails with much of what our Australian research has found as well, and is illustrated in the previous section of this chapter. The nature of the violence is intrinsically dictated by the nature of the group formation. In such a context, bullying may, in some circumstances, be frowned upon insofar as it does not reflect a legitimate avenue for the expression of 'manhood', 'masculinity' and 'machismo' associated with gang identity, peer solidarity and group status.

Indeed, the specific cultures and rituals of gangs must be considered when it comes to determining how violence is perceived and experienced by gang members. For example, gang induction may require initiates to endure a character test in what are called 'beat-downs' or 'jump-ins' (i.e., subjecting initiates to a group beating) [15]. Is this bullying? Not really, since the violence is welcomed by the recipient and interpreted as empowering rather than an imposition of power. Street culture more generally also demands ongoing character tests that involve constant affirmation of dangerousness and ability to fight – essential gang member attributes [16]. In other words, violence within the gang, and on the street, is expected and routinised.

In our Australian research, one young gang member's answer to the assertion that they weren't allowed to hurt each other within the group is particularly revealing:

> No. But usually there was no problems with fights within the group, that would happen on a daily basis – or an hourly basis.... Oh it would just be a big laugh. Everybody else would sit there and watch. It was all right, you know. Whoever was left on the floor bloodied and bruised, they lost. The other guy would go get somebody to hand 'em another drink. And would the one on the ground, would they be seriously hurt? Sometimes. It depends. If it was someone's little brother, yeah, the fight would get stopped half way through, you know. But someone without – usually you go no relation in the group then, yeah, usually you could end up pretty badly hurt.
>
> (18-year-old young man, Canberra)

The motivations for gang violence include such things as retaliation, which is related to the group aspects of violent acts. Groups of young men who are regularly vilified and subject to street taunts and attacks may band together and become a gang for the purposes of protection and symbolic strength. These same people experience racism from teachers at school (subjectively experienced as a form of 'bullying'). On the other hand, rivalries between defined groups may involve 'picking on' a specific individual (from the other side or gang); but this in turn needs to be interpreted not as individualised bullying but part of a collective social dynamic.

Gang violence may thus involve bullying individuals and groups outside the gang. Gang rivalry, for instance, involves mutually recognised antipathy. In this social context, each individual is always seen as gang member, even when alone. An individual's membership of a gang makes them vulnerable when they are not with the gang. They may be vulnerable to bullying not only by other rival gang members but also by young people who are not a member of a gang. Their membership in a gang thus makes them vulnerable to bullying by others, especially when they do not have other gang members around to protect them.

With respect to this, our research suggests that gang members are significantly more likely than non-gang members to report that other students pester or persecute them and that they dread going to school. Moreover, when asked why young people join groups, a significantly greater proportion of gang members than non-gang members reported that they joined the gang for protection. When present in numbers, the gang may provide a defence against being bullied, both by individuals and by other (competing) groups.

The motives for bullying in a gang context may be different from those where an individual is bullied either by a single person or by a non-gang peer group. Gang bullying is not only about degradation or aiming a statement about the worthlessness of the individual; it is a tactic used as part of ritualised violence. It is not persecution *per se* but rather an opportunistic behaviour aimed at asserting physical and thereby social dominance over a rival group. It is interesting in this regard to note that ex-gang members are not usually put into the category of the Other, as indicated in US research that reveals that gang members can normally leave the gang without serious consequences [17].

Although bullying is associated with the reasons why individuals join gangs, the violence *within* a gang is of a different character than that usually described by at least some definitions of bullying. But gang members can and do bully outsiders. Thus there is an association between bullying and gangs, but this is more complicated and layered than it might at first appear.

Explaining gang violence

A social structural explanation for gang violence tends to view the phenomenon in terms of marginalisation of specific population groups (see Chapter 5). This marginalisation may have a number of interrelated dimensions, including economic (e.g., poverty), social (e.g., exclusion from mainstream institutions), political (e.g., little or no representation) and cultural (e.g., minority religious or language group). The level of social disorganisation and extent of social capital are also seen as vital ingredients in the criminality or otherwise of specific neighbourhoods. In effect, brutal and/or highly disadvantageous social conditions provide the groundwork for angry and aggressive people, whose main resource is their body rather than property, finance capital or wages.

A related explanation focuses on social identity as a key variable in explaining group formation and street violence. For example, groups of young people band together for social, cultural and familial reasons. They also do so for protection. Youth group formation, which in some cases may include the evolution of the group into a gang, is thus often intertwined with violence or the threat of violence in the lives of young people. Over time, group identification becomes central to individual social identity, and the fate of the collective is inseparable from the security and social belonging of the individual. In some locales, group membership is accompanied by group rivalry. And violence becomes both 'grouped' in nature (rather than individualised), often around particular constructions of 'ethnicity' or 'territory', and ritualised in content and execution (vis-à-vis times, locations and weapons).

Work undertaken on violence and masculinity demonstrates a strong cultural component to violence, especially for men. Particularly for working-class young men, physical prowess or toughness is a form of social capital. In most social milieu, a young man's reputation depends in part upon the credible threat of violence. Quick resort to physical combat – as a measure of daring, or courage, or defence of status – appears to be a standard cultural expectation, especially for working-class boys and young men. This perhaps explains the widespread nature of violence among school-age male populations. That is, in a context in which 'manhood' is yet to be proven by attainment of paid work, marriage, leaving home or beginning a family of their own, physicality itself, relying upon the body, is one way in which to 'prove oneself' [18]. This would therefore help to explain the prevalence of male violence across the schoolyard, if not the intensity and differences in manifestation.

Various kinds of group formation (e.g., gangs, crowds, peer groups, subcultures) and different kinds of violence (e.g., riots, mob action, street fighting) are linked in the sense that certain key attributes tend to feature across much of what occurs in public spaces, such as city streets [19]. The specific nature of gang violence can thus be linked to broader social developments and trends, including:

- Active use of new communication technologies, such as mobile phones, combined with access to motor vehicles, which allows for quick mobilisation of large groups of people in particular locations – hence the capacity to 'swarm'.
- An emphasis on excitement, thrill-seeking, and taking collective control over particular public areas and local territories – hence an assertion of self and social identity via certain types of activity.
- Defiance and resistance in relation to authority figures, such as the police, and antagonistic, frequently physical and verbal abuse of law-enforcement officers – hence a disregard for normal conventions and laws.
- Events marked by a degree of unpredictability, due to the diversity and anonymity of participants, and the volatile nature of crowd behaviour – hence a general lack of clarity regarding the rules of engagement surrounding the use of violence.
- The media frequently plays a major role in reflexively creating violent events by publicising them in advance, sensationalising them when they occur, and exaggerating the enormity of particular events – hence the stimulation and provocation to violence is to some extent inspired by the mass media.

Access to communication technologies (e.g., mobile phones, social networking sites such as *Facebook* and *MySpace*), and exposure to modelling of risky fighting behaviours through entertainment technologies and the media (e.g., cage fighting), also have a major impact on group decisions and fighting patterns. It is interesting to note in this regard that a recent US study of current and former gang members in Fresno, Los Angeles and St Louis found that 71 per cent of those interviewed reported using a social networking site [20]. The two most prevalent activities were posting videos and watching gang-related videos. The next most prevalent activities were having a gang website and searching for gang-related information online. Less used were recruiting new members online and organising illegal activities online – although arranging a gang get-together can be usefully achieved via online communications. The study found that the gang members committed acts such as illegally downloading music, harassing or threatening people online, and attacking someone on the street because of things that had happened online.

Processual accounts of gang violence

Situational explanations of violence offer a processual account. A processual account of group violence focuses on the specific factors in any given situation that influence the presence or absence of violence. For example, we might examine pre-fight conditions (do people know each other?), fight precipitators (are they teasing or making fun of someone?) and the escalation from verbal abuse to physical contact. We might also examine a range of contextual factors. It is the linking of situational and contextual factors that allows for social analysis of the dynamics of youth violence.

Contextual factors

- factors relating to setting (e.g., time of day/night, location);
- factors relating to situation (e.g., absence of guardians, drugs/alcohol use, presence/absence of peers);
- factors relating to interaction (e.g., exchange of words, bullying, racism, peer pressure, 'being tough');
- factors relating to social structure (e.g., age, class, gender, ethnicity);
- factors relating to local history (e.g., intergenerational gangs, urban stories & legends).

Situational factors

An analysis of situational factors includes consideration of the triggers to violence. For example, violent incidents among school students often occur owing to an escalation of seemingly trivial events, often without premeditation to fight. Although they do not intend the outcome (e.g., a fight), the students suffer the consequences (e.g., direct harm, punishment). The interesting thing about these accounts is that we can distinguish between situational factors pertaining to individuals and those relevant to groups. In other words, non-gang members tend to engage in fights on a spontaneous basis, rather than as part of ritualised violence or ongoing group conflict. Lockwood, for example, discusses school violence in the following terms [21]:

- Disputants know each other.
- The dispute occurs at school or home.
- There are distinctive 'opening moves' (e.g., minor slights, teasing, unprovoked offensive touching, insults).

- A 'character contest' may develop, in which neither party will back down (e.g., an offence requires saving face).
- Verbal attempts are made to influence the other person, escalating into insults, then to violence in the form of fights.
- Violence is justified or excused on the basis of particular values systems within which violence is acceptable. These rationalisations include:

  o retribution – punishing the antagonist for something they did;
  o compliance – convincing the antagonist to desist from an offensive course of action;
  o defence – of one's self or others;
  o promotion – of one's image, by saving face, defending one's honour, or enhancing or maintaining one's reputation.

- Violence is rationalised on the basis of either 'justifications' (e.g., the other disputant had done something to deserve harm) or 'excuses' (e.g., free will was impaired by anger, they were pushed into the incident by aggressors, they did not mean to do it).

By way of contrast, Decker describes gang violence as involving a process in which group violence undergoes a series of ebbs and flows [22]:

- Gang members feel loose bonds to the gang.
- Gang members collectively perceive a threat from a rival gang (which increases gang cohesion).
- A mobilising event occurs, which may or may not be violent.
- Activity escalates.
- One of the gangs lashes out in violence.
- Violence and activity rapidly de-escalate.
- The other gang retaliates.

The group dynamics described here apply to both gang and non-gang groups of young people. However, it is those who identify strongly with a gang who are more likely to respond in this way and to reinforce their identity through such interactions. In many cases, group protection from perceived and actual threats is integral to both group identity and the use of violent means to protect oneself.

The interesting thing about these accounts is that we can distinguish between situational factors pertaining to individuals, and those relevant to groups. In other words, as we found in our Perth youth gangs research, non-gang members tend to engage in fights on a spontaneous basis, rather than as part of ritualised violence or ongoing group conflict.

The role of the bystander is also important to situational accounts. For example, the ways in which groups of young men goad each other on, and how as observers of violence they contribute to the event through encouragement and generating a heightened sense of performance and excitement, are significant to the escalation of violence [23].

A typology of violence would need to consider violence from the point of view of:

- offenders
- victims
- passive observers
- active audience
- authority figures
- venues
- events
- situations

A range of factors need to be taken into account in explaining specific kinds of violence, and in responding to each type of violent episode. In addition to an analysis of particular factors, it is important to bear in mind the ambiguity of many social situations that makes them volatile and unpredictable from the point of view of whether or not violence will occur. Consider for example the following scenario:

What reaction do you have if someone bumps you on the street? This involves *interpretation* of the event (e.g., simply as an accident or as a provocation); *emotionally responding* to the event (e.g., anger, fear, nonchalance); and *acting* in some way to the event (e.g., ignore the bump or view it as an invitation to a hostile response).

Being a gang member, or not being a gang member, can shape responses to street-level situations such as this.

Timeline accounts

A timeline type of account can be used to illustrate the process dynamics of violence. For instance, we can identify the dynamics of violence as these evolve over time, starting from pre-fight conditions, such as the participants knowing each other, through to post-fight conditions and the possibility of ongoing reasons, such as continued hostility, as grounds for further fighting.

* Time 1   *Pre-fight conditions – fight 1* (e.g., know each other)
* Time 2   *Fight precipitators* (e.g., teasing, touching)
* Time 3   *Escalation in verbal abuse* (e.g., insults)
* Time 4   *Violence* (e.g., fight)
* Time 5   *Cessation of immediate violence* (e.g., adult and/or authority figure intervention)
* Time 6   *Post-fight conditions* (e.g., reconciliation, resentment, punishment)
* Time 7   *Pre-fight conditions – fight 2* (e.g., ongoing hostility, antagonism, threat and so on)

Group violence, therefore, is bound up with certain temporal processes, geographical spaces and social factors that shape when, where and why it occurs.

Rituals and meaning of violence

The rituals and dynamics of violence also need to be looked at. Rituals, in the present context, relate mainly to the 'rules of engagement' of violence. These vary depending upon the individual, the group and the social context within which violence occurs. They also imply a familiarity with violence itself.

In the normal course of events, 'Social rules govern violence and these rules render violence intelligible and rewarding for those who participate in it' [24]. Thus, for example, gang-related violence is often guided by rituals of restraint when a gang member fights another member of the same gang, whereas outsiders are more likely to suffer from a no-holds-barred approach.

However, in situations where there are large groups of people, the rules and rituals become less clear. Mcdonald observes that when young people venture outside their local neighbourhoods, they are extremely wary of who they might meet, in part because there does not seem to be any restraint on the level of violence they might suffer if drawn into a street conflict [25]. In other words, violence with strangers is inherently unstable and ambiguous, since neither party knows the rules of engagement.

In the context of a large crowd, the rules become even less defined. Mob rule is precisely about lack of restraint, the unbridled use of force against an opponent. In small-scale fight situations a 'ritual mediator' may step in to end the potential escalation of conflict (e.g., a mate who intervenes to cool things down) [26]. In crowd situations, such mediation is much less likely. Rather, the transformation into the mob precludes such mediation and opens the door to unrestrained violence.

As applied to gangs research, these observations translate into the proposition that affiliation with a gang alters individual behaviour in certain ways. Specifically, it is argued that 'membership in a gang increases the chances of delinquent behaviour such as violence, crime and drug use. Personal actions and responsibility are minimized and replaced with shared responsibility' [27]. When violence occurs in a group context, the 'crowd dynamic' described earlier tends to come into play, and it is the group rather than the individual that actively promotes violent behaviour.

The use of drugs appears to be a factor in gang violence, although in what ways is less than clear. For example, the Perth research found that gang members were more likely than non-gang members to be engaged in poly-drug use. To what extent this is a causal factor in the violence is uncertain. The drug would most probably include methamphetamine (crystal meth, 'ice'), since research tells us that gang members partake in a wider variety of drugs than their non-gang counterparts. This drug has been associated with violent behaviour, although it is not necessarily a direct causal reason for increased violence as such [28]. Gang violence has been related to drug dealing, as part of the dangers and processes associated with criminal transactions. It has also been linked to the individual use of drugs. In the latter case, interviews as part of the national gangs study indicated that sometimes particular members of gangs 'got off their heads' and would get 'aggro' as a result of drug use. Occasionally, where one person did go 'loopy' and pick a fight with strangers, the rest of the gang would intervene on their mate's behalf to either stop the fight or provide group back-up for their comrade. The influence of drugs in relation to gang violent behaviour seems to be more indirect than direct.

The place of violence in society generally, and in the lives of young men in particular, also shapes the propensity for specific violent incidents to occur. In contemporary Australian society, there appears to be a certain 'naturalisation' of violence as an everyday phenomenon, and as a significant form of anger management and conflict resolution. This is especially so for boys and men. We know, for example, that teenage boys have a much higher rate of fighting than girls. Studies also show that early engagement in anti-social behaviour tends to lead to ongoing, long-term involvement in such behaviour among teenage boys [29]. The majority of them are familiar with violence – as perpetrators, as victims, as observers. Violence is not new or particularly disturbing for many boys. For others, however, exposure to violence can have socially toxic effects – for themselves, their families and their communities – with regard to self-esteem, fear, performance at school and building trust relationships.

But violence in groups or involving group action is different from fights between individuals. Group dynamics very much affect the pretext for violence and the outcome of disputes. US research, for example, demonstrates that much gang violence relates to norm violations (e.g., annoying behaviour, defending others), identity attacks (e.g., with regard to the gang or in the Australian context, 'ethnic' identity), and retaliation (e.g., action taken in revenge for some prior wrongdoing) [30]. Australian gangs research likewise highlights the importance of reputation, group identity, social belonging and physical protection in how groups are socially constructed [31]. A threat to the group is enough to warrant violence. And specific types of threat, especially with regard to norm violations, give rise to even greater levels and use of violence. The particular type of group formation (e.g., a gang) will influence what are deemed to be acceptable justifications for violence, and the 'appropriate' sorts of group response in any given situation.

Not only is violence made natural by its very prevalence in the lives of boys and men but in many cases it is an important source of pleasure (see Chapter 8). It is the occasions when 'exceptional' violence occurs that provide the excitement and the break from the ordinary routines of everyday life. From the perspective of cultural criminology, physical violence and other types of anti-social behaviour can be interpreted as meaningful attempts to 'transgress' the ordinary [32]. In a world of standardised diversity and global conformities, it is exciting and pleasurable to break the rules, to push the boundaries and to engage in risky and risk-taking activities. To transgress is to deviate. It is to go beyond the ordinary, to seek that adrenaline rush that pushes the boundaries of emotion and convention.

Related to this, we also have to account for the inherent attractions of violence, as violence, in its own right: 'many people feel drawn towards violence because it can give pleasure' [33]. From one point of view, force or violence may be viewed as rational behaviour to the extent that it is designed to effect change in the target of violence. For example, many young people fight not because of an absence of values but because of values that hold such behaviour to be a justifiable, commonsense way to achieve certain goals [34]. This is especially understandable in the context of concerns about masculine identity, and violence that relates to the defence of 'male honour'. But the rationale behind the violence need not be simply due to cues or triggers imposed externally. There is increasing evidence, including recent gangs research, that violence also stems from the efforts of young people themselves to engineer situations and events with the intended aim of increasing the likelihood of violence occurring [35]. From this perspective, the gang provides a forum or ready-made structure within which to engage in what is felt to be exhilarating activity. Gangs provide an avenue to increase the thrill factor beyond the norm.

The 'will to violence', as Schinkel describes it, provides its own reward [36]. However, this will may be overlooked in social scientific research that looks to external causes (e.g., unemployment, masculinity, social inequality). Or, it may be subject to varying forms of 'denial' at the level of personal engagement. For example, interviews with gang members in Melbourne revealed that in some instances, individuals from ethnic-minority backgrounds did not just fight in order to defend themselves or to confirm their group identity. The research found that periodically some of these young people used the notion of racism as a convenient cover for their own aggression. That is, in some cases the violence was motivated by a desire to engage in the violence itself rather than to respond to racism as such [37]. This phenomenon is not specific to ethnic-minority young men; rather, it is an attribute that finds general purchase across the diversity of ethnic backgrounds, including mainstream Anglo-Celtic. Violence is thus its own attractor, regardless of the techniques of neutralisation that may be invoked to deny responsibility or wrongdoing.

Gang violence thus may be experienced as fun by participants, in the sense that it provides an adrenaline rush and is associated with 'typical' working-class masculine pursuits that define a 'top night out', such as drug taking, drinking and fighting. Not surprisingly, then, 'Groups of men with a history of fighting often evolve into gangs in the Russian context', an observation that has Australian equivalents and that resonates in other cultural and national contexts as well [38]. Why and how this is the case is explored in greater depth in Chapter 8.

Conclusion

As this chapter has demonstrated, specific kinds of violence – and its causes, its dynamics, its protagonists – are bound up with particular social contexts and processes. Different groups of young people experience violence differently, as is especially evident in the different experiences of youth gang and non-gang members. Violence as an act varies greatly depending upon immediate circumstances and proximate triggers. Who engages in violence and why is thus bounded by situational factors and structural contexts.

Fighting can be experienced as fun and be linked to risk, excitement and thrills as opposed to the boredom and routines of the mundane. It can also be linked to social humiliation and perceived majority attacks on communal identity (and manifest as a 'chip on the shoulder' on the part of members of a minority group). Violence can be linked to insecurity and as a source of pre-emptive protection. It can be associated with group dynamics that emphasise masculinity that is informed by certain notions of self-respect and social respect. For many young men, violence exists as the 'normal' form of anger management and conflict resolution – a resort of the first kind. Given the prominent place of violence in the life of a gang, it is worth delving into the nitty gritty of why young men choose to fight the way they do. This is the task of Chapter 8.

8
The Body and Violence

Introduction

An underlying assumption of this book is that in addition to violence *per se* being a crucial dimension of youth gang behaviour, a further vital feature pertains to the gendered nature of that violence. That is, most physical aggression is tied to masculinity and the self-perceptions and self-images of boys and young men, particularly those from the working class. The construction of violence as a working-class phenomenon partly stems from the importance of physicality – the body – in working-class life and culture. Traditionally paid work was largely reliant upon performing physical tasks (in the factories, in the mines, in the trades, in the army).

The centrality of physique and the physical translates into forms of aggressive masculinity that celebrate strength, speed, agility and general physical prowess. At the same time, it is bound up with specific class codes of conduct and permissibility. Solidarity, dependability and co-operation demand strict parameters on what violence is allowed, when, to what degree, involving whom and to what social end. This is perhaps most evident in physical sports. It is also apparent when it comes to the rules and standards pertaining to street fighting.

The study of 'the body' in criminology has generally been related to the analysis of punishment regimes that target the body as the object of control, or to the examination of resistance to control regimes through the use of the body. In the first instance, analysis tends to focus on those strict disciplinary practices that shape how inmates and convicts physically present themselves as well as the contours of daily routine that limit the freedom and scope of prisoners to do what they will with their bodies. Damousi, for example, describes how the female convict represented a 'depraved' form of sexuality; the official response to which was the practice of headshaving, as one means to reduce and minimise potential expressions of the assumed depravation [1]. Meanwhile, Foucault provided a review of the systematic measures employed in prison that reshape the body through a series of spatial, temporal and directly physical means that regiment, organise and 'discipline' the prisoner [2]. The physical and moral body are no longer the prisoner's to order and command. The point of the prison is to restrain and retrain, to enforce from within (via routine and repetition) the docile body.

Against this broad template, however, is the resistance of prisoners to the authority of a highly regulated and structured regime. For instance, a Queensland study explored how young detainees use and experience their bodies in ways that assert their individuality and limited social power [3]. For example, the choice of clothing, hairstyle, body size, necklaces, wristbands, fingernail length, makeup and so on was actively used by the young people to establish some sense of individual identity, membership of particular ethnic groups, and power and prestige relative to both other inmates and detention officers. The manipulation of one's body also extends to self-destructive behaviour: 'The act of cutting could be thought of as attempting to gain a measure of power over one's predicament, of asserting control over one's body. Just as control can be displayed through care of the self, so too can it be seen in self-mutilation' [4]. The ways in which young detainees use their bodies, therefore, is reflective of a culture of resistance to the institutionalised authority of the detention centre.

Analysis of the body in closely monitored or confined settings reveals the fundamental importance of the body to human interaction and wellbeing. It is the site of contestation between authority figures and those resisting authority. It is the means of suppression and repression, as well as the key to resistance and expression. By bulking up in prison, the male inmate and the female juvenile detainee alike create fear, intimidation and anxiety among their captors. By 'bronzing' (i.e., covering themselves in their own excrement), the inmate demonstrates that they too have something to say. The body cannot be ignored; the body ensures that people will not be ignored.

The other strand of criminological consideration of the body, albeit generally rather outmoded, consists of attempts to make a link between the body and criminal behaviour [5]. It is this broad orientation that is the main substance of this chapter. Similar to punishment studies of the body, however, analysis of the body in this context reveals interesting ambiguities and fascinating insights into the dynamics of everyday life. It also very much raises perennial questions about 'essentialism' and the ways in which observed social patterns may, or may not, be explained through reference to certain biological traits. How the body is presented and controlled continues to be of theoretical and practical interest, especially in discussions that see the body as inextricably linked to considerations of violence. As this chapter demonstrates, there are indeed close connections between physicality and violence; but these connections themselves warrant close consideration of the interplay between the biological, the social and the cultural.

The social context for violence

Some kinds of violence are disapproved of more than others. When we think of violence, we tend to think of male violence. And when we think of male violence, we usually think of working-class male violence. This is reflected in media images and moral panics over youth gangs and street crime. Conversely, it is rare to find comparable treatments of, for instance, racist violence or preventable industrial deaths (even though the latter accounts for the same number of, or more, deaths per year than homicide). It is assumed that working-class, and especially working-class indigenous men, are more violence prone than other identifiable groups. It is also assumed that their crimes of violence are more serious than other forms of violence.

It is also taken for granted that some forms of violence are legitimate while some are not. State legitimised violence and structural violence perpetrated by the police and correctional officials (as evident, for example, in deaths in custody figures) is generally viewed as a legitimate part of everyday life and institutional practice. Violence is seen as normal and legitimate when aggression is channelled in socially approved directions, such as war, the sports field, work, policing and punishment. Violence of this nature is meant to be discrete, socially instrumental and purposive.

Violence that engenders formal coercive state responses is most closely identified with the working-class male experience. The construction of violence as a working-class phenomenon is related to everyday social processes. Fights outside the pub, for example, are a normal occurrence that reflects the 'protest masculinity' of the working-class man at leisure [6]. Using the body in this particular way provides a class-based acknowledgement of social identity as well as pleasure. We shall explore these ideas in relation to youth gangs shortly.

The propensities for aggression can become exaggerated for some young men. This is especially so in circumstances where violence is not only closely tied instrumentally and affectively to the rules of the (sports, military, occupational, leisure) game but permeates social life. This is perhaps most evident with regard to members of the so-called underclasses of society. The very poor are forced to eke out an existence in a context of increasing residential ghettoisation, economic marginalisation and political disenfranchisement [7]. So, too, identifiable ethnic minority and indigenous communities may be subjected to chronic racism that can generate aggressive social reaction as well as anti-social behaviour within communities [8]. Poverty and economic disadvantage are not the sole reasons why violence occurs but they do engender a social landscape that is conducive to certain types of aggressive behaviour.

Given a lack of financial resources, the body may literally be one of the only ways in which to secure an income – through prostitution, fighting, stealing and mugging. It can be both commodity (i.e., to sell to another) and instrument (i.e., to secure something for oneself). In the context of violence, how the body is viewed and used is, in turn, frequently (although not exclusively – see Chapter 10) tied to particular conceptions of masculinity.

Masculinities differ considerably according to ethnic differences, generational differences, class patterns and sexual preferences, but often these are subordinated to the dominant definition of what it is to be a man. The dominant or hegemonic conceptions of masculinity prescribe male behaviour in very particular ways. Real men are those who are tough, competitive, public, heterosexual and active. Real men see themselves as having higher social status than, and authority over, women. The maintenance or attainment of this notion of manhood, however, depends not only on the idea of what it is to be a man but also on the material resources to do so [9].

Opportunity, choice and group affinity all have an impact on how individuals construct or attempt to construct a masculine identity for themselves. The specific social context of the individual is crucial to understanding how different groups of men attempt to negotiate, reconcile or oppose the masculine ideal in the light of the actual resources at their disposal. For those men who traditionally established their masculine credentials via paid work, but who are now unemployed, homeless or generally marginalised from mainstream institutional life, the expression of masculinity has to take on different and potentially much more anti-social forms. A lack of institutional power and accredited social status often leaves little alternative than physicality itself as the main form of self-definition – whether this manifests itself as self-destructive behaviour or as violence directed at another. Much of the violence is in fact directed at other young men, many of whom are likewise in vulnerable social positions.

Groups of young people band together for social, cultural and familial reasons. They also do so for protection. Youth-group formation, which in some cases includes the evolution of the group into a gang, is thus often intertwined with violence or the threat of violence in the lives of young people. Over time, group identification becomes central to individual social identity, and the fate of the collective is inseparable from the security and social belonging of the individual.

The institutional racism and economic marginalisation experienced by ethnic-minority young people is directly linked to group formations that function in particular ways to sustain a sense of identity, community, solidarity and protection (see Chapter 3). The assertion of identity, and the 'valorisation of respect in the face of marginalisation', manifests itself in the form of group membership and group behaviour that privileges loyalty and being tough (individually and as a member of the identified group) in the face of real and perceived outside threats [10]. It also sometimes takes the form of contempt for 'Aussies' (or whatever the dominant social group is) and wariness of other ethnic-minority groups that likewise are struggling to garner respect and reputation in a hostile environment. Marginalisation is thus associated with the idea of 'dangerousness'.

Disadvantage, racism and prejudice can frequently exist as precursors to violence, as well as being forms of structural violence in their own right. However, much fighting and gang formation cuts across actual colour or religious divides; more often than not it is primarily about territory and neighbourhoods. This, too, is intertwined with particular constructions of masculinity and public displays of manhood.

With regard to territoriality, for example, young men basically protect themselves by posing as dangerous and 'bad', and by behaving and dressing aggressively. Ironically, how they do so may well tap back into wider racial and ethnic stereotypes. For instance, 'In street culture, negative stereotypes from mainstream society can provide protection and status...symbolic signs associated with the category "foreigner" can be conceptualized as a form of *embodied* street capital.' [11]. Gangster images combined with ethnic markers and aggressive physicality may well provide group protection in what are generally hostile social environments for minority groups.

Specific activities are associated with specific types of group formation. For example, fighting is definitely a male thing, although our gangs research did find that certain identifiable young women frequently engaged in fighting as well (see Chapter 10). In general and in most cases, however, while there was a place for young women in the gang scene, this tended to be on the periphery and to mainly involve socialising elements. Criminal acts, such as armed robbery and assault, as well as group fights, seemed to be pretty much the domain of the young men.

Masculinity as expressed on the street is very much constructed in terms of toughness and being manly. It also includes notions of loyalty to the group and to each other, to courage and fearlessness, and to mutual protection:

> these days it's about all muscle and people in our group – some of 'em are big and some of 'em have courage like as in if somebody swears to 'em they'll come back at 'em… They wish to be all big and strong and if anyone swears to you or says something about your mum, you go bash 'em and this and that.

> (Lebanese young man, Sydney)

Ironically, it is the very lack of options that may reinforce the worst aspects of hegemonic masculinity. That is, marginalised young men often display a strong compliance with the negative features of hegemonic masculinity as a last resort to status. This manifests itself in the language of emasculation and effeminisation which often accompanies attempts to humiliate others – 'no balls', 'poofter', 'sissy-boy'. Even the notion that weapons are for wimps (see below) encapsulates the idea that one is a lesser man by having to rely upon such aids.

Gang violence and the body

The Australian research we carried out showed that the contours of gang violence involve different types of social engagement whose character was fundamentally shaped by ethnic affiliation. A crucial difference in gang-related behaviour between different groups of young people related to the physicality of the young people involved – the size and shape of their bodies, the cultural context within which they use their bodies, and the circumstances under which violence occurs. Moreover, the material and ideological basis of group activity included important aspects of family and cultural group socialisation processes, and different social constructions of what constitutes 'fun' and the enjoyable.

While everyone we interviewed mentioned fighting, the nature and dynamics of fighting varied depending upon social background. Conflicts occurred within groups and between subgroups, as well as between identifiable ethnic conglomerations. The latter refers to instances when 100 or more young people would travel outside their local area, usually into the city centre. Inevitably this type of swarming would result in some kind of group punch-up. Many of the young people also mentioned occasional fights involving members of their immediate social group. In other instances, the fighting was intracommunal, involving different groups from the same ethnic-minority community – for example, Vietnamese fighting Vietnamese.

The nature of the violence, and in particular the attitude towards and actual use of weapons, varied greatly according to the distinct ethnic group. This is what is of particular interest, since it is this that reveals some crucial underlying differences in how features of everyday life are embodied by the participants. Some young men were reluctant and seemed regretful about having to carry weapons. Their logic was that if everyone carries weapons, then everyone has to:

> It's for show – yeah. Fuck man – why do a lot of people carry? 'cause the streets are getting rough these days man. Fuck everyone's carrying these days. So fuck everyone has to get strapped man. That's why they carry.
>
> (Samoan-Australian young man, Sydney)

For others, weapon use was associated with a graduated learning experience. The idea is that, depending upon age and experience, one progresses to different types of weapon use:

> Usually like before you fight with poles. Before that you fight with hands, but then you fight with poles, and then comes the machetes. After than, nowadays, you know, once you get older, you mostly do it with guns and that... 'cause say when you're young, you know, you don't know nothing about guns, you know what I mean, all you know is how to hold something and just whack 'em with it, you know what I mean, like a baseball bat or something – yeah. But then that's only going to give 'em a bruise and this and that. But when you get a bit older, you go 'All right. I'll use a knife' you know what I mean. 'I can cut 'em and make 'em bleed'. You know what I mean it's more effective than maybe a baseball bat, you know, you can slice people. In nowadays like when you get older, you know, you're thinking 'Oh man, these guys, you know, they're using machetes on me'. You've gotta use a gun to protect yourself 'cause most older people these days are all holding guns.
>
> (Vietnamese-Australian young man, Sydney)

This progression varies, however, depending upon whom you talk with. For example, some interviewees said that it was mainly the older young men who handled the guns and/or used them. Others, by contrast, said that it was the younger individuals – those around 15 and 16 years of age – who used guns to impress others around them. The older ones in fact had 'matured' and gone beyond the need to 'put on a show'.

Among the sample, it was the 'Asians' who were most associated with weapon use. In fact, other groups, such as the Lebanese and Samoans, were disdainful of the generalised use of weapons on the streets. For some Vietnamese, the use of weapons was intrinsically tied to body size:

> Maybe 'cause we small people you see and the other ones they're so big. If you fight by hand you can't win.
>
> (Vietnamese-Australian young man, Sydney)

The question of physical size also emerged in relation to two other types of weapon-carrying street-present youth. Drug users were identified as weapon users due in no small part to the impact of substance use on their bodies and their need for additional forms of protection:

> Nowadays, if I know I'm going to get in a conflict with someone I'd have a – I'd have a machete or a knife in my pocket, you know, and weapons are involved now. Whereas back then, it wasn't so much weapons, it was fist to fist. But now you get a heroin user who is so unhealthy, that skinny, and can't fight – they need a weapon. So now the more drugs that are coming into Canberra, the unhealthier people are getting in here, the more weapons are coming out because that's their only, umm, safety or means of hurting someone.

What about weapon use? Has that changed? Is it more or less?

> More as you get into drugs. If you get into the drug scene you get into weapons, you get into all that sort of shit. They're the sort of people that carry that shit right. So if you don't get into that lifestyle, you don't see it.
>
> (25-year-old young man, Canberra)

The other type of weapon carrier did so mainly due to their physical size, similar to our earlier Vietnamese example. Size does matter, but here it is the physical size of the individual and not just related to their ethnicity:

The majority of the time one of us has got a weapon on us in case something does happen... I normally carry my little bat – my little steel iron bar – stick it in the inside of my pants and a knife in my – my six inch bayonet blade in my back pocket. It's only 'cause I'm small. The bigger boys, they'll just wear their steel caps. I normally wear steel caps in my jeans as well... It's too hot in the city to carry stuff round. But a cigarette lighter can inflict some damage.

(15-year-old young man, Adelaide)

But there is more to the character and dynamics of street fighting than just body size. It also has to do with the specific 'culture' surrounding the body. Some sense of cultural difference is provided in the following observation by a young Samoan-Australian man:

Well if you fight with Asians all right expect to have knives chucked at you and if it is – this is how it is race based all right. The Samoans are guaranteed to have a good fight one on one – fist to fist. If it's Lebo's guaranteed to have every family down on you flat. If it's Asians get ready to have everything – every knife you've seen in your life.

(Samoan-Australian young man, Sydney)

Physicality is directly related to ethnicity. This takes the material form of different body sizes and shapes. For example, the Samoan young people tend to be heavier and more thick-set than the Vietnamese, who are of slighter build. The physical body is also the site for cultural construction. Every Samoan young person who was interviewed said that they had played rugby (rugby union or rugby league). Many of the Lebanese young people likewise had experience of playing rugby, or engaging in contact sports, such as boxing. The Vietnamese, if they played a sport, tended to pick basketball or martial arts. It was clear from the interviews that the Samoan young people, in particular, really enjoyed the physicality – the roughness, the aggressiveness and the body pounding – of their chosen sport.

Consideration of the intersection between ethnicity and class as this relates to the body helps us to understand the quite different perceptions regarding weapon use and masculinity, which vary according to social background. It is generally acknowledged that being tough and putting one's bodily integrity at risk is associated with traditional working-class male culture. Matters of physique and the physical have been central to working-class forms of aggressive masculinity that celebrate strength, speed, agility and the ability to withstand pain. Those young men who are socialised into experiencing, and enjoying, more brutalising forms of contact sport are more likely to favour violence that tests their physical prowess in some way. Those who do not share these experiences or whose physical size limits their ability to engage in unarmed combat are derided by those who 'can do':

> they can't do bitches – they can't fight with their fists.
>
> (Lebanese-Australian young man, Sydney)

Translated: weapons are for those who can't or won't fight. They are for 'wimps'. This was a recurring theme across cities, and across diverse ethnic groups around the country. Typical comments included:

> I don't know. I reckon they just don't have the balls to throw fists – use their fists. That's mainly with my group we never – we hated like – hated guns and we hated.

> I reckon if people wanna use a weapon, they can't fight.

> I've noticed more people who have [weapons]. I've noticed a lot more than when I was younger. Like when you go to Manuka and that, the fucking wogs, they all carry knives there... If they get in fights and that, they'll pull 'em out 'cause they won't fight... They won't go one on one. They just do it all together.

> What do you think of people carrying weapons? Dickheads, soft, can't fight with their fists. And why do you think people carry weapons? 'cause they think they're tough and they just wanna knock – knock the shit out of someone for no reason. It's stupid.

Importantly, there was some suggestion in the interviews that those young men who adopted this kind of attitude were also those most likely to enjoy fights as a form of recreation and fun. They were also most likely to resort to violence as a 'normal' and first reaction to conflict. Fighting for these young men is 'naturally' enjoyable, and a 'natural' part of their everyday life. They don't even think twice about resolving an argument by 'giving 'em a smack'. It is an ingrained reflex into which they have been socialised – at the neighbourhood level, at home and in sports. Fighting is fun precisely because of its physicality and the adrenaline rush that accompanies it.

> Oh we love fights, smoking up and drinking and girls.
>
> (Samoan young man, Sydney)

I knocked a guy last year for being a racist... He just walked past me and he just said 'Yeah, you black shit.' So I broke his nose. I broke his nose and shit and broke his jaw.

(Samoan young man, Sydney)

Thus violence is not only made natural by its prevalence in the lives of boys and men, but in many cases it is an important source of pleasure. It parallels experiences of the physical in pursuits such as sports, yet offers a different way in which to vent aggression, passion and emotional angst. Violence is desirable because it can and does offer pleasure, for some people, for some of the time.

Violence was also tied up with group identity and group protection. One young man was asked how he would feel if he was not part of a group. He replied: 'Scared... I expect that I'd feel lonely, feel powerless, weak.' Interestingly, in the neighbourhoods where this particular interview was carried out, the largest group tended to consist of Lebanese-Australian young men. It was this ethnic-minority group that was also seen by the non-Lebanese young men as the most aggressive, in school and on the street, and to instigate fights the most often. They were considered cocky and arrogant, even by friends and allies (such as the Samoan-Australian young men). Violence was considered by almost all the respondents as something that permeated their lives and that, for many, made them fearful about going out without their mates.

Essentialism and violence

One difficulty raised by these accounts is the problem of essentialism. Is it possible or desirable to speak about masculinity as something that is not essential to the very being or nature of men? While there is no doubt that the contours of masculinity do change over time, and from culture to culture, there nevertheless remains a strong essentialist flavour to much of the current writing about men (and women). The descriptions of male behavioural traits identified in the literature on men's criminality (and other areas) often reinforce the idea that somehow men, by virtue of being men, are innately more prone to such things as violence and aggression [12]. This leads to certain tensions in analysis and action.

On the one hand, male behaviour is sometimes reduced to hormones and testosterone levels; on the other, biology is often ignored when it comes to devising strategies for reform. The precise relationship between biological given and cultural process is a conundrum which requires further research and evaluation. Is it legitimate or fruitful to ask, as do some feminists about womanhood, whether there is a 'true male self' underlying the socially constructed 'masculine self'? Or are we best served by moving beyond an endless nature–nurture debate, to assume that whatever the biological ground, it is social relations which invest male biology with its substantive meaning and content [13]?

After all, it is by no means clear that all aspects of women's and men's behaviour can be neatly separated from biological processes (e.g., the capacity to have children does have meaningful social consequences which are, to some degree, linked to female biology). Further to this, there may well be certain features of being male and being female which are not cross-transferable in the sense that fundamental differences may exist between the two sexes which, in the end, cannot be ignored at a social and cultural level (e.g., physical size).

Yet we also know that what is deemed to be a desirable or undesirable quality (in the case of both masculinity and femininity) is subject to diverse interpretation (e.g., depending upon class, gender and ethnic background). It is also highly variable in terms of the meaning and consequences of specific social practices under particular social circumstances (e.g., the definition of what an appropriate quality is partly depends upon immediate needs and desires at any given moment). Nevertheless, doubts can be raised about whether or not it is possible to analytically construct a non-essentialist model of masculinity (i.e., one which posits that there are no core or innate biological/cultural differences between men and women), and thus whether it is possible to frame an explanation of contemporary social behaviour that can bypass the biological.

The idea that there is a link between the (male) body and certain types of behaviour is certainly not new to criminology. From the days of Lombroso onwards, the presumption that bodies matter forms a key part of biological explanations for criminality. The 'science' of phrenology was popular in criminology, for example, for a number of years around the beginning of the 20th century. For instance, a study undertaken in 1912 by the University of Melbourne was conducted on 355 male inmates at Pentridge Prison. The skulls of the prisoners were examined and estimates of the cubic capacity of their brains were made in an attempt to correlate the size of skull to intelligence. It was concluded that cattle stealers had the least brain capacity, while forgers and embezzlers had the greatest [14].

Of particular interest to the present work is the type of study that looks to physiology or body structure as the determinant of criminal behaviour. William Sheldon is a key figure [15]. It was he who proposed a theory based on body build (somotype). He wished to establish a link between different body types and criminality. According to him, human body types can be classed into three broad categories: endomorphic (soft and round), mesomorphic (muscular and strong) and ectomorphic (thin and fragile). Each body type was associated with a particular temperament: endomorphic (relaxed, sociable and fond of eating), mesomorphic (energetic, courageous and assertive) and ectomorphic (brainy, artistic and introverted). It was further argued that mesomorphs were most likely to become criminals. In other words, there was a positive correlation between body type and criminal activity.

Biological explanations of this kind imply that crime is the result of something essential to the nature of the individual. Thus we are born with certain biological attributes that we cannot change but that may lock some of us into a life of crime and anti-social behaviour. Certain groups are seen to be more predisposed to crime than others because of biological and social environmental factors.

There remains a continuing tendency among some researchers to reduce the reasons for criminal behaviour to a single cause, either biological or psychological [16]. Such work assumes that adult behaviour and personality are overwhelmingly determined and reducible to single overarching factors (e.g., a violence gene). This reductionism to a single cause can lead to both racist and sexist conclusions. Where offending is linked to biology, the logical extension of the line of reasoning can lead to attempts to correlate certain people (e.g., Aboriginal people, poor people) with certain 'biologically determined' traits (e.g., intelligence as measured by IQ) and so to criminal offending. Without adequate discussion of the assumptions underlying positivist research of this sort, the search for the causes of criminal behaviour leads inexorably to racist and unwarranted conclusions. Are the Samoan young men in our study innately more prone to violence than other young men because of their physical build? Or are there other, non-biological reductionist, ways to explain differences in the social behaviour of similarly positioned young men?

A recent biological reductionist explanation is found in reference to the so-called warrior gene allegedly found among Maori men. Media reports explained that the monoamine oxidase (MAO) gene was dubbed the warrior gene by US researchers due to its links to aggressive behaviour. Speaking at the International Congress of Human Genetics in Brisbane, Australia, in August 2006, genetic epidemiologist Rod Lea of the Institute of Environmental Science and Research, based at

Wellington in New Zealand, went one step further [17]. He said that his research showed that 60 per cent of Maori men have the MAO gene, compared with only 30 per cent of men of European descent. Thus the movie *Once Were Warriors* translates into 'Still Are Warriors' in the real world of genetically determined behaviour. Extrapolating from this scenario, one might wonder whether the Samoan young people we talked with were somehow biologically predisposed to like fighting. Aggression linked to genetic make-up thus provides fertile ground for explanations that conveniently blame the biology rather than the social environment.

And yet we cannot ignore the body in social explanations for certain types of behaviour either. As indicated above, body size and shape do matter, in conjunction with how one is socialised in the use of one's body, and in the type of activity in which one engages.

Explanations at the individual and relationship level look to biological and psychological factors to explain engagement in violence and anti-social behaviour. Yet not all men are violent, and some are more violent than others. Some women are violent, while many are not. This implies that while there is a general socio-cultural context that means that some societies are generally more violent than others, and that some groups within society are more violent than others, there are nevertheless individual factors that contribute to who, specifically, engages in which kinds of violence.

Psychological factors include such things as temperament, learned social responses, social and communication skills, and perceptions of rewards or penalties for engaging in violence. These are influenced by family upbringing and neighbourhood context, as well as being mediated by things such as alcohol and drug use, arousal levels (related to stimulation) and emotional state. There are also biological factors that have an influence on general propensities toward violence. Testosterone in young men, for example, impacts upon potential behaviours. While not reducing behaviour to a simple matter of biology, one's biological and physiological make-up does have a bearing on specific frequencies and types of engagement in violence. Certain neurobehavioural traits – that is, capacities determined by status at birth, trauma and ageing processes such as puberty – may be associated with certain kinds of behaviour. Likewise, transient neurobehavioural states, which describe temporary conditions associated with emotions and external stressors, can influence violent behaviour [18].

As mentioned, recent scientific research on genetics and anti-social behaviour has shown an association between certain types of genes (e.g. the MAO gene) and a propensity toward physical violence. Generally speaking, however, while there is evidence that both genetic and environmental factors contribute to anti-social behaviour, violence *per se* cannot be reduced to a single genetic factor. Certain genetic and neurobehavioural traits may also provide the grounding for why alcohol affects some people more dramatically than others vis-à-vis intoxication and propensity towards violence [19].

The combination effect of different factors is also apparent in other ways. For example, alcohol is the only psychoactive drug that in many individuals tends to increase aggressive behaviour temporarily while it is taking effect. However, factors at other levels – behaviour patterns when people are not drinking, the setting in which people drink and local drinking customs, for example – influence the strength of this relationship [20]. In effect, researchers have suggested a biological predisposition to violence (based upon genetic and hormonal factors) and to alcohol use (related to blood sugar levels), but these, in turn, are influenced by cultural norms and social settings. Biological drivers (genetics, biochemistry) and social determinants (situational triggers, cultural contexts) are each, in their own right, grounded in the body.

The body and desistance from fighting

For some gang members, some types of violence are fun. This is especially the case where certain conditions apply: the fight takes the form of fist fights; where the rules of engagement for the violence are clear; where physical prowess can be displayed to others; where the participants have a history of engagement in sports and martial arts; and where the young people are familiar with violent behaviour at an everyday level.

The thought of violence can also be very attractive insofar as there are constant cultural affirmations of the thrills associated with violence (via movies, DVDs, computer games, *YouTube*). In many different ways, recent years have seen the routinisation and naturalisation of violence in everyday life. It is more often than not seen as the first resort with regard to conflict resolution, and as an important expression of loyalty and mateship. Violence can make one feel powerful. It also provides a ready outlet for anger, resentment and aggression.

But when does the fighting become less than fun? This is an important question because it, too, bears some relation to the place of the body in explanations of male group and individual violence. In the Sydney interviews a number of the Samoan young men commented that they no longer played football. The reasons for this were twofold: either they were too aggressive and kept going beyond the rules of the game and thus were asked to leave; or they smoked too much 'weed', to the extent that they lost fitness and thus could not maintain a standard that was sufficient to engage in prolonged contact sport. To some extent the latter is also a matter of how boys 'age' into becoming young men. The earlier one starts smoking (of whatever substance), the quicker one is likely to lose match fitness. Over time this will also impact upon the ability to fight and engage in strenuous physical activities.

The bifurcation of weapon use – the relatively young and the relatively older – can be partly explained in terms of fitness and the extent to which the individual is drawn into the life of crime. Weapons are only for wimps in cases where fighting itself is the key object of the activity. If status is the core concern, then weapons may be used to artificially enhance social status (relative to older and bigger individuals). If crime has become central to life experiences, then fighting is no longer the focus. Rather, weapons become more important for young adults who, in essence, become 'criminals'. Street presence recedes, as do large group conflicts. When income is at stake, then the most potent weapons are those that provide the most purchase when it comes to money-earning. Weapons are not for fun.

The effect of the ageing body is also reflected to some degree in the fact that many interviewees in our sample talked about leaving the 'gang shit' behind them. The thrill of fighting loses its appeal as people settle down to families (and tired nights) and jobs (and variable shifts). Changes in home and work affect energy levels and social priorities. Hanging out tends to be more of a teenage thing; when adulthood creeps into the young people's lives, the demands on the body change, as does the ability to use the body as previously. Getting serious means having the baby, securing the job and deciding once and for all to be 'bad' or not. To some extent, these social processes are likewise socially patterned by ethnic considerations: the place and role of the family, the place and attitude towards paid work, and the capacity to earn a living through legitimate and illegitimate means are contingent upon community traditions, resources and opportunities.

Fear is embodied. Being afraid is a physical, emotional and psychological phenomenon. Flight and immobilisation may result due to the perceived consequences of street interactions (such as losing a girlfriend or a job) and the uncertainties associated with these (such as the unpredictability of much street violence). Ironically, fear can also propel individuals to carry weapons, and thus increase the potential harm on the streets:

> I think there's two reasons why people carry weapons. One is so they can feel stronger and tougher and feel more like dominant to everyone else because they have a weapon. And I think some people actually carry weapons to avoid confrontation. So like if someone tries something and they pull out a weapon, they're automatically stronger and they go 'no, there's no fights here man'. So it's good bluff material? Yeah definitely and I think if someone is not prepared to use the weapon they're carrying, they shouldn't be carrying it because if they didn't carry it – I mean they can pull it out and it can get taken from them and used against them.
>
> (14-year-old young man, Canberra)

> Well I think they're too scared to use their own two fists to tell you the truth. They're too scared to cop a hiding. They'll king hit you, they'll bowl you or they'll stab you. They'll do something 'cause they're too scared to cop a hiding. It's not going to last forever. It's going to last for a day or two and the pain's gone. They're weak and they're scared.
>
> (20-year-old young man, Hobart)

The complexities of youth-gang violence suggest that strategies intended to reduce or end violence must incorporate a range of elements. These include everything from the need for alternative sources of adrenaline rush and structured violence (e.g. boxing and football) through to development of exit strategies for those wanting to leave a group and changing the group orientation away from street fighting into other kinds of competition. Challenging the dominant culture surrounding violence in Australian society is fundamental to any change strategy. This demands an analysis of specific types and forms of violence – outside pubs, gangs, schools, drug-related, racism, homophobic – and adoption of a multipronged approach.

Conclusion

The structural violence of dispossession, exploitation and marginalisation feeds the situational violence of the streets and the home. Popular media images of violence concentrate on the poor ('feral kids'), the black ('troublemakers') and the alien ('ethnic youth gangs'). These images are important symbolically and ideologically in separating these groups out from the mainstream, in reinforcing the division between 'us' and 'them'. They are also grounded to some extent in actual street realities pertaining to these groups.

These kinds of social division are further entrenched through biological reductionist explanations that focus on physical traits. As we have seen, there has been talk of a 'violence gene' which supposedly is a key mechanism behind personal violence. Thus the violence is attributed solely or mainly to biological factors (for which there is no easy solution or cure). More than this, given the over-representation of minority groups in official crime statistics (especially African-Americans in the US, Maori in New Zealand, Aborigines in Australia), the genetic explanation clearly has racist applications. The problem is seen as intractable and as originating in the people themselves. Yet depending upon the group in question, there is nonetheless a link between the biological and the social as these interact to foster certain types of desire, want and emotion at the level of the body. While not reducing behaviour to the body, the body still constitutes a crucial medium through which the social is actively constructed. What we do with our bodies, what we must do with our bodies and what we like to do with our bodies are intertwined, and these are matters of cultural significance and practical socialisation.

Social structures and social being thus shape broad propensities in a society, and individual life circumstances are reflected in, and reflective of, identifiable social patterns. Certain kinds of violence are linked to marginalised young men, who rely upon their bodies to exercise authority, with or without the use of weapons. Other kinds of violence are linked to business executives, who have the financial resources to ignore physical means as a way to exert their power and will. In either case, the violence reflects the material realities of each group. As this chapter has demonstrated, how people use and perceive their bodies is grounded in distinct physical, social and cultural contexts. Violence is neither natural nor normal. It is fired up in the crucible of lived experience and shared realities. This has implications for both how we understand phenomena such as gang violence, in its specific manifestations, and how social responses to this violence might best be constructed.

9
Gang Interventions

Introduction

If one focuses a lot of attention on a problem, then the problem will more often than not seem to be real and to grow in importance. This is one of the dilemmas of gangs research. For those who see gangs as a *bona fide* area of public concern, the recognition of gangs is a basic starting point for intervention and crime prevention. For those who view gangs discourse itself as part of the problem, then the agenda is very different indeed. In particular, the stigmatising impact of gang labels and the potential for unwarranted group profiling on the part of justice authorities are seen to be especially problematic. Yet in some instances and localities, there are in fact significant problems pertaining to youth violence, and distinct youth gangs are both real and problematic in certain communities. How we intervene to deal with this is as contentious as how the originating problem is defined.

From the beginning, effective and appropriate responses to youth gangs require a thorough assessment of local communities and neighbourhoods, and careful appraisal of the nature of the problem. As Howell observes,

> Both denial of gang problems and overreaction to them are detrimental to the development of effective community responses to gangs. Denial that gang problems exist precludes early intervention efforts. Overreaction in the form of excessive police force and publicizing of gangs may inadvertently serve to increase a gang's cohesion, facilitate its expansion, and lead to more crime. [1]

This latter point is especially important. For example, certain types of police intervention run the risk of making things worse and reinforcing gang identification and solidarity. On the other hand, the issue of desistance from gang membership and activity needs to acknowledge that there is indeed a problem, and that very often this is related to questions of masculinity, class inequality, racism and violence.

Comprehensive approach to gangs

Most comprehensive attempts to address gang issues involve some combination of coercive and developmental measures. A key matter of concern is the weight given to particular measures within the context of an overall strategy. While not mutually exclusive, the main message of a criminological analysis of youth crime and gang life is that comprehensive community-based approaches are preferable to narrowly focused coercive strategies [2]. This is because gang issues ultimately reflect wider political, economic and social processes (generally relating to structural issues of racism, inequality, blocked opportunities, poverty and oppressive regulatory practices), and, as such, they can be curtailed, but not fully addressed, by reliance upon coercive measures.

Another consideration is what young people themselves have to say about gangs and possible anti-gang strategies. It is notable in this regard that the young people in the 1990s Melbourne youth gangs research generally emphasised the need for proactive and developmental strategies to deal with youth gangs and gang-related behaviour [3]. They spoke of the need for more support services, youth-employment programmes, greater dialogue between youth and authority figures, and positive strategies that provide young people with constructive ways in which to use their time and energy. In essence, the young people identified a range of services and strategies that they felt would improve the situation for themselves and their friends, and which would provide for positive social outcomes. Specific groups also had specific needs. For example, it is clear that newly arrived individuals require greater and different levels of social and community support than those who are already well established in Australia. The particular perceptions and suggestions of the different sample groups have to be assessed in the light of the broad social experiences and social position of that group, particularly in relation to the migration-settlement process. The Melbourne youth gangs research highlighted the importance of dealing with the youth-gang phenomenon across a number of dimensions, taking into account the very different social histories and socio-economic circumstances of the young people.

It is also essential to consider the policy implications of gangs research with regard to the institutional measures that might be designed and utilised to curtail gang formation and gang-related activities. The starting point for policy development and formulation of intervention strategies is careful analysis of what precisely 'the problem' is. Canadian researchers and US criminal justice agencies emphasise the importance of local community-based anti-gang programmes based upon an appreciation of the diversity of youth-group formations, as well as the dynamics of opportunity structures and communal relations (especially in relation to ethnic-minority groups) [4]. Similarly, South African commentary on gangs and anti-gang strategies is particularly critical of one-dimensional, coercion-based methods [5]. Rather, the answer is seen in strategies that do not criminalise gangs, and in better understanding where young people are coming from. It is clear that the prevention of criminal youth gangs must be broad-based and developmental in orientation, rather than simply coercive and reliant upon law-enforcement measures.

Australian, UK, Canadian, European, South African and US recommendations regarding anti-gang strategies share common concerns. These are summarised in Box 9.1.

Box 9.1: Key elements of a comprehensive approach

Identifying the problem – The construction of group behaviour as a problem hinges upon wider community recognition of a particular group as a gang, and the group's involvement in enough illegal and/or violent activities to get a consistent negative response from law-enforcement personnel and neighbourhood residents. Effort should be made to establish various contributors to the construction of the gang phenomenon, and this can be contrasted with the perceptions of the young people at issue. In particular, perceptions of the nature and extent of youth-gang activity and young people's activity generally can be gauged from the perspective of young people, the general public, public space regulators (e.g., police, shopkeepers and security guards), teachers and youth workers.

Identifying the source of the problem – This involves definition and classification of different groups and different types of activity, and examination of the immediate local context and socio-structural factors that foster gang-related behaviour. As intimated above, it is imperative to note that the perceived problem may actually differ substantially from reality. Hence there is a need

---

Box 9.1: (Continued)

to examine problem sources from a variety of perspectives. For instance, there are some indications that differential policing practices as they are applied to young people lead to mutual distrust and disrespect. Thus both police perspectives on young people's collective use of public space and young people's perspectives on the regulation of their public space usage need to be examined.

Developing general strategies to reduce group conflict and the propensity to commit crime – These would include measures designed to address social and economic marginality, racism, educational strategies, job training and placement, dealing with inadequately supported family systems, health service provision and development of social and economic infrastructure.

Programmatic approaches at the community level – These would include the development of specific strategies to discourage gang membership and to provide young people with avenues for positive pro-social group formation, and development of measures designed to minimise any hero worship of gang leaders (e.g., through support for and endorsement of alternative mentors and role models).

US evaluations of youth-gang programmes have indicated that the approaches deemed to be most effective from a law-enforcement perspective included (i) community collaboration (information exchange or gang awareness education); (ii) crime prevention activities (modification of environments and opportunities); and (iii) suppression tactics (street sweeps) [6]. Different approaches are seen to be effective in chronic or longstanding versus emerging or more recent gang-problem cities. Thus, for example, the provision of social opportunities is seen to be more effective at sites with chronic gang problems, while community mobilisation of resources to specifically address gang problems is seen as the most effective way to deal with emerging gang problems.

A clear message from international gangs research is that any intervention should be based upon close and careful examination of local conditions and youth-group formations. Rather than making assumptions about youth gangs, or drawing upon media and other stereotypes of gang life, it is essential to undertake a comprehensive and systematic assessment of a perceived gang problem. This assessment must take into account a range of views and perceptions, including, and especially, those of local young people themselves.

In addition, it is very clear from the literature on youth gangs, as well as the general sociological literature on the nature of juvenile offending, that any strategy to reduce gang activity will necessarily have different dimensions and strands [7]. For instance, analysis of 'risk factors' relating to gang membership show that multiple issues influence potential gang membership, ranging from neighbourhood level (availability of drugs, number of young people in similar troubled situations) through to the level of personality and individual differences (hyperactivity, poor refusal skills).

However, risk-based analysis and interventions have been criticised for their unfounded generalisations about the normalisation of certain types of behaviours regardless of social context, their imprecision in relation to how difference risks interact in specific individual circumstances, and their tendency to reduce major social problems to matters of individual deficiency and/or responsibility [8]. Certainly a simple checklist approach to risk is insufficient to do justice to the social processes that underpin youth-gang formation and gang-related behaviours.

Depending on the focus of the strategy – whether it is directed at structural change and immediate situations, chronic gang problems or newly emergent ones, specific groups of young people or entire neighbourhoods – a range of approaches will need to be canvassed in order to select the most appropriate to deal with the issue at hand. Each community can undertake a systematic needs assessment so that it can make informed decisions as to what can be done with the resources available. This can include a profile of current youth activities and community services in a neighbourhood, as well as establishing planning teams, setting priorities among needs and developing a consensus regarding what ought to be done.

Parents and families

When it comes to issues pertaining to gangs and families, youth and community workers attending a youth gangs workshop in Glenorchy, Tasmania, in July 2002 identified three concerns as requiring close attention [9]:

> *Family feuds and the need to diminish conflict* – The question of 'whose problem it is' was raised in relation to how family feuds tend to carry over and affect all family members regardless of gang membership

or involvement. One suggestion is to approach peripheral family members as an entry point to core family members. In order to diminish conflict, there is a need to deal with both inter- and intrafamily violence. This would involve working separately with each family. In particular, it is important to sell the possibilities and benefits for the children if peaceful resolution of conflicts (including longstanding family feuds) could be achieved. Doing it for the sake of the children could be an important emotional lever for change. While working separately with each family, it was considered important to stress the commonalities and similar interests across families as part of this intervention.

More and more practical parenting support – One of the biggest problems is that social problems themselves tend to be intergenerational. Difficulties in parenting give rise to difficulties in parenting; gang activity gives rise to gang activity; alcohol and drug abuse give rise to more of the same in the next generation. The age of different parents is also an issue, with some being mature adults, others only 16 or 17 years old. Rather than 'lectures' or 'theory', these families need down-to-earth practical skills. They simply have never experienced positive alternative forms of parenting in their own lives. What they want, and need, is an understanding of how to deal with actual issues within their own families, how to deal with their own children, and how to respond to real incidents that affect their lives and the lives of those around them.

Improve parent access to services – While many parenting programmes and projects already exist, it is often those most in need who are least likely to utilise them. This is so for a number of reasons. Poor access can be due to illiteracy; perceptions or experiences of bureaucratic red tape; or reluctance to engage services due to fear and suspicion about the government. The issue is how to access parents via some kind of 'parent outreach'. One possibility is through the juvenile justice system, although this still represents a reactive approach and implies that a young person must come to the attention of criminal justice officials before anything can be done. New models of delivery are also required, given the reluctance of many parents to use mainstream parent support services.

The role of parents, parenting and families is crucial in the development of young people. However, there is no single model of parenting or family life that can be used as a template for good practice. Rather, personal, family and community relationships are intertwined in complex ways, and particular circumstances and contexts give rise to a multitude of family forms. The development of appropriate and effective strategies in relation to the family and parents, therefore, will be contingent upon the particular styles, cultures and resources pertaining to specific groups in the community [10].

Nevertheless, it is apparent that much public policy entrenches social differences based upon class and ethnic background. This occurs in the area of family policy, as it does in other areas. For example, Jamrozik observes that it is mainly working-class families who get caught up with 'child welfare' services that operate largely through the identification of problems such as neglected and at-risk children and that offer coercive or compulsory solutions [11]. By contrast, the issue for middle-class families is 'child care', where the problem is constructed more in terms of rights and entitlements and where intervention is positive, developmental and voluntary. He argues that there is a dichotomy between how the rich and poor are treated in family policy, and that this has increased by the recent policy of shifting the services of the 'welfare' category to the non-government sector, thus changing the nature of services from 'entitlement' to 'charity', bringing again to life the distinction between the 'deserving' and 'undeserving', while the services that are used mainly by the affluent are claimed as 'a right' [12].

Regardless of the merits or otherwise of this argument, it is relevant to ask how recipients perceive the services to which they are exposed. In particular, if some types of service provision or state intervention are seen and experienced as intrusive and/or unfair, then this will have a marked impact upon the families most vulnerable to these processes. Needless to say, the Northern Territory 'intervention' warrants extra special critical scrutiny in this regard.

Educational and school-based strategies

Any discussion of crime and gangs must also take into account the role played by schools in shaping the social resources and social identities of young people. For example, student alienation within the school context can lead to detachment from the institution, feelings of resentment or failure on the part of the young person, the turning towards alternative peer groups (such as gangs) for support and identity networks, and active resistance to what the school has to offer [13]. What happens at school to, and with, individuals and groups has a major bearing on youth behaviour. Factors such as early anti-social behaviour at school, lack of commitment to school and academic failure are all associated with delinquency. So too is absenteeism, particularly that associated with truancy. Bullying also has a major impact on school experiences and in-group and between-group activities (see Chapter 7). These kinds of issue have a profoundly negative impact on school students and those who absent themselves from school. In response, attention needs to be directed at improving whole-of-school environments, and in dealing with school 'troublemakers' and 'truants' in ways that keep them in-system rather excluded from schools and educational opportunities.

In our early youth-gangs work a number of general educational strategies that might help to address gang-related issues were recommended [14]:

- It is essential that young people in general be provided with **specific education in cross-cultural issues** in order that the backgrounds, cultures and patterns of life pertaining to specific ethnic groups be better understood by all concerned.
- Attention must also be directed at the provision of **anti-racist education**, so that issues of discrimination, prejudice and unequal power relations can be analysed and discussed in an enlightened, informative and empathetic manner.
- There should be developed at the local, regional and state levels a series of **youth reconciliation projects** that will promote the diversity of cultures among young people, aim to reduce violence between them, and give young people from diverse cultural and ethnic backgrounds the practical opportunity to get to know each other at a personal and a group level.
- Attention must be directed at providing **quality educational facilities and services** for young people, particularly those which are based upon a multicultural curriculum and atmosphere, where students are provided with adequate individual and group support, and where anti-racist strategies and practices are applied across the whole school population.
- Concerted action is needed on the specific issue of school bullying so that appropriate **conflict resolution and anti-violence strategies** can be put into place in order to reduce the number of such incidents and to reassure students of their safety and security within the educational institution.
- **Special provisions** are needed for those young people who, due to their bullying or gang-related behaviour, might normally be excluded from school, but who still require community support and appropriate educational programmes to ensure that they have the chance to contribute positively to society, rather than to be marginalised even further from the mainstream.

For specifically anti-gang programmes in schools, it has been suggested in US research that three types of strategy should be included at any one time. These are in-school safety and control procedures; in-school enrichment procedures that make the school experience more meaningful, effective and enjoyable; and formal links to community-based programmes [15]. Importantly, any programme development ought to rest upon extensive collaboration between school and community agencies, and with parents and students.

US research has determined that the most cost-effective approach to reducing serious youth and adult gang crime is to discourage children and young people from joining gangs. In this regard, the Gang Resistance Education and Training programme has been touted as one of the more promising schemes [16]. It involves uniformed law-enforcement officers teaching a nine-week course to middle-school students. However, some researchers are sceptical that such programmes can make much of a difference given the repressive gangs agenda informing them and the failure to address the adverse social conditions that give rise to gangs [17]. This is borne out to some extent in formal evaluations which have found limited success in such programmes in keeping young people out of gangs or reducing their delinquent behaviour [18]. In an Australian context, projects such as this raise interesting possibilities for, and questions about, relevant 'Police In Schools' programmes, particularly in relation to curriculum matters. There is also consideration to be given to whether or not the introduction of such a scheme in the Australian context, in which gangs research and gangs 'moral panics' are less prevalent than in US jurisdictions, might not inadvertently foster the formation of gangs. By granting attention to the phenomenon, it could well encourage some young people to become interested in gang membership.

Another type of school and community intervention involves the use of adult and peer mentors. Designated and trained mentors can provide guidance and assistance to younger cohorts. Closely related to this is the use of peer mediators – students whose role is to work through co-operative ways to resolve and reduce conflicts within school settings. The point is to make 'gang stuff' unattractive as a peer-group option. As Gordon emphasises,

> Anti-gang programming appears to be most effective when it is aimed at the supply of new gang and group members, rather than existing and well-established street gang members. Programs in high schools can reduce fear and intimidation, dry up the source of gang

personnel, and help generate a broader, negative perspective of gang membership, especially among younger adolescents [19].

According to experienced youth and community workers, realistic anti-gang strategies have to start where the young people are coming from, rather than solely reflecting the interests or thinking of service providers, including teachers and police [20]. School strategies must likewise be sensitive to these concerns, and include active input from young people.

Community-based approaches

One of the limitations of coercive and repressive approaches to gang activity is that, as noted in Chapter 2, very often gangs occupy a rather ambiguous position within local communities. In the light of the connections between community circumstances that give rise to gangs and community relations that sustain them, it would appear that community processes are also most likely to provide the best opportunities for their transformation.

Community-based approaches have a number of dimensions that include both direct service provision and efforts to build pro-social relationships at the local level. Some are directed at youth specifically; others are designed as whole-of-community strategies that benefit people across the local area in a variety of ways.

An example of youth-oriented strategy is the employment of detached youth and community workers to provide supervised recreation and leisure activities, and after-school programmes. These workers go to where the young people are, and they intervene in a low-key supportive fashion that is founded upon trust and mutual respect. US research has demonstrated the importance of detached youth worker programmes in influencing individual gang membership and group processes [21]. Significantly, some of this work has shown that the intervention of practitioners can itself lead to gang cohesion by fostering joint activities, common identification and overall group cohesiveness [22]. Whether it is welfare or suppression programmes, the inadvertent effect of direct intervention with street groups is to increase gang cohesiveness. This is problematic insofar as 'The more cohesive the gang usually is the more criminally involved' [23]. Youth and community detached work is most strategically effective, therefore, when merged with wider community development types of intervention and citizen participation.

Another example is having youth facilities available that provide young people with safe places in which to hang out, while simultaneously providing an opportunity (through adult and youth mentors) to develop an alternative sense of belonging, identity and self-worth compared with the gang. This is a youth service approach, in which the young people come to the centre (which, to attract a diversity of youth, must cater to their specific needs and interests).

With regard to services for youth, whether intended to be youth-specific or for the community as a whole, it is also important to cater to particular social differences within communities. For example, specific spaces and facilities should be reserved, perhaps at designated times, exclusively for certain young people (e.g., swimming pools, rooms that could be used for prayers), in order that religious and cultural practices can be acknowledged and respected in a dignified and inclusive manner [24].

Community-based approaches also include those that involve large-scale, and often non-youth specific, measures. Urban renewal projects and community empowerment programmes, for example, are meant to increase work opportunities for and civic participation amongst local residents. The intention of such interventions is to change the material situation and infrastructure of specific sites and neighbourhoods (e.g., by building a skateboard ramp), and to change perceptions and attitudes among residents and non-residents about these areas (e.g., by fostering participatory activities such as sports or card-player clubs). Low neighbourhood attachment, economic deprivation and adversity, and limited community organisation are implicated in the constitution of crime-prone areas, so any solution will have to address these kinds of issue.

The development of pride in one's place can be important in changing negative attitudes and anti-social behaviours into more positive, pro-social directions. Community reputation, especially if accompanied by stigma associated with gangs, crime and anti-social activities, has a dramatic impact on life within particular locales. Young people who live in stigmatised areas are more likely than others who live elsewhere to suffer the consequences in the form of reduced job opportunities and difficulties in moving out of the neighbourhood [25]. A 'bad' community reputation may occasionally translate into a gang mentality based upon defensiveness and reassertion of worth in the face of a hostile 'outside' world. Changing the community's reputation through communal development is one way in which to address these issues.

An essential principle underpinning a community approach to gang problems is that investment in people is the best way to reap social rewards. A community strategy (focussing on human beings) ought not to be confused with a neighbourhood approach (focussing on geographically defined physical environments), although the two are obviously interrelated. It has been noted that 'Regeneration priorities need to emphasise the personal development of residents of disadvantaged communities, as physical regeneration alone has been demonstrated to have little impact on the conditions nurturing social exclusion' [26]. Changing local social environments is ultimately what counts, and this means engaging and involving young people and their communities in finding solutions to their own problems, with the support of expert advice and contributions by each tier of government.

Also essential to this task is paying particular attention to those young people who are particularly at risk of becoming gang members or who are currently gang members, so that they too have a meaningful role to play within the regeneration of their neighbourhoods [27]. But how we do this is itself subject to question.

Risk analysis and social profiling

A major source of public consternation about young people, and the key site where perceptions of gang activity and youth gangs occur, is the street. What happens on the street is therefore important both to diminishing anti-social and gang-related behaviour, and to reducing fear of groups of young people in public places.

Street-based interventions

In specific circumstances it may be necessary to institute coercive measures to deal with groups or situations that have got out of hand. In the US, for example, specific city sites (hotspots) and specific youth-group formations (identifiable gangs) have been targeted for aggressive street policing. In Dallas, Texas, for instance, three main suppression strategies were employed:

> *Saturation patrols/high-visibility patrols in target areas* – The patrols stopped and searched 'suspected gang members' and made arrests as appropriate.
> *Aggressive curfew enforcement* – In the USA, many local jurisdictions enacted youth curfew laws and, where these were in effect, ordinances were strictly enforced whenever suspected gang members were encountered.

Aggressive enforcement of truancy laws and regulations – This involved close collaboration between schools and police [28].

Aggressive street policing and zero-tolerance approaches have been criticised, however, for unduly restricting the rights of young people, being linked to racist assessments of who gets targeted for intervention, for creating resentment amongst young people towards authority figures and for sending the wrong message about how best to resolve social conflicts. The more general critique is that repression actually does very little to solve the problem of gangs. This is mainly because gang suppression not only fails to address the social causes of gang formation but also is itself a contributor to gang formation – this is especially so with regard to mass incarceration policies, such as in the US, that fertilises gang proliferation from within as well as outside the prison walls [29].

Nevertheless, even the critics agree that selective use of coercive measures is warranted in specific situations and is an appropriate tactical measure when applied judiciously. For example, a shopping centre in Cairns, Queensland was experiencing major problems with a small group of teenage boys who frightened patrons and caused persistent damage to the premises. For a short time only, the management worked with police and security guards to 'stamp out' the offending group, and with it the offending behaviour. Afterwards, the management strategy no longer relied upon coercive threat but instead much more friendly and interactive forms of social regulation [30].

At a legislative and policy level, attempts to restrict the street presence of gangs have taken the form of youth curfews or anti-loitering statutes. Curfews are used extensively in the US, although the specific features of each vary considerably in terms of times, activities, target populations and enforcement. The evaluation of curfews has indicated that their success is best guaranteed when coercive measures are accompanied by opportunity-enhancement measures, such as leisure and recreation, educational activities and musical forums. Big issues remain, however, with regard to the overall effectiveness and purposes of curfews, and whether they may inadvertently criminalise youth behaviour that is in and of itself not illegal or criminal [31].

'Street cleaning legislation' has long been linked to efforts of the establishment to deal with the most destitute sections of the population. In particular, the history of vagrancy laws in the UK, Australia and the US is a history of social control over selected population groups – the poor, the unemployed, the ethnic minority, the indigenous and the transient [32]. Such measures are nonetheless seen to be 'weak' tools in the overall struggle to diminish gang membership and activity. Rather, much greater faith is put in community involvement and community-wide strategies since these go to the heart of the gang problem.

The issue of weapons also looms large in any discussion of gangs and gang-related behaviour. There are several ways to deal with weapons:

- conduct **community education campaigns** to discourage young people from carrying offensive implements;
- **enact and enforce laws** that prohibit the carrying of offensive weapons and that allow for the confiscation of knives that are clearly being carried for unlawful purposes;
- assure young people in policy and practice, especially those who feel vulnerable to attack from other groups, that they will be **protected by the police** and therefore do not need to arm themselves in self-defence;
- negotiate with communities about the presence and place of weapons among young people and the community generally, with a view to **discouraging parental approval and encouragement of weapon carrying**.

How weapons issues are dealt with in practice has major implications for police–youth relations, and for the consolidation of group identities. For example, as with similar cases in the UK, the lack of police protection can lead some young people to adopt the stance that 'self-defence is no offence' and thus to arm themselves against racist attacks. Concern about the carrying of weapons not only justifies even more intense police intervention, it feeds media distortions about the problem of 'ethnic youth gangs'. Moreover, the enforcement of anti-weapon laws can affect large groups of young people in negative ways by constantly being stopped and searched by police for no apparent reason [33]. This phenomenon – pre-emptive intervention in relation to identifiable groups – warrants further discussion in its own right given that it is frequently constructed and justified in terms of specific identifiable young people who are seen to constitute a greater risk than others.

Risk-based profiling

The conceptual perspective that is often used to frame youthful deviance, including gang-related activity, is the developmental perspective and especially its narrower version, the risk paradigm. This generally involves the charting of specific risk and protective factors that are seen to influence how individuals negotiate particular transitions and pathways in their lives. Multifactoral analysis of specific factors is statistically correlated with certain types of behaviour and certain types of people. The implication is that if certain factors are added together, there will be a predictable certainty that deviancy (or pathology) will result [34].

This kind of forward-looking risk assessment is finding increasing favour in the juvenile justice field [35]. It is being used not simply as a diagnostic tool (i.e., to pinpoint a person's specific needs and deficits – the classic 'at risk' youth) but also in a prognostic manner to determine which young people are most likely to offend (i.e., which youth poses a risk). The construction of specific types of youth is thus achieved via the formulation of categories based on combinations of dynamic risk factors, and the accumulation of information about particular individuals. Profiles of individual young people are also constructed whereby all young people within a certain range of empirical indicators (e.g., age group, school record, type of family, previous criminal record) are dealt with according to the risk that they (presumably) pose now and into the future. It is a process of homogenisation wherein all people with certain similarities are treated similarly.

By their very nature, such tools reinterpret certain characteristics as representing the failings of individuals. This is because they are constructed on the basis of individualised data rather than analysis of, for example, how state policy affects particular groups. The formation of specific kinds of group and specific kinds of individual, as the outcome of inequality, discrimination and the absence of opportunity, is basically lost in such analysis. In its stead it is the consequences of these processes that are central to who is, or who is not, deemed to be at risk [36].

Ethnicity is an important component in this process. For example, being an indigenous person is counted as being a risk factor in some assessment processes [37]. When this occurs, one's heritage and community identity is degraded through its assessment as a contributing factor to youth deviancy. From the point of view of youth gangs research and intervention, similar issues are apparent. Ethnicity and community ties are frequently construed as core elements of what goes into the making of a gang member (as evident in moral panics about 'ethnic youth gangs'). Strong ethnic identification can thus be considered a risk factor when it comes to group deviancy, as evidenced in the discussion of young people of 'Middle Eastern appearance' in Chapter 4.

The identification of at-risk youth typically involves three steps: (i) the identification of specific indicators of the problem; (ii) the use of indicators to identify a target group; and (iii) the implementation of an intervention to bring the target group into line with the mainstream [38]. This popular policy process overlooks the ways in which institutions and policy processes themselves contribute to social problems involving young people, and instead focusses on changing the young people. The paradoxical element of this process is that the 'at risk' come to be stigmatised, adding to their sense of difference and marginality. Moreover, the phenomenon of 'false positives' means that individuals may suffer the negative consequences of unwanted and unneeded intervention solely due to their membership of a 'high risk' group rather than due to their individual risk profile or actual behaviour [39].

When applied to gangs, such risk analysis takes the form of social profiling. This involves constructing a matrix of variables and matching individuals to the variables described in the gang matrix. Such a process tends to be descriptive, and does little to provide a basis for understanding why and how specific groups of young people experience problems or find meaning in their lives.

Social profiling in the name of risk assessment assumes certain things about 'normality' and the inherent correctness of the *status quo*. In effect, the tools can also resort to stereotypes. It is useful in this regard to compare and contrast two types of social profiling – one based upon actual criminal incidents, the other on predictive factors (see Table 9.1) [40].

The first type of profiling acts as a funnel, to sift individuals until a small number of suspects are identified and against whom police can then proceed to take action. The second type of profiling, however, is geared to expanding the suspect terrain. As more variables are added to the list of key identifiers, the process tends to widen the scope of surveillance and intervention.

The second form of social profiling identified in Table 9.1 is especially problematic from the point of view of youth gangs intervention. This is because there is often confusion between identification of a gang and those who engage in 'gang-related behaviour' (see Chapters 2 and 3). This opens the door for extensive net-widening vis-à-vis social profiling. For example, in practical terms there is frequently a conflation of youth gangs and ethnicity in that each may share in the identity of the other, even though they are quite different social constructs. There is also often confusion surrounding the link between gang status and fighting. In this instance, groups of youths who engage in street fights may be perceived to be members of a gang even when not part of a youth gang as such.

Table 9.1   Two types of social profiling

Funnelling	Net-widening
Focus: Criminality Criminal Act – Specific offence	Focus: Gang association Group membership – General behaviour
Process: Reactive – Action after something has occurred	Process: Pre-emptive – Action before anything has happened
Evidence: Based on crime scene investigation and flowing outwards from there	Evidence: Based on loose descriptors, stereotypes and local reputation
Movement from individual event/person to group of suspects, then back to particular matching profile	Movement from identification of group as a whole to inclusion of more and more selected individuals as having (at least some) attributes of the target group
Consequence: Narrows the range and number of suspects around specific criminal cases, based on crime scene investigation findings	Consequence: Increases the range of those potentially placed under surveillance and subject to possible intervention

Increased surveillance and intervention, based upon association, and reinforced through social profiling, can lead to a greater likelihood of the young people adopting a gang identification and thus engagement in violent and/or criminal behaviour. For example, we know that identification shapes involvement in gang-related activity: young people behave in accordance with who they say they are [41]. If police and other authority figures intervene in ways that bolster a particular form of identification over other possible identities (e.g., ethnic youth gang versus 'ordinary' member of the community), then greater likelihood of group violence and anti-social behaviour is sure to follow. Inappropriate intervention can thus generate the very thing it is meant to preclude – namely, the formation and intensification of gangs and gang activity. Patterns of policing can be evaluated in the light of this revelation.

Ethnically targeted policing

How police respond to ethnic-minority youth is linked to personal attitudes as well as operational policies. In many day-to-day interactions there are in fact few problems in the relationship between police and ethnic-minority young people. They may not always get along, but it is not usually open warfare either. Moreover, when media stories flare up regarding presumed ethnic criminality and deviancy, it is frequently the police spokespeople who do their best to provide a calm and reassuring voice in counterpoint to the sensationalist stereotype. Nonetheless, friction often does exist between mainstream police and many ethnic minorities. In part this is due to the predominance of certain ways of working rather than others. This is evident in research which has documented police–youth relations generally [42].

Police–youth relations are circumscribed by the status and position of ethnic-minority youth as young people, and by their standing as members of particular ethnic-minority groups. Police perceptions of young people in general will colour how and when they intervene in young people's lives. Their perceptions and attitudes towards particular ethnic minorities likewise have an influence on how they use their discretion, and the manner in which they will intervene in relation to particular individuals and groups.

In our 1990s Melbourne research the police were seen to play a pivotal role in the affairs of young people. A number of issues were highlighted. In particular, it identified that police harassment, unfair policing and racist policing played significant roles in the relationship between ethnic-minority youth and the police [43].

Most of the Pacific Islander background young people who participated in the research, for example, complained of police harassment. They were also conscious of 'public disapproval' by other people in public places, experienced harassment from private security guards and had trouble with shopkeepers. As one of them said,

> Police'll always pull ya up, no matter what to do, no matter who you're with, they'll always pull ya up and check ya, search ya, strip ya. And you don't want that. You want to be able to walk down the street and the coppers just drive past ya and look at ya and look away.
> (Pacific Islander-Australian young man, Melbourne)

The young people spoke of being hassled, searched and threatened by the police. A number also said that they had been subjected to physical abuse.

Many young people can handle what police do, but what they cannot handle is the experience that they are being treated unfairly by the police. For instance, Turkish-Australian young people had generally had a bad experience consisting of one of two kinds of interaction. First, a number said that they were hassled, searched on the street or threatened by the police. They did not think that this was fair. As a young Turkish respondent saw it,

> Every time we hang around with groups they try to disperse us and treat us as if we're just nothing. One day we were hanging around at the shopping centre with friends and talking there and one of the shop owners must have complained and the cops came and just kicked us out of there.
>
> (Turkish-Australian young man, Melbourne)

Another said:

> Not knowing what the police is going on about and just keep interrogating you for some reason where you get 'pissed off' and you're like 'What are you asking me for? What's the problem, what's the drama?' And then when the police 'arse' up a bit and then the situation could get out of control you know, which depends on you know, what you're feeling at the time – whether you want to put up with it, just co-operate, or whether you really don't want to co-operate and feel that your rights are being impeded on.
>
> (Turkish-Australian young man, Melbourne)

Second, a number of the respondents had been caught by the police while committing a crime or associating with someone else who was committing a crime. The issue was not the police intervention *per se* but how they intervened. The abuse does not have to be simply physical:

> The cop that took me to County Court [abused me], not physical-wise, like not in hurting me wise, but mentally, like the way he talked to me, charged me, the way he was harassing me during the court case 'You're gonna go to jail, that's it.' He was laughing at me.
>
> (Turkish-Australian young man, Melbourne)

The problem here is less that of the police doing their job, and rightfully enforcing the law, than that of not treating the young people with respect and dignity in the course of performing their legal duties.

Most of the young people in the Melbourne study spoke (sympathetically) about how Asians are on the receiving end of media racism. According to the Vietnamese background young people, this was no less true when it came to police relationships with Asian young people:

> They tease you about your culture, the way you look, your eyes and that. And then they beat you.
>
> (Vietnamese-Australian young man, Melbourne)

> Sometimes we're too scared to walk on the streets because of the police. They do body searches on the street and strip searches in houses. Police are racist. They swear at you and tell you to 'go back to your own country, you smelly dog'. They break into the house, bash us for nothing, then wreck the door, mess everything up and then leave without cleaning up or nothing. Food, rubbish, clothes chucked all over the floor, like they're burgling us.
>
> (Vietnamese-Australian young man, Melbourne)

These findings are consistent with other research that has examined Vietnamese-Australian youth and police relations in places such as Sydney and Melbourne. That is, young Asian people tend to be key targets of unnecessary, and often racially offensive, police intervention [44].

A key issue here is that the perceptions of policing in general are based upon very negative experiences and images. These, in turn, have a major impact upon whether or not the young people have confidence in, or are fearful of, the police. Regardless of actual face-to-face experiences, the problem of how perceptions influence social activities also warrants greater attention. Even those young people who do not have much direct contact with the police may feel antagonistic towards them – and vice versa with regard to police attitudes and perceptions of particular ethnic-minority groups. The more you harass and target specific groups, and the more resentful and unco-operative they become, the more likely it is that they will be perceived as outsiders generally and the more likely they will act in ways that 'justify' further police intervention.

Aggressive street policing of a zero-tolerance nature is especially evident in the case of young Muslim- and Arab-Australians living in the western suburbs of Sydney. In the national youth gangs research carried out in the mid-2000s, young people in Bankstown were asked about the nature of their contact with the police. Typically, the responses from Lebanese background young people were highly negative, and at times highly combative. A common complaint was that they were constantly being harassed:

They walk up to me like I'm some kind of – some kind of terrorist. I'm sitting down, smoking or something and they come and ask questions. Why I don't know, maybe my haircut, maybe my dress – the way I get dressed up. They say: 'What are you doing here?" or 'What's your name?' 'Give me your ID?', 'Where have you been for the last half an hour or an hour?' Like what am I going to say? 'I've been sitting here for half an hour, waiting for the bus or some shit.' I don't know. It's getting bad and it's getting hectic.

(Lebanese-Australian young man, Sydney)

The same young person then mentioned a brawl along the riverfront. 'It was practically Lebos – a whole group of Lebos – 30 or 40 against the coppers – all in a brawl.' The antagonistic nature of the relationship between the young people and the police is also captured in the comment of another respondent:

We contact – what it means like – well me and my mates are being smart to the coppers, you know what I mean. They'll come to us, they'll warn us 'If we see you here again, we're going to take you in'. You know what I mean? Me and my mates say "fuck 'em" We'll stay here". You know what I mean? The coppers come back after two minutes and see us here and they end up saying 'You're under arrest' and then we have a struggle. We have a wrestle with 'em. You know what I mean?

(Lebanese-Australian young man, Sydney)

Another young person made the link between the nature of police intervention and subsequent conflicts:

Most of the time it's because they see a big group of Lebos hanging out and they just walk up 'What are you doing here? Why? Go home. Shouldn't you be at home? Shouldn't you be at school?' And they check up your details and like I remember one time a police officer asked me if I had a record and I never had it – me I didn't know I had a record. I just thought – I got into a fight a few weeks before and I thought it was just a caution and I said 'No.' And usually when you say 'No' they walk off, but this guy checked up and after that, you know, started 'Fuck you. Lying to the police and you fucking this and fucking that', and pushed me against a wall and that and one of my friends came from behind him, you know, as soon as he put his hand on the police officer another cop came and started elbowing him in the back and then, you know, after that it ended up in a sort of scuffle between us and them.

(Lebanese-Australian young man, Sydney)

Street violence of various kinds, including violence involving the police, featured strongly in the lives of these young people. The material basis for this street violence lies in the disadvantages and injuries of social inequality. The public images of ethnic-minority youth are further shaped by racialised media portrayals, and by the manner in which police intervene in their lives. They are also influenced by actual incidents of violence, such as fights between groups of young people on the street.

Institutionalised racism (in the form of restrictive life chances and the dominance of monocultural norms), economic marginalisation (in the form of unemployment and poverty) and reliance upon particular notions of masculinity (in the form of reliance on physical and symbolic markers of toughness) put these young people into a particularly vulnerable and volatile social situation. This, in turn, is associated with a central paradox in the lives of ethnic-minority youth. Specifically, the assertion of identity and collective social power via membership of street groups and engagement in fighting, while forged in the context of rejecting racism and threats from outsiders, simultaneously reinforces the subordinate or outsider position of, and negative social reaction directed towards, these same groups of young people. In effect, the spectre of 'ethnic criminality' is effectively bolstered by the actions of youth ethnic-minority youth themselves, as they struggle to negotiate their masculinities, ethnicities and class situations [45].

Leaving the gang

A key question in developing appropriate anti-gang strategies is: What are the social processes involved in the movement of individuals and groups from one type of group formation towards (or away from) a gang formation? European work on this question provides insights that are relevant to Australian gangs research. For example, as Bjorgo points out, street gangs have usually emerged out of something else, such as a play group, a clique of friends or a loose subculture [46]. Significantly, he describes how an immigrant youth gang (the Warriors) in Copenhagen emerged in response to White Power gangs. Australian research, as discussed in this book, has highlighted the ways in which racism permeates the lives of ethnic-minority youth and that group formation, and street

Table 9.2 Entry factors in relation to extremist youth subcultures

Attractions to join
Ideology and politics
  Provocation and anger
  Protection
  Drifting
  Thrill seeking
  Violence, weapons and uniforms
  Youth rebels go to the Right
  Search for substitute families and father figures
  Search for friends and community
  Search for status and identity

Incentives to stay
Positive characteristics of group, such as friendships
  Fear of negative sanctions from the group
  Loss of protection against former enemies
  Nowhere to go
  Fear that career prospects are already ruined

Table 9.3 Exit factors in relation to extremist youth subcultures

Push factors
Negative social sanctions
  Lose faith in the ideology and politics of group or movement
  Disillusioned with inner workings and activities of group
  Losing confidence, status and position in group
  Become exhausted and can no longer take the pressure

Pull factors
Longing for the freedoms of a 'normal' life
  Getting too old for what they are doing
  Jeopardise their career prospects and personal futures
  Establish a family with new responsibilities for spouse and children

fights, are directly linked to issues of protection, social status and group identity.

Analysis of factors affecting entry to and exit from youth gangs is important here, as indicated in Tables 9.2 and 9.3. A mapping out of such factors for specific groups at a local level in Australia is important to understanding the nature, dynamics and attractions of youth gangs. The figures are taken from Bjorgo's work on extremist youth groups and gangs in Europe [47].

Issues of entry and exit are nonetheless complex. They are also highly specific to particular social contexts and particular types of youth-group formation. US and South African research on membership processes, for example, challenge the notion that individuals face difficulties in either entry or exit [48]. In most instances, young people can refuse to join gangs without reprisal, and gang members (especially marginal members) can typically leave the gang without serious consequences. One implication of this is that if gang entry and exit is fluid, and if individuals tend not to remain gang members for long periods of time, then members can be drawn away through the provision of attractive alternatives.

It is important in consideration of anti-gang strategies to bear in mind the positive features of gangs for many young people (and, in some cases, for their parents and other family members). This is one of the key points of Chapter 6, which pointed out that gangs frequently comprise family members. Gangs can provide support and security for vulnerable groups of young people. They can provide opportunities for status, group identity and excitement. They provide a mechanism for young people to cope with oppressive environments, and represent one response or option to chronic marginalisation and social exclusion. All of these features point to the importance of peers and peer networks in the lives of young people but leave open the matter of the social content of youth-group formation. The problem is not with youth groups as such; it is with what youth groups do. This, in turn, is determined by the context within which they form, behave and react.

An important part of strategic thinking is that any policy or intervention should be considered and evaluated in the light of the baseline information generated in other facets of gangs research (e.g., identification of youth-group formations, processes of group transformation). Knowledge of how and why particular groups disintegrate is also essential. Key factors in gang disintegration include:

- growing out of gang life through natural maturation and new priorities in life;
- defeat of the group by external use of force;
- loss of external enemies or threat;
- loss of identity, status and image;
- decay of group cohesiveness, solidarity and attraction value;
- fragmentation of the group into smaller units which may be too weak to survive [49].

There are also issues pertaining to personal wellbeing, and changes and challenges to this over time, that impact upon individual participation in gangs. Specifically, in interviews with gang members it became apparent that many begin to experience violence as frightening. For example, they start to get tired of the constant threat of being a target:

> What kinds of things do you think would help to make you happier? Less violence on the streets and knowing that I can walk out my door without getting bashed by somebody I know and stuff.
>
> (18-year-old young man, Canberra)

> Are there any bad things that arise from being a member of your group? Yeah 'cause if like other people from elsewhere don't like somebody in the group and they know you're friends with him, so they'll start on you too if they see you alone. That's happened to me too.
>
> (18-year-old young man, Canberra)

In other cases, while the gang was perceived to provide some form of protection from violence, it nonetheless had the impact of limiting opportunities and personal options into the future:

> What are some of the good things about being a member of a group? You don't get bashed. Yeah like if you're with big people, big people wouldn't – you know you don't wanna mess with them. Are there any bad things? You get dragged into everything... Actually, I'd be better off I reckon than I am right now. Honestly I do. Like yeah, if I hadn't hung around like the group I'm hanging around with, I honestly – like I might get a job or something and I wouldn't have chucked in school. I coulda kept going.
>
> (18-year-old young man, Canberra)

The culture of violence was also scary for some. Issues such as not knowing the rules of engagement, the escalating use of weapons, the large number of combatants, and actual injury and harm associated with street fighting are collectively a cause of alarm:

> 'cause young people – if there's nothing much to do, they just get in trouble and then these days, there's a lot of violence on television and all that, gang movies and they just want to be a gang and that. It was like me, I always used to want to be in a gang and that, then I just hated it. It was what they used to do to me to see if I was strong enough. They just used to bash me. Do you think there were good things at the time when you joined? Oh yeah, I used to

love the violence – yeah, but things have changed. People have been killed...They're professionals and if they do something, they won't get caught.

(14-year-old young man, Canberra)

Why did you like to hang out together? 'cause we were unstoppable together. No one could touch us. And what kind of things did you have in common? That we all fight really well and we all liked to get drunk and that's about it...We all grew up together. He says he doesn't want to hang out with most of them anymore. Why? Because they're crazy and they like to hurt people beyond real hurt and once you get to a certain age you start to think about the fact that, shit, someone's half dead...I was the youngest, I was 14.

(19-year-old young man, Melbourne)

Then there is the sheer stupidity of the violence:

Umm, most people, they've grown up out of it and people have just started thinking of positives and just doing the right things because I have a friend who stabbed someone and he went to gaol so that was a message to everyone, a wake-up call...Well, pretty much now everyone's grown up so most of the people they don't hang out, they are trying to survive and make a life, so pretty much in their spare time, they try and get a job...I guess it was just stupidity, just like someone would look at you and you'd be like 'what are you looking at?' And you'd just start fighting over nothing.

(24-year-old young man, Melbourne)

Leaving the gang therefore is often generated 'from within' rather than due to external drivers and state intervention. Nevertheless, planned exit strategies ought to be in place that can facilitate the movement of individuals out of the gang and into a new life course, when their time has come to leave.

Conclusion

Regardless of the realities and myths surrounding youth gangs in Australia today, three key intervention issues stand out. First, the perception that youth gangs exist and are a danger to the community will almost inevitably generate action on the part of the authorities, regardless of what is happening at the grassroots level. Second, analysis suggests that the political and economic conditions for potential growth in gang-related behaviour currently exist, and that action is required now in order to forestall future problems. Third, the discourses of gang have largely been racialised in most places around Australia, with ethnic-minority youth the main subject of such public discourses. These observations require sensitivity to the implicit and explicit social issues that inevitably accompany any consideration of police and community responses to youth-gang-related behaviour and to ethnic-minority young people generally.

Existing research highlights the importance of dealing with the youth-gang phenomenon across a number of dimensions, taking into account the very different social histories and socio-economic circumstances of young people. While youth gangs as such are not a major problem in Australian society at present, there is no doubt that without constructive proactive intervention, they could emerge as an issue of substantive public concern. The pre-conditions for more serious types of gang formation are becoming more entrenched in the Australian context – poverty, high levels of youth unemployment, precarious job markets, and ghettoisation in our larger cities. It is these pre-conditions that need to be addressed if we are truly serious about addressing youth-gang issues.

10
Beyond Gangs

Introduction

This book is ostensibly about youth gangs in Australia. It has acknowledged debates and controversies surrounding the definition and interpretation of youth gangs. It has drawn upon extensive empirical research into the life worlds of street-frequenting young people around the country. This research has been carried out over the course of almost 20 years, and has taken the form of face-to-face interviews, survey questionnaires and document analysis. The book has tried to be sensitive to the voices and concerns of the young people, as well as providing a conceptual lens through which to understand what is being said and why.

Yet the enigmas and ambiguities remain. Questions such as 'What is a youth gang?' and 'What do youth gangs mean for young people, their communities and for society as a whole?' seem even more difficult – or more simple – to answer today than when I first embarked upon youth gangs research in the early 1990s. To me, this implies several things.

First, when it comes to youth gangs, there is no set recipe or trait analysis that can adequately capture the flow and dynamics of everyday life. In social studies of this kind, we tend to find what we look for – 'youth gangs' and 'violent young men' – as if these exist in themselves outside other aspects of young people's lives. As discussed in Chapter 2, however, a different cut of the data, a different methodological emphasis – from the group to the individual, from the gang-related activity to the totality of mundane day-to-day activities – reveals far more complicated pictures of how these young people live their lives. The gang does not have to be an overwhelming influence in their life, dominating all relationships and all emotions. Nor does gang-related aggression have to

178

take centre stage everywhere and at all times. There is peace, and giving, and solidarity, and love, and affection, too. If we look for the positives, of gangs and of those who join them, then these, as well, can be found. It all depends upon where and how we turn our analytical gaze.

Second, it is important to raise doubts about whether or not youth gangs are really the central problem anyway. Across the youth gangs literature, whether as backdrop or explanation, most writers recognise that the young people at the centre of gangs research are disadvantaged and/or abused in some way. These structural features of their lives are crucial to gang formation and youth violence around the world, as discussed in Chapter 4. Yet so much analysis and commentary continues to be focussed on the young people themselves as the problem as if policy and intervention can ever really make a difference by attempting to change individuals but not the social structures and opportunities that shape their lives en masse. It seems easier to speak about specific projects and specific programmes than to raise fundamental issues of social inequality, racism and repressive state power.

This chapter continues these musings by providing a few final critical reflections on the doing of youth gangs research and interpretations of what it is that we find when doing so. The main attention is on matters pertaining to violence – as seen through the prisms of class, gender and cultural diversity.

Street violence and class conflict

The humiliations and chronic disrespect associated with unequal distribution and access to societal resources manifest themselves in a particular moral economy on the street. Youth violence is frequently portrayed as the search for, and assertion of, social respect, based upon the body (see Chapter 8). But this is only one part of the picture, and a problematic one at that. Understanding why some young men are more violent or engage in violence more than others is not the same as explaining the violence or endorsing this violence.

The empirical situation of members of youth gangs has been described in terms of 'disadvantage', 'poverty' and 'social exclusion' by writers of various political and methodological persuasion. Such descriptions have been a feature of positivist as well as critical criminologists; there is nothing new in the idea, for example, that poverty is somehow linked to crime. Any violence or other anti-social behaviour arising from this foundation, however, is more often than not deemed to be the key issue and, accordingly, the basis for designing policy and intervention strategies. Thus the answer to the 'gang problem' tends to be framed in terms of what to do about or to the gang members (an effect of class inequality) rather than how to tackle the structures that generate poor and rich to begin with (a structural relation of class inequality).

This is illustrated in present government policies, national and state, that attempt to maximise the efficiency of the state in cushioning the community against the impact of social problems, rather than dealing with the generative conditions of these social problems. As Jamrozik puts it,

> Many of the issues that are commonly regarded as 'social problems' are indeed normal conditions in a free-market society. For example, unemployment, poverty, inequality and law-breaking are normal conditions, directly related to and stemming from particular political, economic and social arrangements.... The activities that are provided to ostensibly remedy or alleviate the given problem serve, first and foremost, to legitimise the situation and at the same time alleviate public consciousness by demonstrating that the government cares and aims to remedy the situation. The outcome is usually a demonstration of an inadequacy or fault of the affected population – it is indeed an activity creating a 'blaming the victim' syndrome [1].

Patterns of activity, including youth-gang-related behaviour, are shaped by class position and class relations. Where young people are located in the class structure will influence the kinds of social activity they engage in, the propensity to engage in such activity and the intensity of that involvement (and, of course, whether it will be identified by the state as posing a risk or threat, and whether it will be policed or punished). Responses to youth gangs that do not accept this fundamental proposition can only ever, at best, ameliorate the situation for some or, as is more likely, default into highly coercive forms of suppression.

Understanding the source of the problem, and the limitations of dealing with structural violence through state-sponsored repression, is not, however, the same thing as endorsing or condoning the street violence that occurs. There is nothing romantic, productive or progressive about street crime. Such crime

> divides the working class against itself, deepens the divisions between employed and unemployed, sharpens racial antagonism, confirms ethnic stereotypes, and depreciates the quality of life in working-class neighbourhoods. It helps to recruit 'respectable' residents into

campaigns for tougher 'law and order' measures. Even if crime can be seen to be precipitated by conditions of poverty, marginalization and 'super-exploitation', it provides no solution to these problems [2].

Youth gangs which engage in street violence and crime do so because of the humiliations and necessities imposed by capitalism, but such activities generally constitute little more than an accommodation to the existing order [3].

To put it differently, youth gangs in Australia and worldwide may be spawned by the conditions of life under global capitalism, but this does not justify or excuse thuggish street activities. Expressing anger through street fighting and predation upon other sections of the community are hardly progressive or desirable. Moreover, if those from the most economically and socially marginalised communities can be portrayed as 'deviant' and inherently criminal and evil, then people will be less willing to consider the fact that they constitute the social groups with the highest rates of unemployment and poverty.

How different can things be, however, when those who have been marginalised become politically organised. It is notable in this regard that progressive movements have occasionally been born out of the crucible of gang life. The Black Panthers in the US emerged out of such formations. And it is important to note how youth gangs in the US, when given a voice, have emphasised the systemic processes of exclusion from mainstream educational, economic and social life that have made them what they are [4]. In the Australian context, the persistent marginalisation and scapegoating of young Arab-background and Muslim people in western Sydney likewise opens the door to explicit political organising around progressive themes. As we saw in Chapters 3 and 4, many of the young men in these gangs have sought to valorise their ethnicity (and masculinity) through anti-social forms, such as territorialism and aggressive masculinity. Yet the seeds are there for the formation of specifically political responses to negative police interventions and social inequalities.

Further to this, it is important not to view all street violence as necessarily dysfunctional from a systemic perspective. For example, violence can signal resistance against social hierarchy, racial oppression and structural disadvantage: 'Historical and cross-cultural scholarship has demonstrated that much male violence is an ambiguous form of protest or rebellion against social hierarchies based on social class, caste and racial/ethnic differences' [5]. Symbolic protest and collective cultural resistance can become part of the traditions and experiences of communities under pressure. To whom or what youth-gang violence is directed is, of course, a matter of continuing and considerable concern as this, too, forms part of the politics of male violence.

Ethnic and Aboriginal identity and intergroup conflict

One of the striking things about doing youth gangs research over a number of years, for example, has been the level and intensity of inter-ethnic rivalry and conflict. Exploring this further is worthwhile but first requires an initial detour into methodological considerations before reconsideration of what is going on at the ground level.

Much of the early youth gangs research in Australia tended to be predominantly ethno-specific in focus and orientation (see Chapter 3). Valuable work was undertaken, for example, on Lebanese youth in Sydney, and Italian and Greek youth in Adelaide. The emphasis tended to be on the specific features of a particular group, and social relation-ships and social dynamics were examined from the point of view that these groups are at the centre of the research gaze. As part of this anal-ysis, some very interesting and thought-provoking aspects of identity were uncovered. For example, the Adelaide study showed how Italians and Greeks both came to identify with the signifier 'Wogs' and then sub-verted the negativity of the label by adopting it as a sign of pride and belonging [6]. Likewise, the Sydney research discusses how Syrian-born youth learn to be comfortable being labelled 'Lebanese', since it signi-fies a social connection of meaningful substance for the young people involved. Sydney research also confirmed the hybrid character of ethnic identity – the strategic use of being 'Lebanese', 'Australian' or 'Lebanese-Australian', depending on the immediate social circumstances [7].

These examples of shared and hybrid identification are nevertheless bound by the specific composition of the groups at hand. That is, who is or is not perceived or allowed to be part of the group is broadly shaped by ethnicity (and stereotypes pertaining to ethnicity). Study of these groups tended to focus on in-group relationships and social dynamics. In the case of external relationships, research has tended to look mainly at a group's interaction with Anglo youth or the police, rather than other groups of ethnic-minority youth.

There has also been research that has perhaps been more ethno-general in approach, in that several groups of ethnic-minority youth may be incorporated into an overall study, such as our 1990s Melbourne research. Yet even here the tendency was to carry out research in an ethno-specific way. Specific groups, such as the Vietnamese, Somalian and Pacific Islander, were generally collapsed into one-dimensional categories. Then they were studied solely in terms of the specific (presumed or assigned) group membership itself rather than in relation to other ethnic groups.

One consequence of this approach was that, for example, Pacific Islanders tend to be treated as a unified social group, when in fact there are major social, cultural and historical differences that exist between Maori, Samoan, Fijian and other island communities. This kind of categorisation (based on simple geography) belies the complexity and differences amongst the young people who are included in the artificially constructed group 'Pacific Islander'. It also may not reflect what the young people themselves think about their ethnic or community identification. More generally, little is revealed about how young people from particular ethnic-minority backgrounds relate to similarly positioned young people from other ethnic communities and local neighbourhoods.

Later research associated with the national youth gangs project did capture the inter-ethnic dimension to a greater extent than previous work (see Chapter 3). But some of this research also revealed youth perceptions that were disturbing insofar as they speak of entrenched identities and practices that require further interpretation.

For example, another perspective on indigenous gang formation (see Chapter 6) was provided by non-indigenous young people who were also interviewed for the national youth gangs study. One set of comments came from young Anglo-Australian people in Perth. A common theme was the idea that indigenous youth engaged in a form of reverse racism. This is reflected in the following comments by two separate respondents:

> Like Aboriginals are a better race, that they're better than us and no one's really quite game to fight with them and things like that ... Umm, getting things stolen from me because I was white and my friends have had things stolen out of their bags and they've been ganged up on at school like.

> Most of the Aboriginals stick together. We're still friends with 'em, but they stick together in one group, so sometimes they gang up on white people or treat them like they're lower or something like that. But not – they wouldn't go round bashing 'em up for no reason, yeah, but you can just see it.

Another non-indigenous Perth respondent was asked why they said that if there was ever an incident with an Aboriginal young person and a white young person, the authorities were just going to blame the Aboriginal person straight out:

> I'd have to say it's the Aboriginal's behaviour. Like some of them I reckon are alright, but on the whole when they're in a group, they just break windows and stuff yeah ... Umm, like well Miss X – if I can say that – if there's ever something going on, she'll instantly – I'm not sure if it's just 'cause they're trouble makers – but she'll instantly blame Y and W because they're Aboriginal. It's like even though most of the time it's either me or my other mates that are doing it. We don't deliberately try to get them into trouble or anything, but they instantly just assume it's them. Of course we'd own up, but its weird how they just assume they're the ones responsible.

Perhaps part of the reason why indigenous young people are singled out for being responsible for wrongdoing, whether or not they have perpetrated the trouble, lies in the following observation by another respondent:

> It's not apparent all the time, but [racism] is there between the Aboriginals and the whites and the Asians and the Middle Eastern people. Just general stuff that goes on. Like a lot of people think that it's always the white people that are giving out the racism, but it's actually I've seen more of the other way ... If they start making accusations about other people in the group usually there's a white group involved, and also Aboriginals have this great like capacity to kind of stick up for their race and they've got loyalty. It's a great quality to have usually, but sometimes things get a bit out of hand when there's fights involved.

Other non-indigenous respondents alleged that it was usually indigenous young people who start fights at school; and group loyalty ensures that their presence will certainly be felt regardless of how a conflict originates.

In Darwin, a number of the 'Asian' (e.g., Chinese, Vietnamese, Malaysian-Australians) young people also spoke about the local family-based indigenous gangs. One commented:

> There's nothing to do. They wanna look good. They wanna think they're tougher than other groups. They wanna be superior. They want the attention and they wanna also give the message 'Oh you

can't mess around with us. Don't come onto our territory or anything like that.'

Another pointed to deep resentment, and constant harassment, of Asian young people by indigenous people. Threats to the Asian young people were continuous and in many cases backed up by action. By way of contrast, indigenous young people in Canberra spoke about how they relate to and get along with Indian-background young people. The nature of specific places, and the ethnic and racial composition of specific local populations, influences who hangs around with whom and which groups are in an antagonistic relationship.

These kinds of observation and perception were also mirrored in how non-Lebanese young people in Sydney spoke about Lebanese young people in their neighbourhoods and schools. Large family-based groups, especially if they included young people with apparent 'chips on their shoulder', were seen by those outside them as threatening and highly intimidating.

While one can point to structural and cultural conditions that underpin this kind of group behaviour, such as colonialism and systematic processes of racial vilification (see Chapters 4 and 6), for young people who are not indigenous or Lebanese-Australian, the experience can also have lasting negative effects. Again, the actual behaviour and attitudes of young people at street level can be hurtful and disrespectful at an interpersonal level. Social conflict is an inevitable outcome of inequalities that position identifiable communities differently within the Australian social mosaic. Those who are structurally disadvantaged often 'act out' in ways that make them into their own worst enemy in terms of those beyond their own peer groups and community. While understandable, it is not something that should be applauded. Rather, it needs to be responded to in ways that can break down the barriers separating identifiable communities from each other.

Young women and violence

The vexed question of female engagement in, and association with, youth gangs is complicated by the intersection of gender, class and ethnicity/indigeneity as this is played out on the street and in the school. By and large our Australian youth gangs research did not find much evidence of either specific gangs of young women or young women playing an integral role in the fighting side of male-dominated youth gangs.

However, as always, this statement requires further scrutiny and critical reflection.

For instance, the one major exception to these findings is indigenous young women. Over the years, and in different parts of the country, indigenous young women did sometimes refer to themselves as gangs, and did talk about getting into punch-ups with other groups of young women (including other indigenous young women). In research we undertook in the Northern Territory in the late 1990s, for example, young indigenous women in Darwin talked about their fights with the gang down the road in Palmerston. The reference by these young women to themselves as gangs was quite explicit, as was mention of street fights with other groups of young women.

Sustained discussions with individual young women, however, reveal some of the complexities of self-definition when it comes to the gang label. This is borne out in the interview extract below, which is reproduced at length in order to provide a sense of the nuances and dynamics surrounding public perceptions and group behaviours:

> Her special group is made up primarily of her sisters. There's four of them and four of her friends, so a total of eight. They have all committed various crimes and have records.

Researcher: Does your group have a name?

Interviewee: No but when we used to walk around X High, everyone called us a group – like a gang – and we got sent to the principal's office and they said: 'We don't like having gangs.' And we said: 'Look, we're not gangs. If you want us to be gangs, we'll be gangs, but we're not, so yeah.'

> They are all Aboriginal girls, they all like the same music. The oldest is 22, and the youngest is 15 years old.

Researcher: Do members of your group enjoy participating in illegal or anti-social activities? What kinds of things?

Interviewee: Prostitution. Not selling themselves, but having sex for money. Yeah that's about it. Oh, and selling drugs.

Researcher: So when do you get together with lots of others? Is it for special events?

Interviewee: Friday nights is the drinking night. All of us get maggotted and go to [town] and that. Sort of like 50 of us together.

Researcher: So why do young people like to join groups such as yours? What's the attraction do you think?

Interviewee: The attraction is – we're not a gang, okay. A gang is when you've got knives and guns. People call us a gang, but we're more like a friendly gang. Like people come and people go, okay. But with gangs they can't leave. So we don't care if people come and go, so yeah. People like us – who we are.

Researcher: What are some of the good things about being a member of a group?

Interviewee: Umm, people love you – who you are. You have – no one cares what your opinion is. Like you can say anything you want and no one has got it against you. We have no violence against us – one another.

Researcher: So what are the bad things that come out of being a member of a group sometimes?

Interviewee: Oh well all of us stick together, okay, and if one of us are dobbing each other – like dobbing us in to the police or talking about us – the other tells us and we go against each other and that. One of us put – all of us put a girl in hospital for dobbing us in to the police. We put her in intensive care. You know where you're on the machine for life. Yeah we put her in there, but that hardly happens unless people dob us in.

Researcher: Did she recover?

Interviewee: Yeah, she's out now.

Researcher: Do you ever see large groups in [town]?

Interviewee: We don't see 'em together – like we're together – the only reason we see each other is to fight, okay.

Researcher: How do you know that there's going to be a fight?

Interviewee: Well people – we walk past people in a big gang and they look at us and we go up to 'em like ready to go 'come on, let's go then', and then all their gang comes and that's how we collide.

Researcher: Right, and how often does that happen?

Interviewee: Nearly every day.

Researcher: Why are there regular fights do you think? Is it something to do?

Interviewee: Well mainly it's because we don't like getting stared at, okay. If we're walking around the streets, we don't like people full on staring at us. That's what we don't like.

Researcher: Do you consider your special group to be a gang?

Interviewee: Oh it depends. People call us a gang. Everyone else calls us a gang, but we don't call each other a gang 'cause we're mainly sisters. So we just call ourselves sisters. We call each other – our gang name is Black Rules 'cause we all love blacks, so we say our name is Black Rules and we're just – [our territory is] mainly [town].

They engage in fights, stealing, burglary, graffitiing, drug use or selling, car theft, vandalism and threatening people, and she says their group is mainly concerned with criminal activities. She says her gang only uses alcohol; they don't use any drugs.

Interviewee: I've walked down the street and seen gangs bash one person – like ten of 'em bashed one person, but when the police get involved, like me and my other friend – she done it, but I get the blame for it, so I go to gaol for it. So that's what happens in gangs. You have no choice whether you go to gaol or not, you just have to abide by it since you're in a gang.

The young indigenous woman who we interviewed was 15 years of age at the time and living in Canberra. Her family and relations are her main peer group, and as a group they are publicly perceived to be a gang, a form of recognition that, in turn, brings forth their own name for the group. Violence is a constant and is frequently stirred by street-level interactions with other groups of young women. Solidarity is forged both through family ties and collective engagement in violence and through specific criminal acts.

As stated, very few of the youth gangs that we researched over the years seemed to incorporate young women into the core gang business of assaults, robbery and group fights. However, this finding is partly an artefact of the methods used to investigate youth gangs. While many of the interviews of gang members were carried out by female youth and community workers, the selection of interviewees was influenced both by research criteria (e.g., self-identification as a gang member) and based on the perceptions of the youth and community workers themselves as to which individuals were *bona fide* gang members, which in most instances led to a focus on young men. It needs to be acknowledged that when the research method allows for and is more clearly and closely focussed on young women, the result may well be different.

Certainly US and UK research has provided a more sophisticated picture of young women's roles in youth gangs, although there remain major ambiguities in this literature regarding the precise nature of their role in relation to whether or not it is ancillary or active, involves sexual participation or victimisation, and the young women are encouragers or themselves an agent of violence [8]. Gender inequality appears to be central to understanding the causes, dynamics and consequences of young women's gang involvement. But their involvement varies depending upon the circumstances and the specific nature of the group. Just as one cannot generalise about youth gangs as a specific youth-group formation, so too we cannot generalise with regard to women's gang involvement.

We also need to be careful about what is said about the specific relationship between young women and violence. Compared with young men across the board, there is no doubt that violence is predominantly a 'guy thing'. However, it is a 'girl thing', too, in very specific and particular manifestations. Being a girlfriend to a boy or a young man who is street savvy and street tough generally implies support for activity that reinforces the tough image. In other words, while some young women do not engage in violence themselves, they may still actively encourage and support street fighting.

For other young women, fighting is, indeed, a regular part of their street experience, as indicated in the Canberra quote above. This experience need not be entirely negative. As with young men, there is evidence to suggest that for young women, fighting is likewise motivated by excitement, status and protection [9]. But whether this needs to be conceptualised specifically as gang violence is another question altogether. It is interesting to note, for example, that over half of all female appearances in juvenile court are related to acts intended to cause injury and theft, a much higher proportion compared with male juvenile offending [10]. Looking more closely at this, we find that in Queensland, although young males commit a far greater number of serious assaults, serious assaults comprise about three times the proportion of finalised court matters for girls compared with boys. In relation to less serious assaults by young women, a Queensland survey found that these frequently involved fights between girls in public places, such as shopping centres. In one-third of the cases the victim was another young woman, and in another one-third of the cases the victim was a police officer [11].

All of this adds up to one thing: a need to be conscious of both gender commonalities and gender differences in the experiences and activities of young men and young women, both on the street and in relation to gangs. As always, this will involve a conscious appreciation of how the intersections of class, gender and ethnicity both shape and reflect social relations at the individual, family and neighbourhood levels.

Conclusion

The research projects upon which this book has been based have yielded important insights into the nature of youth gangs in the Australian context. These findings have to be interpreted carefully and contextually, of course. This is because dealing with real or imagined gang problems is necessarily a complex process. It involves many different sorts of intervention, analysis and evaluation. It embodies different ideological perspectives and conflicting viewpoints.

Given the complexity and diversity of youth experiences in relation to being in a gang or engaging in gang-related behaviour, and given the profoundly similar circumstances that underpin such group formations across the globe, it is difficult to accept that the 'gang problem' is or should be the central agenda if we are serious about dealing with street violence and group deviancy.

Deep social and economic problems cannot be reduced to simplistic formulas that in the end serve to pile even more woe onto the backs of identified young people and their communities. It is time to go beyond gangs and to address the substantive issues of inequality, racism and oppression that lie at the heart of structural humiliation. The personal search for meaning and the struggle to attain respect are difficult and alienating for so many precisely because of the systemic limits and pressures on who they are and what they can become.

In the end, without significant social transformation and major improvements in collective life prospects, youth gangs will flourish, and violence – personal, family, structural and state – will dominate social life in 21st-century society.

Notes

1 Doing Gangs Research

1. Hallsworth, S. & Brotherton, D. (2011) *Urban Disorder and Gangs: A Critique and a Warning*. London: Runnymede; Hallsworth, S. & Young, T. (2008) 'Gang Talk and Gang Talkers: A Critique', *Crime, Media, Culture*, 4(2): 175–195.
2. Contrast, for example, the arguments presented in the following publications:

   Pitts, J. (2008) *Reluctant Gangsters: The Changing Face of Youth Crime*. Devon: Willan Publishing; Decker, S. & Weerman, F. (eds) (2005) *European Street Gangs and Troublesome Youth Groups*. Lanham, MD: Alta Mira Press; van Gemert, F., Peterson, D. & Lien, I-L. (eds) (2008) *Youth Gangs, Migration, and Ethnicity*. Devon: Willan; Goldson, B. (ed) (2011) *Youth in Crisis? 'Gangs', Territoriality and Violence*. London: Routledge;
3. For a detailed and personal account of the methods and approaches I have used over the years in undertaking youth gangs research, see White, R. (2011) 'The Challenges of Doing Collaborative Research', in L. Bartels & K. Richards (eds) *Qualitative Criminology: Stories from the Field*. Sydney: Federation Press.
4. For an overview of the debates, see Spergel, I. (2009) 'Gang Databases: To Be Or Not To Be', *Criminology & Public Policy*, 8(4): 667–674.
5. Wacquant, L. (2007) 'Three Pernicious Premises in the Study of the American Ghetto', in J. Hagedorn (ed) *Gangs in the Global City: Alternatives to Traditional Criminology*. Urbana and Chicago: University of Illinois Press; Venkatesh, S. (2008) *Gang Leader for a Day*. New York: The Penguin Press ; Hagedorn, J. (2008) *A World of Gangs: Armed Young Men and Gangsta Culture*. Minneapolis: University of Minnesota Press; Hallsworth, S. (2011) 'Gangland Britain? Realities, Fantasies and Industry', in B. Goldson (ed) *Youth in Crisis? 'Gangs', Territoriality and Violence*. London: Routledge.
6. See also White, R. (2011) 'The Challenges of Doing Collaborative Research', in L. Bartels & K. Richards (eds) *Qualitative Criminology: Stories from the Field*. Sydney: Federation Press.
7. Klein, M.W. (2002) 'Street Gangs: A Cross-National Perspective', in R. Huff (ed), *Gangs in America* (3rd edition). Thousand Oaks, California: Sage.
8. Anderson, E. (1999) *Code of the Street: Decency, Violence and the Moral Life of the Inner City*. New York: W.W. Norton & Company.
9. See, for example, van Gemert, F., Peterson, D. & Lien, I-L. (eds) (2008) *Youth Gangs, Migration, and Ethnicity*. Devon: Willan; Goldson, B. (ed) (2011) *Youth in Crisis? 'Gangs', Territoriality and Violence*. London: Routledge.
10. Hagedorn, J. (ed) (2008) *A World of Gangs: Armed Young Men and Gangsta Culture*. Minneapolis: University of Minnesota Press; Morgan, G. & Poynting, S. (eds) (2012) *Global Islamophobia: Muslims and Moral Panic in the West*. Surrey: Ashgate.

11. This observation is documented and repeatedly made by Hallsworth, S. & Brotherton, D. (2011) *Urban Disorder and Gangs: A Critique and a Warning*. London: Runnymede.

2   Gangs and Identity

1. Howell, J. (2000) *Youth Gang Programs and Strategies: Summary*. Washington, DC: US Department of Justice, Office of Justice Programs, Office of Juvenile Justice and Delinquency Prevention.
2. Hagedorn, J. (2008) *A World of Gangs: Armed Young Men and Gangsta Culture*. Minneapolis: University of Minnesota Press; Hagedorn, J. (ed) (2007) *Gangs in the Global City: Alternatives to Traditional Criminology*. Urbana and Chicago: University of Illinois Press; Hallsworth, S. & Young, T. (2008) 'Gang Talk and Gang Talkers: A Critique', *Crime Media Culture*, 4(2): 175–195; Alexander, C. (2008) *(Re)thinking 'Gangs'*. London: Runnymede Trust.
3. Hallsworth, S. & Young, T. (2008) 'Gang Talk and Gang Talkers: A Critique', *Crime Media Culture*, 4(2): 175–195.
4. United States Bureau of Justice Assistance (1997) *Addressing Community Gang Problems: A Model for Problem Solving*. Washington, DC: Office of Justice Programs, US Department of Justice.
5. Klein, M.W. (2002) 'Street Gangs: A Cross-National Perspective', in R. Huff (ed), *Gangs in America* (3rd edition). Thousand Oaks, California: Sage.
6. Klein, M., Maxson, C. & Miller, J. (eds) (1995) *The Modern Gang Reader*. Los Angeles: Roxbury Publishing; Miller, W.B. (1992) *Crime by Youth Gangs and Groups in the United States*. Washington, DC: US Department of Justice, Office of Justice Programs, Office of Juvenile Justice and Delinquency Prevention; Sanders, W. (1994) *Gangbangs and Drive-Bys: Grounded Culture and Juvenile Gang Violence*. New York: Aldine De Gruyter; Huff, R. (ed) (2002) *Gangs in America* (3rd edition). Thousand Oaks, California: Sage; Howell, J. & Moore, J. (2010) *History of Street Gangs in the United States*. National Gang Center Bulletin No. 4, Office of Juvenile Justice and Delinquency Prevention, US Department of Justice, Washington, DC; Howell, J., Egley, Jr., A. & Gleason, D. (2002) *Modern-Day Youth Gangs*. Juvenile Justice Bulletin, June. Washington, DC: Office of Juvenile Justice and Delinquency Prevention, US Department of Justice; Spergel, I.A. (1995) *The Youth Gang Problem*. New York: Oxford University Press; Howell, J.C. (1998) *Youth Gangs: An Overview*. Bulletin. Washington DC: US Department of Justice, Office of Justice Programs, Office of Juvenile Justice and Delinquency Prevention; Short, J. & Hughes, L. (eds) (2006) *Studying Youth Gangs*, Walnut Creek, CA: AltaMira Press.
7. Gordon, R. (1995) 'Street Gangs in Vancouver', in J. Creechan & R. Silverman (eds) *Canadian Delinquency*. Toronto: Prentice Hall; Gordon, R. (1997) 'Gangs in Vancouver', Justice/Immigration Domain Seminar, Ottawa, 27–28 February; Gordon, R. (2000) 'Criminal Business Organizations, Street Gangs and "wanna-be" Groups: A Vancouver Perspective', *Canadian Journal of Criminology*, January: 39–60; Gordon, R. & Foley, S. (1998) *Criminal Business Organizations, Street Gangs and Related Groups in Vancouver: The Report of the Greater Vancouver Gang Study*. Vancouver: Ministry of Attorney General;

Soulliere, N. (1998) *Youths and Gangs: Various Views, and Varied Strategies.* Ottawa: Research Centre, Canadian Police College; Bjorgo, T. (1998) 'Recruitment and Disengagement from Extreme Groups: The Case of Racist Youth Subcultures', *Paper Presented at 7th International Seminar on Environmental Criminology and Crime Analysis*, 21–24 June, Barcelona; Klein, M., H-J Kerner, Maxon, C. & Weitekamp, E. (eds) (2001) *The Eurogang Paradox: Street Gangs and Youth Groups in the U.S. and Europe.* Dordrecht: Kluwer Academic Publishers; Royal Canadian Mounted Police [RCMP] (2007) *Gang Prevention and Intervention Strategies.* Ottawa: RCMP; Pitts, J. (2008) *Reluctant Gangsters: The Changing Face of Youth Crime.* Devon: Willan Publishing; Decker, S. & Weerman, F. (eds) (2005) *European Street Gangs and Troublesome Youth Groups.* Lanham, MD: Alta Mira Press; van Gemert, F., Peterson, D. & Lien, I-L. (eds) (2008) *Youth Gangs, Migration, and Ethnicity.* Devon: Willan; Goldson, B. (ed) (2011) *Youth in Crisis? 'Gangs', Territoriality and Violence.* London: Routledge; Maclure, R. & Sotelo, M. (2004) 'Youth Gangs in Nicaragua: Gang Membership as Structured Individualization', *Journal of Youth Studies*, 7(4): 417–432; Standing, A. (2005) *The Threat of Gangs and Anti-Gangs Policy*, ISS Occasional Paper 116. South Africa: Institute for Security Studies; White, R. (2002) 'Understanding Youth Gangs', *Trends & Issues in Crime and Criminal Justice*, No. 237. Canberra: Australian Institute of Criminology; White, R. (2006) 'Youth Gang Research in Australia', in J. Short & L. Hughes (eds) *Studying Youth Gangs.* Walnut Creek, CA: AltaMira Press; White, R. (2008) 'Australian Youth Gangs and the Social Dynamics of Ethnicity', in F. van Gemert, D. Peterson & I-L Lien (eds) *Youth Gangs, Migration, and Ethnicity.* Devon: Willan; White, R. (2008) 'Disputed Definitions and Fluid Identities: The Limitations of Social Profiling in Relation to Ethnic Youth Gangs', *Youth Justice: an International Journal*, 8(2): 149–161.

8. Klein, M.W. (2002) 'Street Gangs: A Cross-National Perspective', in R. Huff (ed), *Gangs in America* (3rd edition). Thousand Oaks, California: Sage.

9. Standing, A. (2005) *The Threat of Gangs and Anti-Gangs Policy*, ISS Occasional Paper 116. South Africa: Institute for Security Studies.

10. John Howard Society of Alberta (2001) *Gangs.* Edmonton: John Howard Society of Aberta.

11. Perrone, S. & White, R (2000) *Young People and Gangs. Trends & Issues in Crime and Criminal Justice*, No. 167. Canberra: Australian Institute of Criminology.

12. Miller, W.B. (1992) *Crime by Youth Gangs and Groups in the United States.* Washington, DC: US Department of Justice, Office of Justice Programs, Office of Juvenile Justice and Delinquency Prevention.

13. van Gemert, F., Peterson, D. & Lien, I-L. (eds) (2008) *Youth Gangs, Migration, and Ethnicity.* Devon: Willan.

14. Maxson, C.L. & Klein, M.W. (1989) 'Street Gang Violence', in N. Warner & M. Wolfgang (eds) *Violent Crime, Violent Criminals.* Newbury Park, CA: Sage Publications.

15. Standing, A. (2005) *The Threat of Gangs and Anti-Gangs Policy*, ISS Occasional Paper 116. South Africa: Institute for Security Studies.

16. See, for example, Gordon's typology of diverse youth group formations in Canada (note 7 above).

17. McGloin, J. (2005) 'Policy and Intervention Considerations of a Network Analysis of Street Gangs', *Criminology and Public Policy*, 4(3): 607–636.

18. Kitik, Z. (2009) 'The Gang of 49: A Contemporary Example of the Social Construction of a Gang and the Accompanying Moral Panic', BA(Hons) Sociology Thesis, School of Communication, International Studies and Languages, University of South Australia.
19. Collins, J., Noble, G., Poynting, S. & Tabar, P. (2000) *Kebabs, Kids, Cops & Crime: Youth, Ethnicity and Crime*. Sydney: Pluto Press.
20. Esbensen, F-A., Winfree, Jr., L., He, N. & Taylor, T. (2001). 'Youth Gangs and Definitional Issues: When Is a Gang a Gang, and Why Does It Matter?', *Crime & Delinquency*, 47: 105–130.
21. The figure is taken from White, R. (2008) 'Disputed Definitions and Fluid Identities: The Limitations of Social Profiling in Relation to Ethnic Youth Gangs', *Youth Justice: an International Journal*, 8(2): 149–161.
22. Barry, M. (2006) *Youth Offending in Transition: The Search for Social Recognition*. London: Routledge.
23. Butcher, M. & Thomas, M. (2003) 'Being in-between', in M. Butcher & M. Thomas (eds) *Ingenious: Emerging Youth Cultures in Urban Australia*. Sydney: Pluto Press.

3   Groups and Networks

1. Hagedorn, J. (2008) *A World of Gangs: Armed Young Men and Gangsta Culture*. Minneapolis: University of Minnesota Press; Hagedorn, J. (ed) (2007) *Gangs in the Global City: Alternatives to Traditional Criminology*. Urbana and Chicago: University of Illinois Press; van Gemert, F., Peterson, D. & Lien, I-L. (eds) (2008) *Youth Gangs, Migration, and Ethnicity*. Devon: Willan.
2. Stratton, J. (1992) *The Young Ones: Working-Class Culture, Consumption and the Category of Youth*. Perth: Black Swan Press; Moore, K. (2004) 'Bodgies, Widgies and Moral Panic in Australia 1955–1959', *Paper Presented to the Social Change in the 21st Century Conference*. Centre for Social Change Research, Queensland University of Technology.
3. United States Bureau of Justice Assistance (1998) *Addressing Community Gang Problems: A Practical Guide*. Washington, DC: Office of Justice Programs, US Department of Justice.
4. United States Bureau of Justice Assistance (1998) *Addressing Community Gang Problems: A Practical Guide*. Washington, DC: Office of Justice Programs, US Department of Justice, p. 21.
5. Cunneen, C. & White, R. (2011) *Juvenile Justice: Youth and Crime in Australia*. Melbourne: Oxford University Press.
6. Huff, R. (1998) 'Comparing the Criminal Behavior of Youth Gangs and At-Risk Youths', Research in Brief, October. Washington, DC: US Office of Justice, National Institute of Justice; White, R. & Mason, R. (2006) 'Youth Gangs and Youth Violence: Charting the Key Dimensions', *Australian and New Zealand Journal of Criminology*, 39(1).
7. United States Bureau of Justice Assistance (1997) *Addressing Community Gang Problems: A Model for Problem Solving*. Washington, DC: Office of Justice Programs, US Department of Justice.
8. United States Bureau of Justice Assistance (1998) *Addressing Community Gang Problems: A Practical Guide*. Washington, DC: Office of Justice Programs, US Department of Justice.

9. Moore, J. (1988–1989) 'Changing Chicano Gangs: Acculturation, Genera-tional Change, Evolution of Deviance or Emerging Underclass', *Institute for Social Science Research, Working Papers in the Social Sciences*, 4(24).
10. Howell, J., Egley, Jr., A. & Gleason, D. (2002) *Modern-Day Youth Gangs*. Juve-nile Justice Bulletin, June. Washington, DC: Office of Juvenile Justice and Delinquency Prevention, US Department of Justice.
11. Howell, J. (2007) 'Menacing or Mimicking? Realities of Youth Gangs', *Juvenile and Family Court Journal*, 58(2): 39–50.
12. Aumair, M. & Warren, I. (1994) 'Characteristics of Juvenile Gangs in Melbourne', *Youth Studies Australia*, 13(2): 40–44.
13. Foote, P. (1993) *Like, I'll Tell You What Happened From Experience ... Perspectives on Italo-Australian Experience*. Hobart: National Clearinghouse for Youth Studies.
14. Foote, P. (1993) *Like, I'll Tell You What Happened From Experience ... Perspectives on Italo-Australian Experience*. Hobart: National Clearinghouse for Youth Studies.
15. White, R., Perrone, S., Guerra, C. & Lampugnani, R. (1999) *Ethnic Youth Gangs in Australia: Do They Exist?* [7 reports – Vietnamese, Latin American, Turkish, Somalian, Pacific Islander, Anglo-Australian, Summary]. Melbourne: Australian Multicultural Foundation.
16. Collins, J., Noble, G., Poynting, S. & Tabar, P. (2000) *Kebabs, Kids, Cops & Crime: Youth, Ethnicity and Crime*. Sydney: Pluto Press.
17. Collins, J., Noble, G., Poynting, S. & Tabar, P. (2000) *Kebabs, Kids, Cops & Crime: Youth, Ethnicity and Crime*. Sydney: Pluto Press.
18. For a recent illustration of this process and portrayal, see Windle, J. (2008) 'The Racialisation of African youth in Australia', *Social Identities*, 14(5): 553–566.
19. The figure is taken from White, R. (2008) 'Australian Youth Gangs and the Social Dynamics of Ethnicity', in F. van Gemert, D. Peterson & I-L Lien (eds) *Youth Gangs, Migration, and Ethnicity*. Devon: Willan.

4   Fluidity and Continuity

1. White, R., 2008a, 'Class Analysis and the Crime Problem', in Anthony, T. & Cunneen, C. (eds) *The Critical Criminology Companion*.Sydney: Federation Press.
2. Standing, G. (2011) *The Precariat: The New Dangerous Class*. New York: Bloomsbury Academic.
3. Morris, L. (1994) *Dangerous Classes: The Underclass and Social Citizenship*. London: Routledge.
4. See Morris, L. (1994) *Dangerous Classes: The Underclass and Social Citizenship*. London: Routledge.
5. Pearson, G. (1983) *Hooligan: A History of Respectable Fears*. London: Macmillan Education, p. 159.
6. Pearson, G. (1983) *Hooligan: A History of Respectable Fears*. London: Macmillan Education.
7. On the nature and activities of the 'larrikins', see Finch, L. (1993) 'On the streets: Working Class Youth Culture in the Nineteenth Century', in

R. White (ed) *Youth Subcultures: Theory, History and the Australian Experience*. Hobart: National Clearinghouse for Youth Studies: 75–79; Finnane, M. (1994) 'Larrikins, Delinquents and Cops: Police and Young People in Australian History', in R. White & C. Alder (eds) *The Police and Young People in Australia*. Melbourne: Cambridge University Press; Maunders, D. (1984) *Keeping Them Off The Streets: A History of Voluntary Youth Organizations in Australia 1850–1980*. Melbourne: Phillip Institute of Technology, Centre for Youth and Community Studies; Murray, J. (1973) *Larrikins: 19th Century Outrage*. Melbourne: Lansdowne Press.

8. See Finch, L. (1993) *The Classing Gaze: Sexuality, Class and Surveillance*. Sydney: Allen & Unwin.

9. Grabosky, P. (1977) *Sydney in Ferment: Crime, Dissent and Official Reaction 1788 to 1973*. Canberra: Australian National University Press, p. 70.

10. Morgan, G. (1997) 'The Bulletin and the Larrikin Moral Panic in Nineteenth Century Sydney', *Media International Australia*, 85: 17–24.

11. Murray, J. (1973) *Larrikins: 19th Century Outrage*. Melbourne: Lansdowne Press, pp. 78–79.

12. Grabosky, P. (1977) *Sydney in Ferment: Crime, Dissent and Official Reaction 1788 to 1973*. Canberra: Australian National University Press.

13. Finnane, M. (1994) 'Larrikins, Delinquents and Cops: Police and Young People in Australian History', in R. White & C. Alder (eds) *The Police and Young People in Australia*. Melbourne: Cambridge University Press, p. 9.

14. Pearson, G. (1983) *Hooligan: A History of Respectable Fears*. London: Macmillan Education, p. 159.

15. Murray, J. (1973) *Larrikins: 19th Century Outrage*. Melbourne: Lansdowne Press.

16. Murray, J. (1973) *Larrikins: 19th Century Outrage*. Melbourne: Lansdowne Press, p. 83.

17. White, R. (2006) *Swarming and the Dynamics of Group Violence. Trends & Issues in Crime and Criminal Justice*. No. 326. Canberra: Australian Institute of Criminology.

18. Grabosky, P. (1977) *Sydney in Ferment: Crime, Dissent and Official Reaction 1788 to 1973*. Canberra: Australian National University Press.

19. Lee, M. (2005) 'Public Dissent and Governmental Neglect: Isolating and Excluding Macquarie Fields', *Current Issues in Criminal Justice*, 18 (1): 32–50.

20. Cohen, P. (1979) 'Policing the Working-Class City', in National Deviancy Conference/Conference of Socialist Economists (eds) *Capitalism and the Rule of Law*. London: Hutchinson; Finnane, M. (1994) 'Larrikins, Delinquents and Cops: Police and Young People in Australian History', in R. White & C. Alder (eds) *The Police and Young People in Australia*. Melbourne: Cambridge University Press.

21. Finch, L. (1993a) 'On the Streets: Working Class Youth Culture in the Nineteenth Century', in R. White (ed) *Youth Subcultures: Theory, History and the Australian Experience*. Hobart: National Clearinghouse for Youth Studies, p. 79.

22. Cohen, P. (1979) 'Policing the Working-Class City', in National Deviancy Conference/Conference of Socialist Economists (eds) *Capitalism and the Rule of Law*. London: Hutchinson.

23. Wilson, W.J. (1996) *When Work Disappears.* New York: Knopf; Wacquant, L. (2012) 'A Janus-Faced Institution of Ethnoracial Closure: A Sociological Specification of the Ghetto', in R. Hutchinson & B. Haynes (eds) *The Ghetto: Contemporary Global Issues and Controversies.* Boulder, Colorado: Westview Press.
24. Collins, J., Noble, G., Poynting, S. & Tabar, P. (2000) *Kebabs, Kids, Cops & Crime: Youth, Ethnicity & Crime.* Sydney: Pluto Press.
25. Heitmeyer, W. (2002) 'Have Cities Ceased to Function as "Integration Machines" for Young People?' in M. Tienda & WJ Wilson (eds) *Youth in Cities: A Cross-National Perspective.* Cambridge University Press, Cambridge.
26. Poynting, S., Noble, G., Tabar, P. & Collins, J. (2004) *Bin Laden in the Suburbs: Criminalising the Arab Other.* Sydney: Sydney Institute of Criminology.
27. Poynting, S., Noble, G., Tabar, P. & Collins, J. (2004) *Bin Laden in the Suburbs: Criminalising the Arab Other.* Sydney: Sydney Institute of Criminology. See also: Poynting, S. & Morgan, G. (eds) (2007) *Outrageous! Moral Panics in Australia.* Hobart: ACYS Publishing.
28. Collins, J., Noble, G., Poynting, S. & Tabar, P. (2000) *Kebabs, Kids, Cops & Crime: Youth, Ethnicity & Crime.* Sydney: Pluto Press.
29. Hage, G. (1998) *White Nation: Fantasies of White Supremacy in a Multicultural Society.* Pluto Press: Sydney.
30. Collins, J., Noble, G., Poynting, S. & Tabar, P. (2000) *Kebabs, Kids, Cops & Crime: Youth, Ethnicity & Crime.* Sydney: Pluto Press.
31. Jakubowicz, J. (2006) 'Hobbits and Orcs: The Street Politics of Race and Masculinity', *Australian Options*, No. 44: 2–5.
32. Human Rights and Equal Opportunity Commission (2004). *Ismae – Listen: National Consultations on Eliminating Prejudice Against Arab and Muslim Australians.* Sydney: HREOC.
33. White, R. & Perrone, S. (2001) 'Racism, Ethnicity and Hate Crime', *Communal/Plural*, 9: 161–181.
34. Cunneen, C. (2007) 'Riot, Resistance and Moral Panic: Demonising the Colonial Other', in S. Poynting & G. Morgan (eds) *Outrageous! Moral Panics in Australia.* Hobart: ACYS Publishing.
35. Noble, G. (ed) (2009) *Lines in the Sand: The Cronulla Riots, Multiculturalism and National Belonging.* Sydney: Institute of Criminology, University of Sydney.
36. Poynting, S., Noble, G., Tabar, P. & Collins, J. (2004) *Bin Laden in the Suburbs: Criminalising the Arab Other.* Sydney: Sydney Institute of Criminology.

5 Gangs and the Transnational

1. See, for example, Aldrige, J., Ralphs, J. & Pickering, J. (2011) 'Collateral Damage: and Policing in an English Gang City', in B. Goldson (ed) *Youth in Crisis? 'Gangs', Territoriality and Violence.* London: Routledge; Decker, S. & Weerman, F. (eds) (2005) *European Street Gangs and Troublesome Youth Groups.* Lanham, MD: Alta Mira Press; Duffy, M. & Gillig, S. (eds) (2004) *Teen Gangs: A Global View.* Westport: Greenwood; Hagedorn, J. (ed) (2007a) *Gangs in the Global City: Alternatives to Traditional Criminology.* Urbana and Chicago: University of Illinois Press; Hagedorn, J. (2007b) 'Introduction: Globalization, Gangs, and Traditional Criminology', in J. Hagedorn (ed) *Gangs in the*

Global City: Alternatives to Traditional Criminology. Urbana and Chicago: University of Illinois Press; Hagedorn, J. (2008) *A World of Gangs: Armed Young Men and Gangsta Culture*. Minneapolis: University of Minnesota Press; Huff, R. (ed) (2002) *Gangs in America* (3rd edition). Thousand Oaks, California: Sage; Matusitz, J. & Repass, M. (2009) 'Gangs in Nigeria: An Updated Examination', *Crime, Law and Social Change*, 52(4): 495–511; Pitts, J. (2008) *Reluctant Gangsters: The Changing Face of Youth Crime*. Devon: Willan Publishing; Pitts, J. (2011) 'Mercenary Territory: Are Gangs Really a Problem?', in B. Goldson (ed) *Youth in Crisis? 'Gangs', Territoriality and Violence*. London: Routledge; White, R. (2006) 'Youth Gang Research in Australia', in J. Short & L. Hughes (eds), *Studying Youth Gangs*. Walnut Creek, CA: AltaMira Press; Venkatesh, S. (2008) *Gang Leader for a Day*. New York: The Penguin Press.

2. White, R. (2008) 'Disputed Definitions and Fluid Identities: The Limitations of Social Profiling in Relation to Ethnic Youth Gangs', *Youth Justice: an International Journal*, 8(2): 149–161; Decker, S.H. (1996) 'Collective and Normative Features of Gang Violence', *Justice Quarterly*, 13: 243–264; Esbensen, F-A., Winfree, Jr., L., He, N. & Taylor, T. (2001). 'Youth Gangs and Definitional Issues: When Is a Gang a Gang, and Why Does It Matter?', *Crime & Delinquency*, 47: 105–130; Gordon, R. (2000) 'Criminal Business Organizations, Street Gangs and "wanna-be" Groups: A Vancouver Perspective', *Canadian Journal of Criminology*, January: 39–60; Howell, J.C. (1998) *Youth Gangs: An Overview*. Bulletin. Washington DC: US Department of Justice, Office of Justice Programs, Office of Juvenile Justice and Delinquency Prevention; Klein, M.W. (2002) 'Street Gangs: A Cross-National Perspective', in R. Huff (ed), *Gangs in America* (3rd edition). Thousand Oaks, California: Sage; Klein, M., H-J Kerner, Maxon, C. & Weitekamp, E. (eds) (2001) *The Eurogang Paradox: Street Gangs and Youth Groups in the U.S. and Europe*. Dordrecht: Kluwer Academic Publishers; Miller, W.B. (1992) *Crime by Youth Gangs and Groups in the United States*. Washington, DC: US Department of Justice, Office of Justice Programs, Office of Juvenile Justice and Delinquency Prevention.
   Standing, A. (2005) *The Threat of Gangs and Anti-Gangs Policy*, ISS Occasional Paper 116. South Africa: Institute for Security Studies.

3. Hagedorn, J. (2007b) 'Introduction: Globalization, Gangs, and Traditional Criminology', in J. Hagedorn (ed) *Gangs in the Global City: Alternatives to Traditional Criminology*. Urbana and Chicago: University of Illinois Press, p. 2.

4. Franco, C. (2008) *The MS-13 and 18th Street Gangs: Emerging Transnational Gang Threats?* CRS Report for Congress. Washington, DC: Congressional Research Service, p. 3.

5. Franco, C. (2008) *The MS-13 and 18th Street Gangs: Emerging Transnational Gang Threats?* CRS Report for Congress. Washington, DC: Congressional Research Service; see also Prowse, C. (2012) *Defining Street Gangs in the 21st Century: Fluid, Mobile, and Transnational Networks*. New York: Springer.

6. See Short, J. (2007) 'The Challenges of Gangs in Global Contexts', in J. Hadgedorn (ed) *Gangs in the Global City: Alternatives to Traditional Criminology*. Urbana and Chicago: University of Illinois Press; Hagedorn, J. (2008) *A World of Gangs: Armed Young Men and Gangsta Culture*. Minneapolis: University of Minnesota Press.

7. Hagedorn, J. (2008) *A World of Gangs: Armed Young Men and Gangsta Culture*. Minneapolis: University of Minnesota Press, p. xxiv.

8. Johnson, S. & Muhlhausen, D. (2005) *North American Transnational Youth Gangs: Breaking the Chain of Violence*. Backgrounder No. 1834, 21 March. Washington, DC: The Heritage Foundation.
9. See especially Hagedorn, J. (ed) (2007) *Gangs in the Global City: Alternatives to Traditional Criminology*. Urbana and Chicago: University of Illinois Press; Hagedorn, J. (2008) *A World of Gangs: Armed Young Men and Gangsta Culture*. Minneapolis: University of Minnesota Press; Wacquant, L. (2008) *Urban Outcasts: A Comparative Sociology of Advanced Marginality*. Cambridge: Polity Press; Wacquant, L. (2012) 'A Janus-Faced Institution of Ethnoracial Closure: A Sociological Specification of the Ghetto', in R. Hutchinson & B. Haynes (eds) *The Ghetto: Contemporary Global Issues and Controversies*. Boulder, Colorado: Westview Press; White, R. & Wyn, J. (2013) *Youth and Society*. Melbourne: Oxford University Press.
10. White, R. (2008) 'Class Analysis and the Crime Problem', in T. Anthony & C. Cunneen (eds) *The Critical Criminology Companion*. Sydney: Federation Press; White, R. & Cunneen, C. (2006) 'Social Class, Youth Crime and Justice', in B. Goldson & J. Muncie (eds) *Youth Crime and Justice: Critical Issues*. London: Sage.
11. Wacquant, L. (2007) 'Three Pernicious Premises in the Study of the American Ghetto', in J. Hagedorn (ed) *Gangs in the Global City: Alternatives to Traditional Criminology*. Urbana and Chicago: University of Illinois Press.
12. Decker, S., van Gemert, F. & Pyrooz, D. (2009) 'Gangs, Migration, and Crime: The Changing Landscape in Europe and the USA', *International Migration & Integration*, 10: 393–408.
13. Paul, E. (2009) 'The Political Economy of Violence in Australia', *Journal of Australian Political Economy*, No. 63: 80–107.
    Wacquant, L. (2008) *Urban Outcasts: A Comparative Sociology of Advanced Marginality*. Cambridge: Polity Press.
14. Hagedorn, J. (2008) *A World of Gangs: Armed Young Men and Gangsta Culture*. Minneapolis: University of Minnesota Press.
15. Medina, J. (2010) 'Youth Gangs in a Global Context' in S. Shoham, P. Knepper & M. Kett (eds) *International Handbook of Criminology*. New York: Taylor and Francis.
16. Cohen, S. (1973) *Folk Devils and Moral Panics*. London: Paladin; Poynting, S. & Morgan, G. (eds) (2007) *Outrageous! Moral Panics in Australia*. Hobart: ACYS Publishing; Morgan, G. & Poynting, S. (eds) (2012) *Global Islamophobia: Muslims and Moral Panic in the West*. Surrey: Ashgate.
17. Poynting, S., Noble, G., Tabar, P. & Collins, J. (2004) *Bin Laden in the Suburbs: Criminalising the Arab Other*. Sydney: Sydney Institute of Criminology, University of Sydney.
18. Collins, J., Noble, G., Poynting, S. & Tabar, P. (2000) *Kebabs, Kids, Cops & Crime: Youth, Ethnicity & Crime*. Sydney: Pluto Press; Poynting, S. & Morgan, G. (eds) (2007) *Outrageous!: Moral Panics in Australia*. Hobart: ACYS publishing.
    Poynting, S., Noble, G., Tabar, P. & Collins, J. (2004) *Bin Laden in the Suburbs: Criminalising the Arab Other*. Sydney: Sydney Institute of Criminology, University of Sydney.
19. Decker, S., van Gemert, F. & Pyrooz, D. (2009) 'Gangs, Migration, and Crime: The Changing Landscape in Europe and the USA', *International*

Migration & Integration, 10: 393–408; Johnson, S. & Muhlhausen, D. (2005) *North American Transnational Youth Gangs: Breaking the Chain of Violence.* Backgrounder No. 1834, 21 March. Washington, DC: The Heritage Foundation.

20. Van Gemert, F. (2005) 'Youth Groups and Gangs in Amserdam: A Pretest of the Eurogang Expert Survey', in S. Decker & F. Weerman (eds) *European Street Gangs and Troublesome Youth Groups.* Lanham: Alta Mira.
21. Pakes, F. (2012) 'A Panicky Debate: The State of Morrocan Youth in the Netherlands', in G. Morgan & S. Poynting (eds) (2012) *Global Islamophobia: Muslims and Moral Panic in the West.* Surrey: Ashgate.
22. Decker, S., van Gemert, F. & Pyrooz, D. (2009) 'Gangs, Migration, and Crime: The Changing Landscape in Europe and the USA', *International Migration & Integration,* 10: 393–408, p. 401.
23. White, R. (2008c) 'Australian Youth Gangs and the Social Dynamics of Ethnicity', in F. van Gemert, D. Peterson & I-L Lien (eds) *Youth Gangs, Migration, and Ethnicity.* Devon: Willan.
24. White, R. (ed) (2012) *Youth Subcultures: Theory, History and the Australian Experience.* Hobart: Australian Clearinghouse for Youth Studies.
25. White, R. & Wyn, J. (2013) *Youth and Society.* Melbourne: Oxford University Press.
26. Zilberg, E. (2004) 'Fools Banished from Kingdom: Remapping Geographies of Gang Violence Between the Americas (Los Angeles and San Salvador)', *American Q,* 56(3): 759–780.
27. White, R. & Wyn, J. (2013) *Youth and Society.* Melbourne: Oxford University Press.
28. Hagedorn, J. (ed) (2007a) *Gangs in the Global City: Alternatives to Traditional Criminology.* Urbana and Chicago: University of Illinois Press; Short, J. & Hughes, L. (eds), *Studying Youth Gangs.* Walnut Creek, CA: AltaMira Press; van Gemert, F., Peterson, D. & Lien, I-L. (eds) (2008) *Youth Gangs, Migration, and Ethnicity.* Devon: Willan.
29. Adamson, C. (2000) 'Defensive Localism in White and Black: A Comparative History of European-American and African-American Youth Gangs', *Ethnic and Racial Studies,* 23(2): 272–298.
30. White, R. (2008c) 'Australian Youth Gangs and the Social Dynamics of Ethnicity', in F. van Gemert, D. Peterson & I-L Lien (eds) *Youth Gangs, Migration, and Ethnicity.* Devon: Willan. See also Chapter 3.
31. Hagedorn, J. (2008) *A World of Gangs: Armed Young Men and Gangsta Culture.* Minneapolis: University of Minnesota Press, p. 132.

6   Indigenous Gangs and Family

1. White, R. & Wyn, J. (2013) *Youth and Society.* Melbourne: Oxford University Press.
2. White, R. & Wyn, J. (2013) *Youth and Society.* Melbourne: Oxford University Press.
3. Morrissey, M. (2006) 'The Australian State and Indigenous People 1990–2006', *Journal of Sociology,* 42(4): 347–354.

4. Australian Bureau of Statistics and Australian Institute of Health and Welfare (2005) *The Health and Welfare of Australia's Aboriginal & Torres Strait Islander Peoples*, catalogue 4704.0. Canberra: ABS & AIHW.
5. Cunneen, C. (1994) 'Enforcing Genocide? Aboriginal Young People and the Police', in R. White & C. Alder (eds) *The Police and Young People in Australia*. Melbourne: Cambridge University Press; Cunneen, C. (2001) *Conflict, Politics and Crime: Aboriginal Communities and the Police*. Sydney: Allen & Unwin.
6. White, R. (1999) *Hanging Out: Negotiating Young People's Use of Public Space*. Canberra: National Crime Prevention, Attorney-General's Department.
7. White, R. (1999) *Hanging Out: Negotiating Young People's Use of Public Space*. Canberra: National Crime Prevention, Attorney-General's Department; Ogwang, T., Cox, L. & Saldanha, J. 2006, 'Paint on Their Lips: Paint-sniffers, Good Citizens and Public Space in Brisbane', *Journal of Sociology*, 42(4): 412–428.
8. Palmer, D. & Collard, L. (1993) 'Aboriginal Young People and Youth Subcultures', in R. White (ed) *Youth Subcultures: Theory, History and the Australian Experience*. Hobart: National Clearinghouse for Youth Studies.
9. See, for example, Johnston, E. (1991) *Report of the Royal Commission into Aboriginal Deaths in Custody, Vols1–5*. Canberra: Australian Government Publishing Service.
10. National Inquiry into the Separation of Aboriginal and Torres Strait Islander Children and Their Families (1997) *Bringing Them Home*. Canberra: Commonwealth of Australia.
11. Cunneen, C. & White, R. (2007) *Juvenile Justice: Youth and Crime in Australia*. Melbourne: Oxford University Press, p. 146.
12. For a critical discussion of this issue, see Blagg, H. (2008) *Crime, Aboriginality and the Decolonisation of Justice*. Sydney: Hawkins Press; but also see Kimm, J. (2004) *Fatal Conjunction: Two Laws, Two Cultures*. Sydney: Federation Press.
13. National Inquiry into the Separation of Aboriginal and Torres Strait Islander Children and Their Families (1997) *Bringing Them Home*. Canberra: Commonwealth of Australia.
14. See, for example, Cunneen, C. & White, R. (2011) *Juvenile Justice: Youth and Crime in Australia*. Melbourne: Oxford University Press.
15. Australian Institute of Health and Welfare (2008) *Juvenile Justice in Australia 2006–07*. AIHW Juvenile Justice Series No. 4. Canberra: AIHW.
16. Johnston, E. (1991) *Report of the Royal Commission into Aboriginal Deaths in Custody, Vols 1–5*. Canberra: Australian Government Publishing Service.
    Ogilvie, E. & Van Zyl, A. (2001) 'Young Indigenous Males, Custody and the Rites of Passage', *Trends & Issues in Crime and Criminal Justice*, No. 204. Canberra: Australian Institute of Criminology.
17. Paradies, Y. 2006, 'Beyond Black and White: Essentialism, Hybridity and Indigeneity', *Journal of Sociology*, 42(4): 355–368.
18. Johnston, E. (1991) *Report of the Royal Commission into Aboriginal Deaths in Custody*, Vols 1–5. Canberra: Australian Government Publishing Service.
19. Ogwang, T., Cox, L. & Saldanha, J. 2006, 'Paint on Their Lips: Paint-sniffers, Good Citizens and Public Space in Brisbane', *Journal of Sociology*, 42(4): 412–428.
20. Toohey, P. 2004, 'Gangsters' Paradise', *Bulletin*, 4 February.

21. Memmott, P. (2010) 'On Regional and Cultural Approaches to Australian Indigenous Violence', *Australian and New Zealand Journal of Criminology*, 43(2): 333–355.
22. Ogwang, T., Cox, L. & Saldanha, J. 2006, 'Paint on Their Lips: Paint-sniffers, Good Citizens and Public Space in Brisbane', *Journal of Sociology*, 42(4): 412–228.
23. See Collins, J., Noble, G., Poynting, S. & Tabar, P. (2000). *Kebabs, Kids, Cops & Crime: Youth, Ethnicity & Crime*. Sydney: Pluto Press.
24. Marie, D. (2010) 'Maori and Criminal Offending: A Critical Appraisal', *Australian and New Zealand Journal of Criminology*, 43(2): 282–300.

7   Provocations and Punch-Ups

1. Campbell, A. (1984) *The Girls in the Gang*. Oxford: Basil Blackwell; Miller, J. (2001) *One of the Guys: Girls, Gangs and Gender*. New York: Oxford University Press; Batchelor, S. (2011) 'Beyond Dichotomy: Towards an Explanation of Young Women's Involvement in Violent Street Gangs', in B. Goldson (ed) *Youth in Crisis? 'Gangs', Territoriality and Violence*. London: Routledge; Hallsworth, S. & Brotherton, D. (2011) *Urban Disorder and Gangs: A Critique and a Warning*. London: Runnymede.
2. Krug, E., Dahlberg, L., Mercy, J., Zwi, A. & Lozano, R. (2002). *World Report on Violence and Health*. Geneva: World Health Organization, p. 5.
3. White, R. (2006) 'Swarming and the Dynamics of Group Violence', *Trends & Issues in Crime and Criminal Justice*. No. 326. Canberra: Australian Institute of Criminology.
4. Decker, S.H. (1996) 'Collective and Normative Features of Gang Violence', *Justice Quarterly*, 13: 243–264; Decker, S. H. (2007). 'Youth Gangs and Violent Behavior', in D. J. Flannery, A. T. Vazsonyi, & I. D. Waldman (eds), *The Cambridge Handbook of Violent Behavior and Aggression*, pp. 388–402. Cambridge, MA: Cambridge University Press.

    Howell, J. (2007) 'Menacing or Mimicking? Realities of Youth Gangs', *Juvenile and Family Court Journal*, 58(2): 39–50.

    Huff, R. (1998) 'Comparing the Criminal Behavior of Youth Gangs and At-Risk Youths', Research in Brief, October. Washington, DC: US Office of Justice, National Institute of Justice.
5. Sandberg, S. (2008) 'Street Capital: Ethnicity and Violence on the Streets of Oslo', *Theoretical Criminology*, 12(2): 153–171.
6. White, R. & Mason, R. (2006) 'Youth Gangs and Youth Violence: Charting the Key Dimensions', *Australian and New Zealand Journal of Criminology*, 39(1): 54–70.
7. White, R. & Mason, R. (2006) 'Youth Gangs and Youth Violence: Charting the Key Dimensions', *Australian and New Zealand Journal of Criminology*, 39(1): 54–70.
8. Rigby, K. (2003) 'Addressing Bullying in Schools: Theory and Practice', *Trends and Issues in Crime and Criminal Justice* No. 259. Canberra: Australian Institute of Criminology.
9. Ttofi, M., Farrington, D., Losel, F. & Loeber, R. (2011) 'The Predictive Efficiency of School Bullying Versus Later Offending: A Systematic/meta-analytic

Review of Longitudinal Studies', *Criminal Behaviour and Mental Health*, 21: 80–89.

Bender, D. & Losel, F. (2011) 'Bullying at School as a Predictor of Delinquency, Violence and Other Anti-social Behaviour in Adulthood', *Criminal Behaviour and Mental Health*, 21: 99–106.

Farrington, D. & Ttofi, M. (2011) 'Bullying as a Predictor of Offending, Violence and Later Life Outcomes', *Criminal Behaviour and Mental Health*, 21: 90–98.

10. Rigby, K. (2003) 'Addressing Bullying in Schools: Theory and Practice', *Trends and Issues in Crime and Criminal Justice* No. 259. Canberra: Australian Institute of Criminology.

11. Trimboli, L. (2010) 'Assaults on School Premises in NSW, 2005–2009', *Crime and Justice Statistics Issue Paper No. 50*. Sydney: New South Wales Bureau of Crime Statistics and Research.

12. Decker, S. H. (2007). 'Youth Gangs and Violent Behavior', In D. J. Flannery, A. T. Vazsonyi, and I. D. Waldman (eds), *The Cambridge Handbook of Violent Behavior and Aggression*, pp. 388–402. Cambridge, MA: Cambridge University Press.

13. Hayden, C. (2008) *'Staying Safe and Out of Trouble': A Survey of Young People's Perceptions and Experiences*. Portsmouth: ICJS, University of Portsmouth.

14. Howell, J. (2007) 'Menacing or Mimicking? Realities of Youth Gangs', *Juvenile and Family Court Journal*, 58(2): 39–50.

15. Howell, J. (2007) 'Menacing or Mimicking? Realities of Youth Gangs', *Juvenile and Family Court Journal*, 58(2): 39–50.

16. Anderson, E. (1999) *Code of the Street: Decency, Violence and the Moral Life of the Inner City*. New York: W.W. Norton & Company; Sandberg, S. (2008) 'Street Capital: Ethnicity and Violence on the Streets of Oslo', *Theoretical Criminology*, 12(2): 153–171.

17. Howell, J. (2007) 'Menacing or Mimicking? Realities of Youth Gangs', *Juvenile and Family Court Journal*, 58(2): 39–50.

18. Connell, R. (2000) *The Men and the Boys*. Sydney: Allen & Unwin; Messerschmidt, J. (1997). *Crime as Structured Action: Gender, Race, Class, and Crime in the Making*. London: Sage; Polk, K. (1994) *When Men Kill: Scenarios of Masculine Violence*. Melbourne: Cambridge University Press.; Tomsen, S. (1997) 'A Top Night: Social Protest, Masculinity and the Culture of Drinking Violence', *British Journal of Criminology*, 37(1): 90–102.

19. White, R. (2006) 'Swarming and the Dynamics of Group Violence'. *Trends & Issues in Crime and Criminal Justice*. No. 326. Canberra: Australian Institute of Criminology,

20. Decker, S. & Pyrooz, D. (2011). 'Leaving the Gang: Logging Off and Moving On', Paper Commissioned by Google Ideas: The Council on Foreign Relations.

21. Lockwood, D. (1997). *Violence Among Middle School and High School Students: Analysis and Implications for Prevention*. National Institute of Justice, Research in Brief. Washington, D.C.: Office of Justice Programs, US Department of Justice.

22. Decker, S.H. (1996) 'Collective and Normative Features of Gang Violence', *Justice Quarterly*, 13: 243–264.

23. Decker, S. H. (2007). 'Youth Gangs and Violent Behavior', in D. J. Flannery, A. T. Vazsonyi, & I. D. Waldman (eds), *The Cambridge Handbook of Violent Behavior and Aggression*. pp. 388–402. Cambridge, MA: Cambridge University Press; Howell, J. (2007) 'Menacing or Mimicking? Realities of Youth Gangs', *Juvenile and Family Court Journal*, 58(2): 39–50; Huff, R. (1998) 'Comparing the Criminal Behavior of Youth Gangs and At-Risk Youths', Research in Brief, October. Washington, DC: US Office of Justice, National Institute of Justice.

24. Moore, David (1994) *The Lads in Action: Social Process in an Urban Youth Subculture*. Aldershot, England: Arena, p. 65.

25. McDonald, K. (1999) *Struggles for Subjectivity: Identity, Action and Youth Experience*. Cambridge: Cambridge University Press.

26. Moore, David (1994) *The Lads in Action: Social Process in an Urban Youth Subculture*. Aldershot, England: Arena, p. 76.

27. John Howard Society of Alberta (2001) *Gangs*. Edmonton: John Howard Society of Aberta.

28. McKetin, R., McLaren, J., Ridell, S. & Robins, L. (2006) The Relationship between Methamphetamine Use and Violent Behaviour, *Contemporary Issues in Crime and Justice*, No. 97. Sydney: New South Wales Bureau of Crime Statistics and Research, Crime and Justice Bulletin.

29. Smart, D., Vassallo, S., Sanson, A. & Dussuyer, I. (2004) Patterns of Antisocial Behaviour from Early to Late Adolescence. *Trends and Issues in Crime and Criminal Justice*, No. 290. Canberra: Australian Institute of Criminology.

30. Hughes, L. & Short, J. (2005) 'Disputes Involving Youth Street Gang Members: Micro-Social Contexts', *Criminology*, 43(1): 43–76; Hayward (2002).

31. Collins, J., Noble, G., Poynting, S. & Tabar, P. (2000) *Kebabs, Kids, Cops & Crime: Youth, Ethnicity & Crime*. Sydney: Pluto Press; White, R. (2006) 'Youth Gang Research in Australia', in J. Short & L. Hughes (eds) *Studying Youth Gangs*. Walnut Creek, CA: AltaMira Press.

32. Hayward, K. (2002) 'The Vilification and Pleasures of Youthful Transgression', in J. Muncie, G. Hughes & E. McLaughlin (eds) *Youth Justice: Critical Readings*. London: Sage.

33. Schinkel, W. (2004) 'The Will to Violence', *Theoretical Criminology*, 8(1): 5–31.

34. Lockwood, D. (1997). *Violence Among Middle School and High School Students: Analysis and Implications for Prevention*. National Institute of Justice, Research in Brief. Washington, D.C.: Office of Justice Programs, US Department of Justice.

35. Jackson-Jacobs, C. (2004). 'Taking a Beating: The Narrative Gratifications of Fighting as an Underdog', in J. Ferrell, K. Hayward, W. Morrison & M. Presdee (eds), *Cultural Criminology Unleashed*. London: Glasshouse Press; Schinkel, W. (2004) 'The Will to Violence', *Theoretical Criminology*, 8(1): 5–31.

36. Schinkel, W. (2004) 'The Will to Violence', *Theoretical Criminology*, 8(1): 5–31.

37. White, R. & Perrone, S. (2001) Racism, Ethnicity and Hate Crime. *Communal/Plural* 9: 161–181.

38. Decker, S. H. (2007). 'Youth Gangs and Violent Behavior', in D. J. Flannery, A. T. Vazsonyi, & I. D. Waldman (eds), *The Cambridge Handbook of Violent Behavior and Aggression*, pp. 388–402. Cambridge, MA: Cambridge University Press; Hagedorn, J. (2008) *A World of Gangs: Armed Young Men and Gangsta Culture*. Minneapolis: University of Minnesota Press.

8   The Body and Violence

1. Damousi, J. (1997) *Depraved and Disorderly: Female Convicts, Sexuality and Gender in Colonial Australia*. Cambridge: Cambridge University Press.
2. Foucault, M. (1977) *Discipline and Punish: The Birth of the Prison*. Harmondsworth: Penguin.
3. Ogilvie, E. & Lynch, M. (1999) 'A Culture of Resistance: Adolescents in Detention', in R. White (ed) *Australian Youth Subcultures: On the Margins and in the Mainstream*. Hobart: Australian Clearinghouse for Youth Studies.
4. Ogilvie, E. & Lynch, M. (1999) 'A Culture of Resistance: Adolescents in Detention', in R. White (ed) *Australian Youth Subcultures: On the Margins and in the Mainstream*. Hobart: Australian Clearinghouse for Youth Studies, p. 154.
5. Sheldon, W. (1940) *Varieties of Human Physique*. New York: Harper & Row.
6. Tomsen, S. (1997) 'A Top Night: Social Protest, Masculinity and the Culture of Drinking Violence', *British Journal of Criminology*, 37(1): 90–102.
7. Lee, M. (2006) 'Public Dissent and Governmental Neglect: Isolating and Excluding Macquarie Fields', *Current Issues in Criminal Justice*, 18(1): 32–50; Vinson, T. (2004) Community Adversity and Resilience: the distribution of social disadvantage in Victoria and New South Wales and the mediating role of social cohesion, The Ignatius Centre for social policy and research, Jesuit Social Services, Richmond, Victoria.
8. Collins, J., Noble, G., Poynting, S. & Tabar, P. (2000) *Kebabs, Kids, Cops & Crime: Youth, Ethnicity & Crime*. Sydney: Pluto Press; Blagg, H. (2008) *Crime, Aboriginality and the Decolonisation of Justice*. Sydney: Hawkins Press.
9. Collier, R. (1998) *Masculinities, Crime and Criminology*. London: Sage; Connell, R. (1995). *Masculinities*. Cambridge: Polity; Connell, R. (2000). *The Men and the Boys*. Sydney: Allen & Unwin; Tomsen, S. (2008) 'Masculinities, Crime and Criminalisation', in T. Anthony & C. Cunneen (eds) *The Critical Criminology Companion*. Sydney: Hawkins Press.
10. Collins, J., Noble, G., Poynting, S. & Tabar, P. (2000) *Kebabs, Kids, Cops & Crime: Youth, Ethnicity & Crime*. Sydney: Pluto Press, p. 150.
11. Sandberg, S. (2008) 'Street Capital: Ethnicity and Violence on the Streets of Oslo', *Theoretical Criminology*, 12(2): 153–171.
12. Collier, R. (1998) *Masculinities, Crime and Criminology*. London: Sage.
13. Connell, R. (1995) *Masculinities*. Cambridge: Polity.
14. Brown, D. & Hogg, R. (1992) 'Essentialism, Radical Criminology and Left Realism', *Australian and New Zealand Journal of Criminology*, 25(3): 195–230; White, R., Haines, F. & Asquith, N. (2012) *Crime & Criminology*. Melbourne: Oxford University Press.
15. Sheldon, W. (1940) *Varieties of Human Physique*. New York: Harper & Row.
16. White, R., Haines, F. & Asquith, N. (2012) *Crime & Criminology*. Melbourne: Oxford University Press.
17. See 'MAOA Gene and Maori Violence', *Daily Telegraph*, 8 August; Lea, R. & Chambers, G. (2007) 'Monoamine Oxidase, Addiction, and the 'Warrior' Gene Hypothesis', *The New Zealand Medical Journal*, 120(1250): 2 March.
18. Giancola, P. R., Parrott, D. J. & Roth, R. M. (2006). The influence of difficult temperament on alcohol-related aggression: better accounted for by executive functioning? *Addict Behav*, 31(12): 2169–2187; Roth, J. (1994).

Understanding and Preventing Violence. Research in Brief. Washington, DC: National Institute of Justice, US Department of Justice.

19. Morley, K. & Hall, W. (2003). 'Is There a Genetic Susceptibility to Engage in Criminal Acts?' *Trends & Issues in Crime and Criminal Justice,* 263: 1–6; Tikkanen, R., Sjöberg, R. L., Ducci, F., Goldman, D., Holi, M., Tiihonen, J., et al. (2009). 'Effects of MAOA-Genotype, Alcohol Consumption, and Aging on Violent Behavior', *Alcoholism: Clinical and experimental Research,* 33(3): 428–434.

20. Leonard, K. E. (2005). 'Alcohol and intimate partner violence: when can we say that heavy drinking is a contributing cause of violence?', *Addiction,* 100(4): 422–425; Graham, K. & Homel, R. (2008). *Raising the Bar: Preventing Aggression in and Around Bars, Pubs and Clubs.* London: Willan Publishing.

9 Gang Interventions

1. Howell, J. (2000) *Youth Gang Programs and Strategies: Summary.* Washington, DC: US Department of Justice, Office of Justice Programs, Office of Juvenile Justice and Delinquency Prevention; Howell, J. (2010) Gang Prevention: An Overview of Research and Programs. *Juvenile Justice Bulletin* (December), Office of Juvenile Justice and Delinquency Prevention, US Department of Justice, Washington, DC.

2. See, for example, Bjorgo, T. (1999) 'How Gangs Fall Apart: Processes of Transformation and Disintegration of Gangs', *Paper Presented at the American Society of Criminology Annual Conference,* 17–20 November, Toronto; Greene, J. & Pranis, K. (2007) *Gang Wars: The Failure of Enforcement Tactics and the Need for Effective Public Safety Strategies.* A Justice Policy Institute Report. Washington, DC: JPI; Howell, J. (2010) 'Gang Prevention: An Overview of Research and Programs', *Juvenile Justice Bulletin (December),* Office of Juvenile Justice and Delinquency Prevention, US Department of Justice, Washington, DC; London Safeguarding Children Board (2009) *Safeguarding Children Affected by Gang Activity and/or Serious Youth Violence.* London: LSVB; Home Office, UK (2008) *Tackling Gangs: A Practical Guide for Local Authorities, CDRPS and Other Local Partners.* London: Home Office.

3. White, R., Perrone, S., Guerra, C. & Lampugnani, R. (1999) *Ethnic Youth Gangs in Australia: Do They Exist? Overview Report.* Melbourne: Australian Multicultural Foundation.

4. Gordon, R. (2000) 'Criminal business organizations, street gangs and 'wanna-be' groups: A Vancouver perspective', *Canadian Journal of Criminology,* January: 39–60; United States Bureau of Justice Assistance (1997) *Addressing Community Gang Problems: A Model for Problem Solving.* Washington, DC: Office of Justice Programs, US Department of Justice; United States Bureau of Justice Assistance (1998) *Addressing Community Gang Problems: A Practical Guide.* Washington, DC: Office of Justice Programs, US Department of Justice.

5. Standing, A. (2005) *The Threat of Gangs and Anti-Gangs Policy,* ISS Occasional Paper 116. South Africa: Institute for Security Studies.

6. Howell, J. (2000) *Youth Gang Programs and Strategies: Summary.* Washington, DC: US Department of Justice, Office of Justice Programs, Office of Juvenile

Justice and Delinquency Prevention; Howell, J. (2010) *Gang Prevention: An Overview of Research and Programs*. Juvenile Justice Bulletin (December), Office of Juvenile Justice and Delinquency Prevention, US Department of Justice, Washington, DC.

7. Howell, J. (2000) *Youth Gang Programs and Strategies: Summary*. Washington, DC: US Department of Justice, Office of Justice Programs, Office of Juvenile Justice and Delinquency Prevention.

8. Cunneen, C. & White, R. (2011) *Juvenile Justice: Youth and Crime in Australia*. Melbourne: Oxford University Press; White, R. & Wyn, J. (2013) *Youth and Society*. Melbourne: Oxford University Press.

9. White, R. (2004) Police and Community Responses to Youth Gangs. *Trends & Issues in Crime and Criminal Justice*, No. 274. Australian Institute of Criminology, Canberra.

10. Gelsthorpe, L. (1999) 'Parents and Criminal Children', in Bainham, A., Day Sclater, S. & Richards, M. (eds) *What is a Parent? A Socio-Legal Analysis*, Hart, Oxford; Goldson, B. & Jamieson, J. (2002) 'Youth Crime, the "Parenting Deficit" and State Intervention: A Contextual Critique', *Youth Justice*, 2(2): 82–99; Homel, R., Freiberg, K., Lamb, C., Leech, M., Batchelor, S., Carr, A., Hay, I., Teague, R. & Elias, G. (2006) 'The Pathways to Prevention Project: Doing Developmental Prevention in a Disadvantaged Community', *Trends & Issues in Crime and Criminal Justice*, No. 323. Canberra: Australian Institute of Criminology.

11. Jamrozik, A. (2001) *Social Policy in the Post-Welfare State: Australians on the Threshold of the 21st Century*. Frenchs Forest NSW: Pearson Education Australia.

12. Jamrozik, A. (2001) *Social Policy in the Post-Welfare State: Australians on the Threshold of the 21st Century*. Frenchs Forest NSW: Pearson Education Australia.

13. White, R. (1996) 'Schooling With A Future?', *Just Policy*, No. 5: 44–50.

14. White, R., Perrone, S., Guerra, C. & Lampugnani, R. (1999) *Ethnic Youth Gangs in Australia: Do They Exist?* Overview Report. Melbourne: Australian Multicultural Foundation.

15. Goldstein, A.P. & Kodluboy, D.W. (1998) *Gangs in Schools: Signs, Symbols, and Solutions*. Champaign, IL: Research Press.

16. Howell, J. (2000) *Youth Gang Programs and Strategies: Summary*. Washington, DC: US Department of Justice, Office of Justice Programs, Office of Juvenile Justice and Delinquency Prevention.

17. Hallsworth, S. & Brotherton, D. (2011) *Urban Disorder and Gangs: A Critique and a Warning*. London: Runnymede.

18. Ashcroft, J., Daniels, D. & Hart, S. (2004) *Evaluating GREAT: A School-Based Gang Prevention Program*. Washington, DC: National Institute of Justice, US Department of Justice; Ebensen, F-A., & Osgood, D. (1999) 'Gang Resistance Education and Training (GREAT): Results from the National Evaluation', *Journal of Research in Crime and Delinquency*, 36(2): 194–225; Esbensen, F-A., Osgood, D., Taylor, T., Patterson, D. & Freng, A. (2001) 'How Great is GREAT? Results from a Longitudinal Quasi-Experimental Design', *Criminology and Public Policy*, 1(1): 87–118.

19. Gordon, R. (2000) 'Criminal Business Organizations, Street Gangs and 'wanna-be' Groups: A Vancouver Perspective', *Canadian Journal of Criminology*, January: 39–60; p. 57.

20. White, R. (2004) 'Police and Community Responses to Youth Gangs', *Trends & Issues in Crime and Criminal Justice*, No. 274. Australian Institute of Criminology, Canberra.

21. Howell, J. (2000) *Youth Gang Programs and Strategies: Summary*. Washington, DC: US Department of Justice, Office of Justice Programs, Office of Juvenile Justice and Delinquency Prevention.

22. Klein, M.W. (1995) *The American Street Gang*. New York: Oxford University Press.

23. Klein, M.W. (2002) 'Street Gangs: A Cross-National Perspective', in R. Huff (ed) *Gangs in America* (3rd edition). Thousand Oaks, California: Sage, p. 247.

24. White, R., Perrone, S., Guerra, C. & Lampugnani, R. (1999) *Ethnic Youth Gangs in Australia: Do They Exist? Overview Report*. Melbourne: Australian Multicultural Foundation.

25. Lee, M. (2006) 'Public Dissent and Governmental Neglect: Isolating and Excluding Macquarie Fields', *Current Issues in Criminal Justice*, 18(1): 32–50.

26. Wolverhampton Crime & Disorder Co-ordination Group (2001) *Wolverhampton Youth Safety Strategy: Building Safer Communities*. Wolverhampton City Council, United Kingdom, p. 33.

27. Davis, M. (1990) *City of Quartz: Excavating the Future in Los Angeles*. London: Vintage; Diacon, D. (ed) (1999) *Building Safer Urban Environments: The Way Forward*. Leicestershire: Building and Social Housing Foundation.

28. Howell, J. (2000) *Youth Gang Programs and Strategies: Summary*. Washington, DC: US Department of Justice, Office of Justice Programs, Office of Juvenile Justice and Delinquency Prevention, p. 24.

29. Dixon, D. (1998) 'Broken Windows, Zero Tolerance, and the New York miracle.' *Current Issues in Criminal Justice*, 10(1): 96–106; Hallsworth, S. & Brotherton, D. (2011) *Urban Disorder and Gangs: A Critique and a Warning*. London: Runnymede.

30. White, R. (1998) 'Curtailing Youth: A Critique of Coercive Crime Prevention', *Crime Prevention Studies*, No. 9: 93–113; White, R., Kosky, B. & Kosky, M. (2001) *MCS Shopping Centre project: A Youth-Friendly Approach to Shopping Centre Management*, Hobart: Australian Clearinghouse for Youth Studies.

31. Bilchik, S. (1996) *Curfew: An Answer to Juvenile Delinquency and Victimisation?* Washington DC: Office of Juvenile Justice and Delinquency Prevention.
    White, R. (1996b) 'Ten Arguments Against Youth Curfews', *Youth Studies Australia*, 15(4): 28–30.

32. Brown, D., Farrier, D., Egger, S. & McNamara, L. (2001) *Criminal Laws: Materials and Commentary on Criminal Law and Process in New South Wales*, The Federation Press, Sydney; Santos, J (2001) 'Down On The Corner: An Analysis of Gang-Related Anti-Loitering Laws', *Cardozo Law Review*, No. 22: 269–314.

33. Edwards, J., Oakley, R. & Carey, S. (1987) 'Street Life, Ethnicity and Social Policy' in G Gaskell & R. Benewick (eds) *The Crowd in Comtemporary*. Britain, London: Sage; New South Wales Office of the Ombudsman (2000) *Police and Public Safety Act*. Sydney: NSW Office of the Ombudsman.

34. Farrington, D. (1994) 'Early Developmental Prevention of Juvenile Delinquency', *Criminal Behaviour and Mental Health*, 4: 209–227.

35. Case, S. (2007) 'Questioning the "Evidence" of Risk that Underpins Evidence-led Youth Justice Interventions', *Youth Justice: An International Journal*, 7(2): 91–106.; MacDonald, R. (2006) 'Social Exclusion, Youth Transitions and

Criminal Careers: Five Critical Reflections on "Risk" ', *Australian and New Zealand Journal of Criminology*, 39(3): 371–383.

36. Cunneen, C. & White, R. (2006) 'Australia: Control, Containment or Empowerment?', in J. Muncie & B. Goldson (eds) *Comparative Youth Justice.* London; Sage.

37. Palmer, D. (1999) 'Talking about the Problems of Young Nyungars', in R. White (ed) *Australian Youth Subcultures: On the Margins and In the Mainstream.* Hobart: Australian Clearinghouse for Youth Studies;Palmer, D. & Collard, L. (1993) 'Aboriginal Young People & Youth Subcultures', in R. White (ed) *Youth Subcultures: Theory, History and the Australian Experience.* Hobart: National Clearinghouse for Youth Studies; Priday, E. (2006) 'New Directions in Juvenile Justice: Risk and Cognitive Behaviourism', *Current Issues in Criminal Justice*, 17(3): 343–359.

38. White, R. & Wyn, J. (2013) *Youth and Society.* Melbourne: Oxford University Press.

39. Case, S. (2007) 'Questioning the "Evidence" of Risk that Underpins Evidence-led Youth Justice Interventions', *Youth Justice: An International Journal*, 7(2): 91–106.

40. This figure is taken from: White, R. (2008) 'Disputed Definitions and Fluid Identities: The Limitations of Social Profiling in Relation to Ethnic Youth Gangs', *Youth Justice: an International Journal*, 8(2): 149–161.

41. Esbensen, F-A., Winfree, Jr., L., He, N. & Taylor, T. (2001) Youth Gangs and Definitional Issues: When Is a Gang a Gang, and Why Does It Matter? *Crime & Delinquency*, 47: 105–130.

42. Blagg, H. & Wilkie, M. (1995) *Young People & Police Powers.* Sydney: Australian Youth Foundation; Cunneen, C. (2001) *Conflict, Politics and Crime: Aboriginal Communities and the Police.* Sydney: Allen & Unwin; Cunneen, C. & White, R. (2011) *Juvenile Justice: Youth and Crime in Australia.* Melbourne: Oxford University Press.

43. White, R., Perrone, S., Guerra, C. & Lampugnani, R. (1999) *Ethnic Youth Gangs in Australia: Do They Exist? [7 reports – Vietnamese, Latin American, Turkish, Somalian, Pacific Islander, Anglo-Australian, Summary].* Melbourne: Australian Multicultural Foundation.

44. Chan, J. (1994) 'Policing Youth in 'Ethnic' Communities: Is community policing the answer?', in R. White & C. Alder (eds) *The Police and Young People in Australia.* Melbourne: Cambridge University Press; Doan, V. (1995) 'Indo-Chinese Youth: Issues of culture and justice', in C. Guerra & R. White (eds) *Ethnic Minority Youth in Australia.* Hobart: National Clearinghouse for Youth Studies; Lyons, E. (1995) 'New Clients, Old Problems: Vietnamese Young People's Experiences with Police', in C. Guerra & R. White (eds) *Ethnic Minority Youth in Australia.* Hobart: National Clearinghouse for Youth Studies; Maher, L., Dixon, D., Swift, W. & Nguyen, T. (1997) *Anh Hai: Young Asian Background People's Perceptions and Experiences of Policing.* Sydney: UNSW Faculty of Law Research Monograph Series.

45. White, R. & Perrone, S. (2001) 'Racism, Ethnicity and Hate Crime', *Communal/Plural*, 9: 161–181.

46. Bjorgo, T. (1998) 'Recruitment and Disengagement from Extreme Groups: The Case of Racist Youth Subcultures', *Paper Presented at 7th International Seminar on Environmental Criminology and Crime Analysis*, 21–24 June, Barcelona;

Bjorgo, T. (1999) 'How Gangs Fall Apart: Processes of Transformation and Disintegration of Gangs', *Paper Presented at the American Society of Criminology Annual Conference*, 17–20 November, Toronto.

47. Bjorgo, T. (1998) 'Recruitment and Disengagement from Extreme Groups: The Case of Racist Youth Subcultures', *Paper Presented at 7th International Seminar on Environmental Criminology and Crime Analysis*, 21–24 June, Barcelona.

48. Howell, J. (2007) 'Menacing or Mimicking? Realities of Youth Gangs', *Juvenile and Family Court Journal*, 58(2): 39–50; Standing, A. (2005) *The Threat of Gangs and Anti-Gangs Policy*, ISS Occasional Paper 116. South Africa: Institute for Security Studies.

49. Bjorgo, T. (1999) 'How Gangs Fall Apart: Processes of Transformation and Disintegration of Gangs', *Paper Presented at the American Society of Criminology Annual Conference*, 17–20 November, Toronto.

10 Beyond Gangs

1. Jamrozik, A. (2001) *Social Policy in the Post-Welfare State: Australians on the Threshold of the 21st Century*. Frenchs Forest NSW: Pearson Education Australia.

2. Hall, S. & Scraton, P. (1981) 'Law, Class and Control', in M. Fitzgerald, G. McLennan & J. Pawson (eds) *Crime & Society: Readings in History and Theory*. London: Routledge & Kegan Paul in association with Open University Press, p. 485.

3. Hirst, P. (1975) 'Marx and Engels on Law, Crime and Morality', in I. Taylor, P. Walton & J. Young (eds) *Critical Criminology*. London: Routledge & Kegan Paul.

4. Davis, M. (1990) *City of Quartz: Excavating the Future in Los Angeles*. London: Vintage.

5. Tomsen, S. (2008) 'Masculinities, Crime and Criminalisation', in T. Anthony & C. Cunneen (eds) *The Critical Criminology Companion*. Sydney: Hawkins Press, p. 101.

6. Foote, P. (1993) 'Like, I'll Tell You what Happened from Experience … Perspectives on Italo-Australian Youth Gangs in Adelaide', in R. White (ed) *Youth Subcultures: Theory, History and the Australian Experience*. Hobart: National Clearinghouse for Youth Studies.

7. Noble, G., Poynting, S. & Tabar, P. (1999) 'Lebanese Youth and Social Identity', in R. White (ed) *Australian Youth Subcultures: On the Margins and In the Mainstream*. Hobart: Australian Clearinghouse for Youth Studies.

8. Campbell, A. (1984) *The Girls in the Gang*. Oxford: Basil Blackwell; Miller, J. (2001) *One of the Guys: Girls, Gangs and Gender*. New York: Oxford University Press; Batchelor, S. (2011) 'Beyond Dichotomy: Towards an Explanation of Young Women's Involvement in Violent Street Gangs', in B. Goldson (ed) *Youth in Crisis? 'Gangs', Territoriality and Violence*. London: Routledge.

9. Batchelor, S. (2011) 'Beyond Dichotomy: Towards an Explanation of Young Women's Involvement in Violent Street Gangs', in B. Goldson (ed) *Youth in Crisis? 'Gangs', Territoriality and Violence*. London: Routledge.

10. Cunneen, C. & White, R. (2011) *Juvenile Justice: Youth and Crime in Australia*. Melbourne: Oxford University Press.

11. Beikoff, L. (1996) 'Queensland's Juvenile Justice System: Equity, Access and Justice for Young Women?', Alder, C. & Baines, M. (eds) *And When She was Bad? Working with Young Women in Juvenile Justice and Related Areas*, National Clearinghouse for Youth Studies, Hobart; Ogilvie, E, Lynch, M. & Bell, S. (2000) '*Gender* and Official Statistics: The Juvenile Justice System in Queensland, 1998–1999', *Trends and Issues in Crime and Criminal Justice*, No. 162, Australian Institute of Criminology, Canberra.

Index

CPSIA information can be obtained at www.ICGtesting.com
Printed in the USA
LVOW04*2312080515

437789LV00009B/281/P

9 781137 333841